Dialogue and the Human Image

D1363918

FOR ALEENE
who has given me both

Dialogue and the Human Image

Beyond Humanistic Psychology

Maurice Friedman

SAGE PUBLICATIONS
The International Professional Publishers
Newbury Park London New Delhi

For information address:

SAGE Publications, Inc.
2455 Teller Road
Newbury Park, California 91320

SAGE Publications Ltd.
6 Bonhill Street
London EC2A 4PU
United Kingdom

SAGE Publications India Pvt. Ltd.
M-32 Market
Greater Kailash I
New Delhi 110 048 India

Printed in the United States of America

Library of Congress Cataloging-in-Publication Data

Friedman, Maurice S.
  Dialogue and the human image : beyond humanistic psychology /
Maurice Friedman
        p.   cm.
  Includes bibliographical references and index.
  ISBN 0-8039-4368-7 (hard).   — ISBN 0-8039-4369-5 (pbk.)
  1. Humanistic psychology. 2. Humanistic psychotherapy. 3. Self-
actualization (Psychology) 4. Interpersonal relations.
5. Dialogue.   I. Title.
BF204.F75   1992
150.19'8 —dc20   91-36152
                                                        CIP

FIRST PRINTING, 1992

Sage Production Editor: Judith L. Hunter

Contents

Acknowledgments

For permission to reprint copyrighted material the author and publisher gratefully acknowledge the following:

Boszormenyi-Nagy, I., & Krasner, B. R. (1986). *Between Give and Take: A Clinical Guide to Contextual Therapy*. Reprinted with permission from Brunner/ Mazel, Inc., New York, New York.

Boszormenyi-Nagy, I. (1987). *Foundations of Contextual Therapy: Collected Papers of Ivan Boszormenyi-Nagy, M.D.* Reprinted with permission from Brunner/ Mazel, Inc., New York, New York.

Buber, M. (1965). *Between Man and Man,* translated from the German by Ronald Gregor Smith. Copyright © 1965 by Macmillan Publishing Company. Reprinted with permisson.

Buber, M. (1988). *The Knowledge of Man: A Philosophy of the Interhuman.* (M. S. Friedman, Ed.; M. S. Friedman & R. G. Smith, Trans.). Published by Humanities Press International, Atlantic Highland, NJ. Reprinted with permission.

Farber, L. H. (1966). *The Ways of the Will: Essays Toward a Psychology and Psychopathology of the Will.* Copyright © 1965 by Basic Books, Inc. Reprinted by permission of Basic Books, a division of HarperCollins Publishers.

Lynd, H. M. (1958). *On Shame and the Search for Identity.* Reprinted with permission from Harcourt Brace, New York, New York.

May, R. (1969). *Love and Will.* Published by W. W. Norton & Company, Inc. Reprinted with permission.

Yalom, I. D. (1989). *Love's Executioner and Other Tales of Psychotherapy.* Copyright © 1989 by Irvin D. Yalom. Reprinted by permission of Basic Books, a division of HarperCollins Publishers.

Preface

In August 1988 I took part in a panel at the American Psychological Association annual convention in Atlanta, Georgia, on "After Rogers and Maslow, What?" organized by Professor Al Mahrer of the University of Ottawa. To my surprise, I received many requests for copies of my paper, "Elements of a New Humanistic Psychology," including publication of it in German translation for *Report Psychologie*, which reaches the 9,000 members of the Union of German Psychologists (Friedman, 1989). These responses started me thinking in terms of what has evolved into this book.

It is not merely the passing of Albert Maslow and Carl Rogers that makes this book timely. It is also the fact that the old humanistic psychology has been criticized rightly by Viktor Frankl, Brewster Smith, and me for insufficient tough-mindedness about such central shibboleths as self-realization and self-actualization. In going "beyond humanistic psychology" I do not mean to leave behind what has been of value in that movement. On the contrary, it is my desire to help the movement itself and others who are interested in it to offer a more coherent live option to contemporary psychologists and psychotherapists. In so doing, I do not presume to speak for all humanistic psychologists, some of whom would want a greater emphasis on transpersonal psychology, others on the relation to this or that element of the First and Second Forces in psychology. Nonetheless, the two elements that I put forward in this book—dialogue and the image of the human—may fairly claim to be essential to any psychology that is indeed humanistic in the root meaning of that term. In the past, dialogue and the human image have in many cases been considered peripherally. Now they need to be placed squarely in the center.

A special word needs to be said here about the critique of encounter groups that is contained in Chapter 3, "Aiming at the Self: The Paradox of the Human Potential Movement." This chapter does not represent an up-to-date appraisal of encounter groups as they have evolved in the last 15 years, including their growing use in codependency groups. It is concerned, rather, with illustrating some of the dangers of the human potential movement, which I think has no more vivid illustration than that of encounter groups as I personally witnessed them at Esalen Institute in the 1960s and early 1970s.

I wish to acknowledge the help given me by Thomas Greening, editor of the *Journal of Humanistic Psychology*; Kenneth Newton of the Department of Psychology of the University of Tennessee at Knoxville; and Chris Anstoos of the Department of Psychology at West Georgia College and editor of *The Humanistic Psychologist*, who wrote six pages of suggestions and critiques in response to an early draft of this book. Above all I am indebted to my friend Charles Brice of the Department of Psychology at Duquesne University for a careful reading and editing of the almost final version of this book. His assistance was invaluable at every level.

—MAURICE FRIEDMAN
Solana Beach, California

PART ONE

Introduction:
After Maslow and Rogers, What?

1

Beyond Humanistic Psychology: Dialogue and the Image of the Human

I have criticized humanistic psychology for helping obscure as well as reveal the human image because it tends to make self-realization and self-actualization a goal in itself rather than a by-product of genuine dialogue, or meeting, which is of value in itself (Friedman, 1984). I also have extended this critique from Maslow and Fromm to Carl Rogers, for whom meeting is sometimes seen as an end in itself and sometimes only a means to the end of personal becoming and self-actualization (Friedman, 1985).

In this chapter I want to point to two elements that I believe need to receive a central emphasis in the movement beyond humanistic psychology that, it is hoped, will develop after Maslow and Rogers. These elements are dialogue and the image of the human.

Martin Buber's ontology of the between begins with the premise that "all real living is meeting." The sphere in which person meets person has been ignored because it possesses no smooth continuity. Its experience has been annexed to the soul and to the world so that what happens to an individual can be distributed between outer and inner impressions. But when two persons "happen" to each other, the essential remainder that is common to them reaches out beyond the special sphere of each. That remainder is the basic reality, the "sphere of the between."

In an essential relation "the other becomes present not merely in the imagination or feeling but in the depths of one's substance, so that one experiences the mystery of the other being in the mystery of one's own." The two persons participate in each other's lives not merely psychologically, as images or feelings in one another's psyches, but ontologically, as a manifest, even if not continuous, reality of the between. For such a relationship to be possible, each must be a real person in his or her own right.

The sphere of the "between" comes to its fullness in the life of dialogue. We attain personal wholeness when we respond to the other without thinking of ourselves, and we attain genuine dialogue not by aiming at it, but by allowing the other to exist in his or her otherness and not just as a content of our experience and thought. We can perceive the other person as whole and unique only through the attitude of a partner and not through that reductive, analytical, and derivative look that prevails today.

The between exists not only in the I-Thou of direct meting but also in the "essential We" of family and community. The common reality of human existence that we build together is the foundation for Buber's distinction between "groundless" neurotic guilt (a subjective feeling within a person, usually unconscious and repressed) and "existential guilt" (an ontic, interhuman reality in which the person dwells in the truest sense of the term). True guilt does not reside in the human person but in his or her failure to respond to the legitimate claim and address of the world. Similarly, the repression of guilt and the neuroses that result from this repression are not merely psychological phenomena but are also events between persons. Existential guilt is the "guilt that a person has taken on himself as a person and in a personal situation" (Buber, 1988c, p. 116), an objective dialogical guilt that transcends the realm of inner feelings and of the self's relation to itself. Existential guilt is the corollary of the answerability and responsibility of the self in the concrete dialogical situation. It is failure to respond and, by the same token, failure to authenticate one's existence.

An essential interrelationship exists between the life of dialogue and the image of the human. The image of the human implies a meaningful personal and social direction. It is at one and the same time concern for what is authentic *human* existence and concern for what is authentic for us in particular; for it is precisely in our uniqueness that each of us realizes what the human can become in us. We come to awareness of ourselves as selves not just through our individuality, however, but in our dialogue with other selves—in their response to us and in the way they call us into being. Because we live as separate selves, yet in relation to other persons and to society, past, present, and future, we need an image of the human to aid us in finding a meaningful way of life, in choosing between conflicting sets of values, in realizing our own unique potentialities.

The image of the human distinguishes between our potentiality and the direction we give to our potentiality. Such terms as *self-actualization* and *self-realization* leave unanswered the question of what direction we must take to "realize" or "actualize" ourselves. To give our potentialities direction means to decide—not consciously, but through the response of our whole being—what is the more and what is the less authentic choice in a particular situation, what is the more and what is the less authentic attitude and response, what way is *ours* because it is true for us and we have committed ourselves to be true to it. We become ourselves through each particular action; we choose ourselves in each act of becoming. Our actual resources are inseparably bound up with the direction we take as persons in response to what calls us out in the concrete situation. The image of the human enters into and forms the attitude that makes us ready to meet and respond to any person whatever as someone we stand open to know, respect, perhaps even love. Thus, the image of the human plays an essential role in linking one moment of realized dialogue with another.

The image of the human distinguishes between impersonal and personal guilt. Certainly, purely social and even neurotic guilt exists that is derived from a set of mores and taboos imposed upon the individual by parents and society and incorporated into an internalized "super-ego." But real personal guilt also exists that has to do with our actual stance in the world and the way we go out to relate to other people from that stance. When we are guilty, it is not because we have failed to realize our potentialities, which we cannot know in the abstract, but because we have failed to bring the resources available to us at a given moment into our response to a particular situation that calls us out. Our potentialities cannot be divorced from the discovery of our personal direction, and this comes not in our meeting with ourselves but with other persons and with the image of the human that we acquire through such meeting. Personal guilt is dialogical—the inseparable corollary of our personal responsibility, our being answerable for authenticating our own existence and, by the same token, for responding to the partners of our existence. We are answerable neither to ourselves alone nor to society apart from ourselves but to that very bond between ourselves and others through which we again and again discover the direction in which we can authenticate our existence (Friedman, 1978).

PART TWO

Humanistic Psychology and Beyond

2

Psychology as a Human Science

As Martin Gardner has pointed out in his iconoclastic book *In the Name of Science* (1952), not all that is done in the name of science is properly called science. In the case of the behaviorist approach to psychology, this distinction between scientism and science has been spelled out lucidly by Amedeo Giorgi, a pioneer in the application of phenomenology to experimental psychology:

> Science becomes scientism when methods successful in one area are transferred uncritically to another domain where their legitimacy is at best questionable. Psychology turned to established and more prestigious sciences to imitate them. But the established sciences were physics, chemistry, biology—each of which was developed within an implicit ontology suitable for nature but not for the human person. The natural sciences were never *intended* to study man as a person. One need not leave the realm of science to study man adequately. We need only to broaden science itself. (Giorgi, 1970b)

Giorgi summarizes the main features of the natural scientific approach that is uncritically carried over to psychology as "empirical, positivistic, reductionistic, quantitative, deterministic, verifiable and predictive." These characteristics have

9

been helpful, but their helpfulness is dependent upon their appropriateness to the subject studied. Giorgi follows Thomas Kuhn's *Structure of Scientific Revolutions* (1962) in recognizing the change of world view that underlies each new breakthrough in science. Like Kuhn, Giorgi "tries to account for the activity of science in terms of the process of perception; whereas, psychologists try to account for the presence of perception in terms of the natural sciences" (Giorgi, 1970b, oral record). In the place of a prereflective or truly perceptual presence to the world, psychology substitutes a natural scientific reflective and conceptual apprehension of the world.

> Psychology, in studying perception, mostly considers stimuli in terms of physics and speaks of the body in anatomical terms. Psychology thus transforms our perceived world into the world of natural science and then tries to explain it in natural scientific terms and not in phenomenal or perceptual terms. (Giorgi, 1969, p. 431)

In his book *Psychology as a Human Science*, Giorgi (1970a) states that instead of modeling itself on the natural sciences, the human sciences, including psychology, should have gone directly to the life-world, discovered its questions and methods from there, and only then tried to ascertain to what extent the human and the natural sciences have methods, concepts, and answers in common. The natural scientific approach applies an analytical process that breaks down the whole into its elements or parts, whereas the approach to the human sciences would understand the whole as part of a larger-structured context. The actual and the present would become then the point of departure for uncovering relationships, contexts, and meaning. Natural science considers man as *part of the world* but studies him without reference to his intentional relations *to* the world. The human sciences recognize that man is also one *for whom the world exists*. Natural science derives its theories and hypotheses from a vital level of integration below the human structural level and looks at the human in terms of pathological cases or traditional laboratory studies. The human sciences, being holistic, study man at his highest level of functioning, the unequivocally human, to which facts obtained at lower levels of function are relevant only if a human context is implicitly present.

The human sciences are intersubjective not only between scientist and scientist but also between investigator and subject. Equal in their humanity, they must relate through a non-manipulative structure based upon appeal and cooperation in which research designs will be open-ended, leaving the final closure to the subject. In contrast to the positivist, reductionist, analytic, and quantitative approach of the natural sciences, the human sciences must be concerned with meaning, qualitative differences, intentional relations, and investigating human phenomena in a human way. The meaning that the *subjects* bring to the situation thus becomes co-constitutive of the results (Giorgi, 1970a). This approach does not mean any attack on the "empirical" and the "real," but a broader, more indeterminate understanding of them and of the human image they imply:

> The only problem with empiricism and positivism is that these philosophies define experience and the real too narrowly, and by means of certain *ideas* of experience and the real, which brought closure too rapidly. (Giorgi, 1970a, p. 205)

Another reply to scientism from the realm of psychology itself is Isidor Chein's book *The Science of Behavior and the Image of Man* (1972). At the heart of the issue of the nature of psychology, writes Chein, is the issue of the image of man. Chein contrasts two basic types of image—man as helpless, powerless reagent and man as active, responsible agent, and he opts for the latter. Man does not passively permit himself to be shaped by his environment; he injects himself into the causal process, shaping both what is around him and himself. "If Man is said to respond to his environment, the word 'response' is to be taken in the sense that it has in active dialogue rather than in the sense of an automatic consequence" (Chein, 1972, p. 67).

In place of the image of responding, responsible man there dominates, not only among psychologists but among an astonishingly large number of those concerned with guidance, counseling, and psychotherapy, a "robotic image of man" resting "on the false assumption that . . . every determinant of behavior is either a body fact or an environment fact" (Chein, 1972, p. 22). In powerful reinforcement of our critique of scientism, Chein charges "that psychologists maintain the image of Man as a passive corporeal entity governed by a thermodynamic principle because of their philosophical precommitments and in flagrant disregard of contradictory information" (Chein, 1972, p. 9).

Freedom to Chein rests on the simple premise that volitions—human desires and motivations—have behavioral consequences and are not themselves reducible to variables of physical environment or physiological process. Like the Gestalt psychologists, Chein holds that the unique aspects of a totality do not emerge from the combination of the components, "since the totality plays a role in determining what the components will be" (Chein, 1972, p. 26). The alternative to this image of man, declares Chein, is to reduce psychological science to a concern with "psychological trivia arbitrarily torn out of the context of their natural setting" (Chein, 1972, p. 43). This setting includes the fact that motivation implies a mission, a commitment to accomplish something. Strict behaviorists who avoid inner feeling and emotion as "mentalistic poison" (Chein, 1972, p. 277) pay the price of losing much of the human being and what makes him do what he does. Scientism is committed to a reductionism that goes beyond the parsimoniousness of science to a preselected set of primitive terms and propositions, usually drawn from physics, chemistry, or physiology, which are held to dogmatically in complete disrespect for the "unparsimoniousness of nature" (Chein, 1972, p. 309). In addition, the scientismist limits himself to clearly understandable, verifiable forms even when they do not fit the case, thus betraying the scientific goal and purposes for the sake of maintaining the scientific form.

In contrast to scientism, Chein puts forward a clinicalist image of man. The "clinicalist" is open to human context and human meaning as they are found in the concrete, the particular, and the unique—hence, in the "image of man" as opposed to "human nature" or the "construct of man." His desire to comprehend every instance "in all of its particularity and unique individuality" leads the clinicalist to be suspicious of any fixed scheme of classification, consistent theory, or statistic evidence. "He rejects fiducial probabilities because the very concept abandons the uniqueness of the particular case." "Evidence," to him, is the phenomenal given itself, explained, when necessary, in terms of "the subjective compellingness and fittingness of an account in terms of temporal-situational context" (Chein, 1972, p. 310). Predictability of nontrivial behavior is, to him, "*prima facie* evidence of constraints that distort normal behavior," and he regards laboratory situations as "so abnormal that no generalizations from them are warranted" (Chein, 1972, p. 311). He gains more from reading Dostoievsky, Mann, Proust, and Shakespeare than all of the pages of the *Journal of Experimental Psychology*; for "a good example of seeing human behavior in its complexity may be worth more in developing principles of grasping particularities than scores of statistically significant generalizations about highly circumscribed behaviors occurring under laboratory conditions" (Chein, 1972, pp. 312f.).

Psychology as a human science must begin with the uniqueness of the person, with the concrete relation between experimenter and subject and between therapist and client, and with that bewildering intermixture of personal freedom and psychological precision to which I have pointed in my book *Problematic Rebel* (1970). Speaking like Giorgi and Chein, Frederick J. Wertz has summed up nicely the pitfalls of scientismic psychology and the requisites of psychology as a human science. Psychology has attempted to achieve scientific status not by looking closely at its own phenomena and developing rigorous methods for revealing the characteristics peculiar to this domain, but by mimicking the natural sciences. It has thereby not only placed itself at an insurmountable distance from human reality but has itself fallen guilty of the dehumanizing objectification of man. Psychology conceived as and modeled after natural science is incapable of understanding those everyday situations that here concern us in their intrinsic richness. What is required is the recognition of what man is over and against nature and the institutionalization of a rigorous science based faithfully upon that recognition. This recognition means first the comprehensive description of situations as they are lived by persons and then systematic reflection on the meanings that express what is at stake in these situations for human life (Wertz, 1981, p. 219).

3

Aiming at the Self:
The Paradox of the Human Potential Movement

"I believe," wrote James Agee, "that every human being is potentially capable, within his 'limits,' of fully 'realizing' his potentialities; that this, his being cheated and choked of it, is infinitely the ghastliest, commonest, and most inclusive of all the crimes of which the human world can accuse itself. . . . I know only that murder is being done against nearly every individual on the planet."[1]

As a holistic approach to the person, which sees his future actuality as unfolding from his present possibility, the concept of self-realization represents a decisive step forward toward the human image. Nevertheless, it leaves much to be desired by way of a fully concrete and serious grappling with the problem of finding authentic personal direction. Erich Fromm, for example, defines "a genuine ideal as any aim which furthers the growth, freedom, and happiness of the self" and defines values in terms of "the mature and integrated personality" and "the truly human self." Yet the very meaning of each of these terms depends upon one's image of the human and one's sense of one's own personal direction.[2] Values cannot be based upon self-realization, as Karen Horney does in her ethic of "self realization," with its assumption of an already given "real self" contrasted with the pseudoself erected by neurotic pride and striving for perfection (Horney, 1950, pp. 13-18, 384f., 388-390, 375-378). On the contrary, we cannot define ourselves or our potentialities apart from the direction we give them, apart from what we become in relation to others.[3]

The Viennese logotherapist Viktor Frankl serves as a useful counterbalance to Fromm and Horney on the subject of self-realization. The main cause of neuroses in our age, he suggests, is the existential frustration that arises from not being able to find a meaning in life. The therapist cannot give a meaning to his patient. "It is up to the patient himself to 'find' the concrete meaning of his existence." In conscious opposition to Sartre, Frankl sees this meaning as one that is discovered and not invented. Frankl sees potentialities as inseparable from the demand that life places upon us to make meaningful and valuable and thus existential commitments. The individual has many possible choices, but at any given time only one of them fulfills *the necessity* of his life task. Responsibility and maturity mean choosing one potentiality that shall be actualized, one that is *worth* actualizing, and relegating the rest to nonbeing. *"Thus the problem really just begins when potentialism ends"* (Frankl, 1960).

Although Abraham Maslow is best known for making "peak experiences" and self-actualization the goals of his psychology, he recognized, as Brewster Smith has pointed out, that not only do self-actualizing people tend to be altruists but also that "their basic needs can be fulfilled only by and through other human beings, i.e., society." What is more important, he stated, is that "Self-actualizing people are, without one single exception, involved in a cause outside . . . themselves . . . some calling or vocation in the old sense." That means they did not aim at becoming self-actualizing persons but instead were involved in their work. (It is Maslow who turned the by-product into the goal by identifying self-actualization as the result of a fully human psychology.) We must agree, therefore, with Brewster Smith's conclusion that, "This, of course, is only a restatement of the Christian wisdom that he who would find his life must lose it—that happiness is a by-product that eludes direct pursuit" and with his further assertion that this is an enduring truth about selfhood and its fulfillment that needs to be fitted into a conceptually articulated self-psychology (Smith, 1973, pp. 28, 30).

The road beyond potentialism is the direction-giving human image. Real values, the values that are operative in our lives, are brought into being through our ever-renewed decision in response to the situations we meet. These values become touchstones of reality for us. We carry them forward not as abstract principles but as basic attitudes, as life-stances that we embody and reveal in ever new and unexpected ways. They remain with us, latent in the deepest levels of our being, ready to be evoked and given form by the situations that call us out. These basic attitudes are the images of the human that unite one moment of lived dialogue with another, for it is not abstract consistency of principles or ideals but faithfulness in responding to the present with the touchstones that live in us from the past that gives unity and integrity to our lives as persons. In contrast, therefore, to those psychotherapists who seek to derive a direction-giving image of the human from the concept of "self-realization," we must recognize that self-realization cannot be made *the goal* either of therapy or of life, however indispensable it is as a by-product and corollary of a true life. Self-realization is corrupted into psychologism, in fact, precisely at the point where one aims at oneself. For this is the age-old paradox! We are called upon to realize ourselves, yet to aim directly at so doing is always self-defeating. You *begin* with yourself, but you do not *aim* at yourself, as Martin Buber says in his little classic *The Way of Man* (Buber, 1988b, Book IV). You must recognize the contribution of your inner contradiction to the conflict between yourself and others, yet you must not bog down in being preoccupied with yourself. Of course, it is not enough to say, "Forget about yourself and be nice to others," for we often relate to others mainly as a way of evading ourselves. For all that, once we make ourselves the goal—even if we do so in the hope of becoming more of a person and thereby being able to help other people more effectively—we embark on a path that is not likely to lead us beyond ourselves to genuine dialogue with others. Instead, we are more and more apt to view our relations with others in terms of our progress toward becoming whatever we feel we should become.

If *psychologism* be defined as "the tendency to convert events that happen between ourselves and others into psychological happenings or categories," then we must say that all modern psychology, psychotherapy, and psychoanalysis run the risk of falling into precisely this. The very attempt to look at the person in abstraction from our relations to others, as a more or less isolated psyche, means this. In the analytical psychology of Carl Jung, however, the danger is doubled, because for him self-realization is the goal, and the means toward the goal is a turning inward to a larger-than-life-size Self to be integrated in the depths of the Objective Psyche, or Collective Unconscious. When the person is thus focused on these inward processes, the danger is that everything else and everyone else consciously or unconsciously become the means to the end of *our* individuation, or integration, the function of *our* becoming. The word *psychologism* is in no sense an attack on either psychology or psychotherapy when these observe their proper limits. It is an attack on the tendency to make the reality of our relationship to what is not ourselves—persons and cats, sunsets and trees—into what is essentially *within* ourselves.

Psychologism is a habit of mind. It is the tendency to divide the reality that is given to us into two parts—one is an outer world into which we fit ourselves, and the other is an inner psyche into which we fit the world. This is an understandable division. Much of our lives is conceived in terms of it. The wholeness that is possible for us as human beings can never be found by regarding the outer as a mere reflection of the inner, but only by overcoming the division itself. The real person—and by "person" I do not mean Jung's "persona," the mask, or social role—has to live with that inner brought into relation to the outer. If we have "vocation," a term that Jung also uses, it is because we are called, and that call cannot come to us only from within. Even if the call comes in mystic ecstasy or in a dream, we do not have the right to say that it is simply *in* us. We do not actually exist divided into "inner" and "outer" except for certain useful purposes. In reality we are a whole in every moment in streaming interaction with every-body and everything.

"By never being an end in himself," Lao-tzu said of the "sound man," "he endlessly becomes himself." We cannot ask in all seriousness and concreteness what we mean by the term *self-realization* until we cease to use the term for its emotional value and really care about it, care deeply, like Celia in T. S. Eliot's *The Cocktail Party*, because our lives have some omission, some call we have not answered, because our guilt is not just committing adultery with Edward but our failure to become the persons we were called to become. To exist is not to realize potentiality, it is to make decisions and find direction. What we call our potentiality, we discover only when we are faced with actuality—that is, in the course of making decisions and finding direction in the situations that call us out. We do not really know our resources—our "potential"—in advance of that call. Every one of us knows that in time of crisis we shall find ourselves capable of a great deal more than we now think possible. Most of us also know how often we make the mistake of plotting our futures on the assumption that we will be up to something that we may not be up to at all when it arrives.

In our culture, potentiality is regarded as some sort of solid object that we may take to ourselves as our possession. Actually, our potentialities are not something we even have control over most of the time. They are not *in* us; they are between us and what calls us out. The questioner is just as important as the answerer. A wise person is not a fount of knowledge. On the contrary, he or she is helpless until someone asks a question great enough to evoke a profound response. A person does not *have* wisdom. Wisdom literally happens, comes to be, in the *between*.

The word *self* has no meaning, I submit, apart from the way in which we bring our deep responses to life situations. Jesus said, "He who would find his life must lose it." But if you set out to lose your life *in order* to find it, you will not really have lost it and, therefore, *cannot* really find it. This is the paradox of aiming directly at self-realization as a goal instead of allowing it to come as a by-product of living itself. If I follow Fromm and other psychologists who tell me it is important to have good relationships with other people so that I may be a mature and productive person, then the relationships are merely functional, and I shall not become even the person I aim at being. Only when I forget myself and respond with *all* myself to something not myself—only then do I even have a self, for only then does my true uniqueness emerge.

By robbing us of these simple contacts with what is not ourselves and the touchstones that merge from them, psychologism robs life of its finest reality. This is a reality that we cannot sustain and maintain, to be sure, a reality that does not relieve us of the task of working with and on ourselves when we are brought back to ourselves. Nonetheless, the possibility exists of finding real life, not by leaving our inwardness behind but by bringing it with us as a whole in our response to whatever comes. This is not a question of "inner" versus "outer." We need all our inwardness, for it is an integral part of our wholeness as persons. Our wholeness is not a state of being but a presence, an event, a happening that comes into being again and again in our contact and response.

At the end of a one-day seminar that I led, I suggested that the people present break up into small groups, one of which I joined as a participant-observer. In that small group were two people, a woman and a man, who had the same complaint—that they continually observed themselves in all that they were doing and, therefore, never did anything freely, spontaneously, with their whole being. "My problem is that I am really a very good psychological analyst, and I know it," said the woman. "I bring it to all of my relations in life," she added, "and therefore I never feel anything that catches me up." She brought to my mind Virginia Woolf confessing with shame in her diary that she could never meet a friend without thinking, How can I use her in my novels? The man leading the small group asked her, "Is there any place where you do, in fact, come out of this?" "Yes," she answered, "if I go to a ballet, or if I get angry." Here at least—caught up by beauty or taken over by anger—she forgot herself and broke out of the vicious circle!

Even this hope seemed denied to the man in question. After my talk to the group as a whole, he had asked me, "Isn't the most important thing to discover your conflicts, your defensiveness, and work on that?" "Yes," I replied, "that is true. Yet you may never get beyond that." He had been with enough groups, he continued, to become aware that he was a defensive person. His problem, he realized, was that he did not hear things as they were said and respond to them spontaneously but heard them only in reference to his own feeling of being vulnerable. He wanted to get out of this by focusing on the fact that he was defensive. But this was equally self-preoccupation. The story he told our small group—of his one and only encounter, in which he got everyone so angry that they stripped him naked and threw him into the hall!—was told so matter-of-factly and impersonally that even this sharing could not break him out of the circle. He was wrapped up in his image of himself.

I am not attacking self-realization as such, therefore, or the desire that people in our day have for a true life. I celebrate life too. I wish we could have joy, feeling, touch, expanded consciousness, true community. Yet, setting out directly to attain these things leads to a planned spontaneity that again and again defeats itself and abstracts us from the real situation in which we are set. Techniques abound for dieting, for playing the piano, for dance, but no true techniques exist for self-realization. Self-realization should not be our concern.

One of the most important claims that encounter and marathon groups make is that they promote the achievement of true, intimate human contact through mutual self-disclosure, emotional expression, and acceptance of self and others—all of which leads to further development of the capacity to love and be loved. Carl Rogers attributed the phenomenal growth of the intensive group experience to the discovery by ordinary people "that it alleviates their aloneness, and . . . brings persons into real relationships with persons." Freed to become aware of isolation amid affluence and the mask-meeting-mask character of most of his life, a person learns also that this tragedy of life is *not necessary*, that he or she can modify existential loneliness through an "intensive group experience," perhaps the most significant social invention of this century (Rogers, 1970, p. 157). One wonders if many people in the encounter movement do not confuse the reciprocal release of pent-up emotions and deeply repressed feelings with genuine relationships. Openness in communication is an important part of genuine dialogue, to be sure, but many encounter leaders seem to be concerned mostly about each person's expressing feelings honestly and expect real mutuality to emerge of itself from this self-expression.

In the encounter movement, too, the search to bring the human image out of hiding not seldom leads only to greater eclipse. I have myself witnessed poor, insensitive, or authoritarian leadership dovetailing with cliché demands and expectations on the part of participants plus the tendency of leaders and participants alike to rely on *techniques*, as opposed to moment-by-moment awareness of the concrete situation. Carl Rogers criticized "the manipulative, interpretative, highly specialized expertise which appears to be more and more prominent in the training of group leaders" and "'exercises' which have become such a large bag of tricks for many group leaders" (Rogers, 1970, p. 157). The authoritarianism on the part of such leaders may mesh with a corresponding authoritarianism on the part of participants who not only suspend their own responsibility in the leader's favor but use what they take to be the rules as clubs with which to attack one another. "Group work offers infinite opportunities to slip into a well-disguised, smoothly rationalized authoritarianism," writes Thomas C. Greening, especially on the part of trainers and participants eager to pursue a predetermined goal of emotional intensity and sensual awakening (Greening, 1971, pp. 84f.).

Basic encounter groups seem to offer many people who are intellectually detached or in some other way cut off from their emotions the hope of getting back to what they "really feel." Actually, many such people are as cut off from the feelings of others as their own, and they are programmed to listen for cues and to put other people on pegs rather than really to hear them. They not only miss the feeling with which and out of which the other speaks; they miss the plain meaning of what one says, the standpoint from which one says it, and not infrequently the very words one utters. No wonder that in trying to cure this condition people not only turn *to* feelings but *away* from words. The danger of this emphasis on feeling *at the expense of thought* is that we may cease to struggle for the word and take it seriously. Few places are left for the person who cares about the *whole human being*, the person who brings oneself and wrestles with the word. What such a person says is all too often reduced by those who have jumped on the bandwagon of "Feeling = reality" to "Those are just words" or "You intellectuals always think in terms of labels." Those who do this, I have often observed, act as if *their* words are really feelings, whereas the words of those they are attacking are "merely words."

Our feelings are important, of course. We must go back to them and start there. But many people today seem to want to end there. When we have a deep and perhaps violent emotional breakthrough, it is a revelation of something hidden in the depths of our souls, something heretofore perhaps entirely unsuspected. This revelation can mislead us into seeing the emotions that are thus brought to light as the *only* reality and into depreciating what was accessible to the conscious mind before. An equal and corollary danger is to see the breakthrough as complete in itself, instead of seeing it as a little light lighting up a long, dark road up a mountain and down into a canyon—a road that you have to walk in your everyday life before this "breakthrough" can be made lasting and meaningful.

The concentration on feeling most often means the concentration on individual feeling, the feelings experienced within us and expressed to others. This dualism between "inner feeling" and outer "facade" raises serious questions about the claims that are made for the carryover of encounter group experiences into everyday life. In many encounter groups we are taken out of our world and are identified with feelings that we can express only outside of any situation that places a demand upon us as active persons working together with other persons.

The result of the location of feeling within is that experienced encounter-goers and even experienced encounter leaders often tend to see the expressions of others as mere "feedback" that will enable us to "get in touch with" our inner feeling. From this tendency it is only one short step to a solipsistic hell in which we imagine that feelings are only *in* ourselves and that the feelings of others concern us at most only as reflections or projections of our feeling. You may be my "anima," to use Jungian terminology, and I may be your "animus," but no direct contact can take place between us as real persons. It is true that we *can* feel things within that no one else can feel equally well, but we do so as persons whose thoughts and feelings are tied up in the most immediate fashion with other persons.

One of the virtues of the encounter group is that it has room for hostility and anger, as well as for "positive" emotions, and does not trap people into repressing the negative because they think they *ought* not feel it. Yet, even in the encounter group a hidden morality often exists that leads one to say to oneself, "I *ought* to feel gut-level hostility," or to say to someone else, "You can't be for real. You haven't expressed any anger or hostility." Even in the rare case in which a leader, like Carl Rogers, is willing to allow a participant to remain on the periphery, the group often will force the issue.

> As time goes on the group finds it unbearable that any member should live behind a mask or front. . . . The expression of self by some members of the group has made it very clear that a deeper and more basic encounter is *possible*, and the group appears to strive intuitively and unconsciously toward this goal. Gently at times, almost savagely at others, the group *demands* that the individual be himself, that his current feelings not be hidden, that he remove the mask of ordinary social intercourse. (Rogers, 1970, pp. 27f.)

How can one know that at this particular moment it is the right time for that person to get so involved? Maybe he or she is very sensibly protecting himself or herself against being murdered psychologically. He or she may have taken the true measure of this group and know intuitively, if not consciously, that it does not have the resources to confirm his or her otherness, whatever its rules, aspirations, and stated intentions. Although I would not assume with Bernard and Constance Apfelbaum that holdouts *always* "express the inevitable presence of *real* risk in a group," my own experience as a member of a family therapy team leads me to agree that the "holdout" may sometimes be the "identified patient" in the family therapy sense, that is, the one who is carrying the burden for the whole group and who, if helped sympathetically, also may help rescue the whole group. What the group member needs, first of all, is to trust, not the group, but himself. Only if the leader helps him see that his reactions to the group contain a grain of truth will he have a ground upon which to stand, a ground from which "self-disclosure would no longer be so risky." How can encounter leaders assume, they ask, "that if a group member is uninvolved and guarded, it is his problem and not the group's"? Does not this imply an unstated assumption that *"if you can learn to trust the group first, then it becomes trustworthy"*? If this assumption is held, then a strong pressure is upon the facilitator to urge members "to take the risk, whether it be in the name of mental health, moral commitment, the courage to be—or just not to let the rest of the group down" (Apfelbaum & Apfelbaum, 1973, pp. 61-65).

The temper of the particular group and the emphases of the facilitator inevitably affect our *attitudes toward* our own emotions so that what we express is not the raw emotion but the emotion shaped by our attitudes as members of *this* group. A particular social matrix exists for the feeling that makes it different from what it would be if we were alone or with a friend or a member of the family. What we feel about our wives or husbands, for example, is going to come out modified by the context of this group or by the leadership style of this facilitator. Our sense of the group's attitude in general and of the attitude of some or all of its members toward us in particular will affect the form, intensity, and even content of the feelings we express. This influence seldom is recognized. Instead, feelings, like potentialities, are treated as a substantive reality that is *in* us and needs only to be brought *out*. The distortion that this causes has been recognized by Sara Kiesler (1973) in her research on conformity and on emotion in groups. The group climate is otherwise often characterized by ambiguity and frustration, for even while a supportive climate is encouraged, "each member of the group wonders if he will be accepted if he acts as 'openly' as expected."

> There is social pressure to be supportive and loving; there is social pressure to give negative feedback and to disconfirm others' self-perceptions. There is pressure to be "real." At the same time, one

should experiment with new behaviors. Members try to grow and learn, but the leader fails to supply clear cues, goals or rewards. The very stirred-up state creates a need for cognitive explanation, but no one explanation is obvious. The person must look to the group for emotional labels, and . . . the emotional state will vary drastically according to the group situation. (Kiesler, 1973, p. 25)

Foremost among the factors that can prevent an encounter group from being real are the expectations that some participants bring with them of instant enlightenment, revelation, and joy. Such insistence upon outcome and result means, quite simply, the unwillingness to start from where the group is and by the same token the impossibility of finding a genuine direction of movement in the present.

We cannot avoid the route of feeling, yet expecting and demanding feeling can get in the way of true spontaneity, of our really being open and really meeting one another. It may lead, indeed, to that supreme contradiction in terms—"planned spontaneity." It takes the most sensitive listening to distinguish between those feelings that really grow out of the group's being together and those that arise as part of the effort to be "groupy." It takes a great deal of listening to allow what happens to come forth spontaneously—not inhibited by the self-images of the participants, which tell them in advance what their strengths and weaknesses are supposed to be, but *also* not inhibited by the group pressure to get down to the "true self" and to express the sort of emotions that the group holds to be "real." Putting the paradox another way, to deal directly with feelings is often to deal indirectly with them. Talking *about* feelings does not necessarily mean expressing them.

Rogers recognized this danger of hothouse spontaneity quite explicitly and linked with the "old-pro" phenomenon those veterans of previous encounter groups who "feel they have learned the 'rules of the game,' and subtly or openly try to impose these rules on newcomers."

> Thus, instead of promoting true expressiveness or spontaneity, they endeavor to substitute new rules for old—to make members feel guilty if they are not expressing feelings, or are reluctant to voice criticism or hostility, or are talking about situations outside the group

relationship, or are fearful to reveal themselves. These "old pros" seem to attempt to substitute a new tyranny in interpersonal relationships in the place of older conventional restrictions. To me this is a perversion of the true group process. We need to ask ourselves how this travesty of spontaneity comes about. (Rogers, 1970, p. 55)

What began as a chance to recover the freshness of being together with others without performance expectations and with the possibility of making mistakes is in danger of becoming an institution, William Coulson points out, "with new rules of procedure, recognized centers for doing it, gurus, formulas, known truths, hierarchies in charge, and credentials for being a practitioner. To be frank, encounter groups are now drowning in gimmickry" (Coulson, 1972, pp. 5, 56, 165).

We would like to live more intensely, more vitally, more fully. We would like to touch and contact others. We would like to share love and joy. Sometimes within encounter groups this is exactly what happens. But the more we *aim* at this goal, the more one part of us will be looking on from the sidelines, anticipating and measuring results, and for that very reason not living fully in the present. Our problem is that we are divided within ourselves, that we are not in genuine dialogue with one another, and that we live immersed in a deep existential mistrust. These sicknesses of our human condition cannot be overcome simply by the *will* to wholeness, openness, and trust, or by the magic of technique.

It makes no sense to talk of pure spontaneity, for structures are necessary and without them we would not have that margin within which spontaneity can arise. But an all-important difference exists between the structure that *makes possible* spontaneity and the structure that takes its place. Nothing is wrong with planning as long as we do not try to plan the spontaneity itself or, what amounts to the same thing, bring such strong expectations of specific results that one type of event is reinforced and another is played down or ignored. It seems to be our human fate that again and again the structure goes over from something that is life-promoting to something that gets in the way of life. Here we touch again upon the paradox that some of the very things that we try in order to reveal the hidden human image hide it still further. Rogers saw the encounter movement as "a growing counterforce to the dehumanization of our culture." Yet, as he himself recognized, it may, in fact, promote that dehumanization because of the tendency to turn structures that arise organically out of a unique group in a unique situation into omnicompetent techniques that may be carried over to any occasion. Sensitivity training is no substitute for sensitivity, openness, and responsiveness, and that always means to the unique, concrete situation in all its fullness and not just to what one is looking for. True sensitivity is wedded to the moment. Coulson, in this spirit, chides a fellow facilitator for suggesting a risk to two people rather than allowing it to be produced *between* them and quotes Buber's statement in *Between Man and Man* that "every living situation has, like a newborn child, a new face, that has never been before and will never come again. It demands of you a reaction that cannot be prepared beforehand. It demands nothing of what is past. It demands presence, responsibility; it demands you" (Coulson, 1972, pp. 18, 20).

By far the most forceful and eloquent statement of the paradox of the hidden human image as it has been manifested in many encounter groups is that of the psychologist and educator Sigmund Koch (1971). Koch attacks the debasing, schematizing, and vulgarization of language that the encounter movement has produced and still more "the reducing and simplifying impact upon the personalities and sensibilities of those who emerge from the group experience with an enthusiastic commitment to its values." Even more than behaviorism he sees the "entire, far-flung 'human potential' movement" as "a threat to human dignity," which obliterates the content and boundary of the self by transporting it into "public space." Self-exposure *functions* as a therapeutic absolute in the work of the movement, he claims, whatever the leaders consciously intend. The threads that Carl Rogers identifies in the encounter process are really "a kind of Pilgrim's Progress toward the stripping of self," such as cracking masks, positive closeness, here-and-now trust, and feedback. The uncritical approval of any kind of feedback, says Koch, makes "the chances for simpleminded, callow, insufficiently considered or reductive shaping" of the individual by the group high. Given the common factors of an adventitiously assembled face-to-face group, the encouragement by the leader of frank, direct, and uninhibited feedback, and the assumption that self-disclosure as facilitated by trust leads to the enhancement or realization of "human potential," these criticisms must apply, says Koch, not just to some but to *all* encounter approaches. Although not denying that some approaches or leaders are "less 'bad' than others," he sees the danger in all encounter groups of "simplistic lexicons" through which joking or wit is interpreted as evasiveness; sleepiness, boredom, or torpor as withdrawal; a raised voice as hostility; blocking as defense; and abstract statement as intellectualist concealment, or "mind-fucking" (Koch, 1971, pp. 112-116, 121, 123, 126f.).

In a reply to Koch, Gerard Haigh, past president of the Association for Humanistic Psychology, suggests that encounter groups do not necessarily violate the uniqueness of persons because they are not programmed to fit a predetermined model. Although Rogers and others predict what *may* happen in encounter groups, "the humanistic approach to leadership is not to make the group process happen as predicted but rather to let it happen as it will." Although group facilitators in training often try to make things happen as a way of assuaging their anxious uncertainty about their own effectiveness, and some "old hands" even employ techniques that have proved effective in the past, most leaders, Haigh holds, are nearer the "facilitating-awareness" pole of the continuum. They approach their task "in the spirit of discovery, trying to allow the participants to unfold in their own way, or not to unfold, if they wish. The beauty of encounter groups, approached in a spirit of discovery, is that they provide an endless opportunity to revise, expand, and deepen our image of man and our ways of growing toward it" (Haigh, 1971, pp. 129-132). Unfortunately, the paradox of our attempts to bring the hidden human image out of hiding cannot be resolved as simply as Haigh does, because he focuses upon the leader's intentions and aspirations rather than upon the climate of expectation. But neither can it be resolved by Koch's insistence that *all* encounter groups are necessarily self-defeating!

To what extent does the human potential movement represent what Martin Buber has called "the lust for overrunning reality"—a lust for instant life, instant joy, instant intimacy, instant relationship? It is salutary, in the midst of our heightened mobility, to realize that life has an organic tempo, that not all human realities can be poured into an atomic crucible and transmuted with the speed of light, that some suffering and sorrow and pain must be lived through for *its* duration and not at the "souped-up" speed that we willfully will.

Only an experienced facilitator and a group of people coming in touch with what is deeply genuine and meaningful in themselves and each other can break through the facade of "group games," "I-Thou jargon," and "peak experiences" to the real person inside, says Greening. Although the pressure to experience awareness undoubtedly exists, an effective group "will encourage deep and sustained confirmation of the authenticity of the awareness rather than hastily praise its semblance." It is "from one man to another that the heavenly bread of self being is passed," Greening quotes Buber. The challenge of the future, says Greening, will be "to create a world in which encounter will no longer have to be an encapsulated, specially arranged event." Too often in everyday life the gestures of self-disclosure and humanness go unnoticed or are rejected, as a result of which people develop a self-fulfilling prophecy that says existential risk-taking is useless. Greening recognizes that no guarantee is given that mutual confirmation will happen in encounter groups. The encounter group *can* be, as Greening himself concludes, a way toward the realization of what I call the community of otherness: "Few social inventions can equal encounter groups as a method for enabling people to learn from their differences and discover or create their unity" (Greening, 1971, pp. 101f.).

William Coulson also points to the community of otherness in his recognition that what matters is not so much whether words hit or miss the mark as whether the members of the group really care for one another. He also recognizes the all-important difference between providing an *occasion* for encounter groups and *structuring* the encounter itself. An encounter group goes better when the leader yields to the process and shares in its suffering, vulnerability, and surprise. What is primary and healing, according to Coulson, is not professional training but the relationship itself. Coulson makes an important distinction between the irresponsible release of possibilities that characterizes some groups and the proving of one's humanity through the responsible return to the people given in one's life situation. If the leader becomes involved in the suffering of the group activity, he or she is less likely to stimulate the group into being overwhelmed by new possibility and more willing to wait attentively and discover what he or she wants in gentle interaction with others. The facilitator helps others meet, not by arranging a cautious experience as opposed to an experimental one, but by providing an occasion for meeting, and *arranging* nothing at all. The foremost learning of an encounter group, states Coulson, is that one can call on people. Encounter is not *useful*. "It is at most a celebration of the mystery that lies between us."

The value of the special encounter group is "getting people relating again person-to-person rather than function-to-function." The humanizing need within institutional life is for occasions for genuine meeting; it is out of such meeting that real community will arise. Community means mutual teaching and learning, influencing and being influenced, letting others have a say and asking them to let you in, taking the time necessary to build up close, human, trusting relationships, helping each other to speak personally (Coulson, 1972, pp. 39, 41, 64, 66f., 76-79, 95, 152-154, 157-159, 171, 173f., 181).

I have myself again and again attempted to guide encounter groups in the direction of meeting through establishing a third type of structure, which I call a "basic encounter-discussion group." This structure makes spontaneity possible without taking its place. One of its purposes is to encourage a return to wholeness beyond the tragic split between thought and feeling that marks our culture. Even *this* holistic structure cannot be imposed. But it is a goal toward which one can move, refusing to accept the split as a permanent one or as a description of how things are.

Another aspect of the "basic encounter-discussion group," and potentially of any encounter group, is that it will help avoid the danger of looking at the interactions of the members of the group only in terms of the feelings they produce *within* each person and not as real events in themselves. The very notion of coming together in order that each might realize his or her *potential*—as if this were a fixed substance within one that needs only to be liberated by some catalytic agent—promotes this turning away from real response to events and persons toward a focus on the impact of the group happenings on the individual psyche. When this turning takes place, the true meaning of the "here and now"—the sphere of the between that transcends all individual feelings and psychic aftereffects—is screened out of awareness and often irreparably injured.

Even the term *group process* obscures the concrete reality of what has come to be in *this* group that will never again exist in any other. If we take our "potential" seriously, we shall discover that it is neither *in* us as something that we possess nor waiting to be pried out of us by one or another technique. It is what comes to be in the two-sided event, the grace that comes from both sides of the happening, from within and from without. Often, it is true that all that is present in an encounter interchange is mutual projection, which entirely obscures the unique person we are confronting in favor of some person or persons in our past. But we must not rule out a priori the possibility that many other things can take place. Perhaps two persons will break through to each other and then really oppose each other because each stands on a fundamentally different ground. This, too, is meaningful encounter and confrontation. But I have observed also that when an interchange that began in hostility and anger changed into one in which one of the parties sensed the sorrow of the other from within, the group leader cut it off in favor of expressions of anger and hostility on the part of others in the group.

We can and do experience the other side of the relationship—looking into each other's eyes, touching each other's face, involving ourselves deeply with another's suffering, pain, or anger. Even when two people cannot stand each other, they can glimpse for a moment what it is like to be the other person. This glimpse is fully as real a part of the feeling aspect of encounters as those self-referring feelings that we entertain within ourselves and tend to make our goal. I would claim, in fact, that the deepest feelings arise not when we are focusing on our own feelings but when we are really responding to someone else. Is it really worth our while discovering that we can feel and touch if we do not use our feeling and our touching for real contact at this moment? The very notion of touching means touching what is not yourself. If instead we focus on *having* experiences of touching or on *having* feelings, we cut off our contact with real otherness and isolate ourselves still more.

Without time spent in working out mutuality and "gradually gaining knowledge of each other, there can be only blind guesswork, a mechanical forcing of one person on the other, in which both will be diminished" (Coulson, 1972, p. 55).

We can grow in the strength to be there for another, really there, so that we are not at all concerned at that moment about whether we are realizing our selves or our potentiality. All great self-realization is a by-product of being really present in the situation in which we are involved. If we come to an encounter group with the concern, How may I grow through this? or, What can I get out of it? we will not grow at all. The concern will stand in the way of our really being spontaneously and unselfconsciously present for the other members of the group. Carried far enough, we will miss the trip entirely; for the present will be seen only as a means to the end, the future, and the group event will never seem real enough to call us out in our wholeness.

What is really called for is a faithful response to the situation, including the otherness of the people in it. Then, in really meeting these people, in really being present for one another, our "shadows" also come into play, and we begin to understand the reality of the interhuman more deeply than before. Such understanding includes a caring about the others for themselves, a caring that is sometimes strong enough to bridge the gap between one lonely person and another. If, in contrast, we look at the others merely as sources of "feedback," then we regard each person's words, gestures, and actions as useful bits of information about ourselves without any genuine response to them seeming called for. Thus, the emphasis upon realizing our possibilities may profane the situation by turning it into a function of a self-becoming, which is not true self-becoming because it does not grow out of faithful listening and response to the call that comes at every moment. Our resources for responding come into being as we are called out by the depth of our caring about someone or something not ourselves. "By never being an end in himself, he endlessly becomes himself" (Lao-Tzu).

4

Carl Rogers and Martin Buber: Self-Actualization and Dialogue

Healing Through Meeting

In a discussion of Ludwig Binswanger's "The Case of Ellen West," which he entitles "The Loneliness of Contemporary Man," Carl Rogers (1980, pp. 164-180) points to Martin Buber's "healing through meeting" as the center of therapy. Ellen West was written up at great length by Ludwig Binswanger, only Binswanger never treated her; he just gave a phenomenological description of her case. The greatest weakness of Ellen West's treatment, in Rogers's opinion, is that no one involved in it seems to have related to her as a *person* whose inner experience is a precious resource to be drawn upon and trusted. She was dealt with as an object and was helped to *see* her feelings but not to *experience* them. She herself recognized that the doctor could give her discernment but not healing. She uttered a desperate cry for a relationship between two persons, but no one heard her.

"She never experienced what Buber has called healing through meeting," writes Rogers. "There was no one who could meet her, accept her as she was." Rogers draws from the case of Ellen

West the lesson that whenever or however the therapist makes an object of the person—"whether by diagnosing him, analyzing him, or perceiving him impersonally in a case history, he stands in the way of his therapeutic goal." The therapist is deeply helpful only when he relates as a person, risks himself as a person in the relationship, experiences the other as a person in his or her own right. "Only then is there a meeting of a depth which dissolves the pain of aloneness in both client and therapist" (Rogers in Friedman, 1991, pp. 484-485).

In *Client-Centered Therapy* (1951), Rogers states that the role of the counselor in "nondirective" therapy is not, as is often thought, a merely passive laissez-faire policy, but rather an active acceptance of the client as a person of worth for whom the counselor has real respect. Client-centered therapy stresses above all the counselor's assuming the internal frame of reference of the client and perceiving both the world and the client through the client's own eyes. It is important in the process of the person's becoming that the person experience understanding and acceptance by the therapist—an active experiencing with the client of the feelings to which expression is given, a trying to get *within* and to live the attitudes expressed instead of observing them. This implies, at the same time, a certain distance and absence of emotional involvement—an experiencing of the feelings from the side of the client without an emotional identification that would cause the counselor to experience these feelings as his or her own. Finally, it implies a laying aside of the preoccupation with professional analysis, diagnosis, and evaluation in favor of an acceptance and understanding of the client, based upon true attitudes of respect that are felt deeply and genuinely by the therapist (Rogers, 1951, pp. 20-45, 55). Rogers is willing to extend this respect and trust even to a patient in danger of committing suicide or one who has been institutionalized.

> To enter deeply with this man into his confused struggle for selfhood is perhaps the best implementation we now know for indicating the meaning of our basic hypothesis that the individual represents a process which is deeply worthy of respect, both as he is and with regard to his potentialities. (Rogers, 1951, p. 45)

A corollary of client-centered therapy is the recognition that good interpersonal relationships depend upon the understanding and acceptance of the other as a separate person who is "operating in terms of his own meanings, based on his own perceptual field" (Rogers, 1951, p. 521). Rogers sees the recognition of the separateness of others as made possible through a relationship in which the person is confirmed in his or her own being. A person comes to accept others through self-acceptance, and this, in turn, takes place through the acceptance of the child by the parent or of the client by the therapist. The real essence of therapy, correspondingly, is not so much the client's memory of the past, explorations of problems, or admissions of experiences into awareness as it is the client's direct experiencing in the therapy relationship.

> The process of therapy is, by these hypotheses, seen as being synonymous with the experiential relationship between client and therapist. Therapy consists of experiencing the self in a wide range of ways in an emotionally meaningful relationship with the therapist. (Rogers, 1951, p. 172)

As early as 1952 Rogers defined the person as a fluid process and potential in rather sharp contrast to the relatively fixed, measurable, diagnosable, predictable concept of the person that is accepted by psychologists and other social scientists, to judge by their writing and working operations. The person as process is most deeply revealed, Rogers wrote, in a relationship of the most ultimate and complete acceptance, a relationship Rogers described, in Martin Buber's terms, as a real I-Thou relationship, not an I-It relationship. The person moves in a positive direction toward unique goals that the person can but dimly define (Rogers, 1961).

In his book *On Becoming a Person*, Rogers (1961) tells how he changed his approach to therapy from the intellectual question of how he could treat the patient to the recognition that changes come about through *experience* in a *relationship*. He found that the more genuine he was in a relationship, the more aware he was of his own feelings, the more willing he was to express his own feelings and attitudes, the more he gave the relationship a *reality* the person could use for his or her own personal growth. He also found that the more he could respect and like the client, showing a warm regard for the client as a person of unconditional self-worth while accepting each fluctuating aspect of the other, the more he was creating a relationship the client could use. This acceptance necessarily includes a continuing desire to understand the other's feelings and thoughts, which leave the other really free to explore all the hidden nooks and frightening crannies of his or her inner and often buried experience. This includes, as well, complete freedom from any type of moral or diagnostic evaluation.

As a therapist, Rogers (1961) writes,

> I enter the relationship not as a scientist, not as a physician who can accurately diagnose and cure, but as a person entering into a personal relationship. Insofar as I see him only as an object, the client will tend to become only an object. I risk myself, because if, as the relationship deepens, what develops is a failure, a regression, a repudiation of me and the relationship by the client, then I . . . will lose . . . a part of myself. (pp. 201-202)

The therapist conducts the therapy without conscious plan and responds to the other person with his or her whole being, that is, total "organismic sensitivity."

> When there is this complete unity, singleness, fullness of experiencing in the relationship, then it acquires the "out-of-this-world" quality which therapists have remarked upon, a sort of trance-like feeling in the relationship from which both the client and I emerge at the end of the hour, as if from a deep well or tunnel. In these moments there is, to borrow Buber's phrase, a real "I-Thou" relationship, a timeless living in the experience which is *between* the client and me. It is at the opposite pole from seeing the client, or myself, as an object. It is the height of personal subjectivity. (Rogers, 1961, p. 202)

Through the therapist's willingness to risk and his or her confidence in the client, the therapist makes it easier for the client to take the plunge into the stream of experiencing. This process of becoming opens up a new way of living in which the client feels "more unique and hence more alone," but at the same time the client is able to enter into relations with others that are deeper and more satisfying and that "draw more of the realness of the other person into the relationship" (Rogers, 1961, p. 203).

In 1967 Rogers placed an even stronger emphasis upon the centrality of healing through meeting than in any of his earlier writings, claiming that it is the "existential encounter which is important, and that in the immediate moment of the therapeutic relationship consciousness of theory has no helpful place" (Rogers, 1967b, p. 189). Healing through meeting occurs when the meeting between therapist and client is the central, as opposed to the ancillary, aspect of the therapy. Practically every therapist sees the relationship as having some importance as structure, or support, but only when the relationship is the *central* factor in the healing is it properly called "healing through meeting." From this definition we can see how strong a place Rogers occupies in healing through meeting.

Thinking about theory during the relationship itself, as opposed to afterward, is detrimental to the therapy because it leads the therapist to be more of a spectator than a player, writes Rogers, who believes that theory "should be held tentatively, lightly, flexibly, in a way which is freely open to change, and should be laid aside in the moment of encounter itself" (Rogers, 1967b, p. 190).

In 1967 Rogers published a brief statement that can serve well as a summation of his own view on healing through meeting.

> I find that when I am able to let myself be congruent and genuine, it often helps the other person. When the other person is transparently real and congruent, it often helps me. In those rare moments when a deep realness in one meets a deep realness in the other, it is a memorable I-Thou relationship, as Buber would call it. Such a deep and mutual personal encounter is experienced by me as very growth-enhancing. A person who is loved appreciatively, not possessively, blooms and develops his own unique self. The person who loves non-possessively is himself enriched. (Rogers, 1967c, pp. 18-19)

Self-Actualization and Dialogue

For Rogers, healing through meeting works both ways. Meeting is seen sometimes as an end in itself and sometimes only as the means to the end of personal becoming and self-actualization. This ambiguity comes through particularly clearly in Rogers's most recent book, *A Way of Being* (1980), in which he puts forward two different and in some ways incompatible touchstones of reality—self-actualization and the I-Thou relationship. In one place Rogers writes of the actualizing tendency as the fundamental answer to the question of what makes an organism tick. In another he writes:

> In those rare moments when a deep realness in one meets a deep realness in the other, a memorable I-Thou relationship, as Martin Buber would call it, occurs. Such a deep and mutual encounter does not happen often, but I am convinced that unless it happens occasionally we are not living as human beings. (Rogers, 1980, p. 9)

Although they reside comfortably together in Rogers's thought, these two touchstones of reality are not really compatible. *Either* the I-Thou relationship is seen as a function of self-actualization, and the real otherness of the Thou is lost sight of in the emphasis on the development of the organism, *or* the I-Thou relationship is seen as a reality and value in itself, in which case self-realization becomes a by-product and not a goal and, what is more, a by-product that is produced not through a pseudobiological development, but rather through the meeting with what is really other than the self.

The Buber-Rogers Dialogue

The issues that arose in the dialogue between Martin Buber and Carl Rogers that I moderated at the University of Michigan in 1957 are subtle ones. Rogers began with a description of his own approach to therapy and ventured that it was, as he himself had often written, an I-Thou relationship.

I feel that when I am being effective as a therapist I enter the relationship as a subjective person, not as a scrutinizer and not as a scientist. I feel too that when I am most effective that somehow I am relatively whole in that relationship. To be sure, there may be many aspects of my life that are not brought into the relationship, but what is brought into the relationship is transparent. There is nothing hidden. When I think too that in such a relationship I feel a real willingness for the other person to be what he is, I call that acceptance. I don't know that that's a very good word for it, but my meaning there is that I am willing for him to possess the feelings he possesses, to hold the attitudes he holds, to be the person he is. But then another aspect of it that is important to me when I think of those moments when I am able to sense with a good deal of clarity the way his experience seems to him. Really viewing it from within him, yet without losing my own personhood or sacrificing in that. And then, if in addition to those things, on my part, my client or the person with whom I am working is able to sense something of those attitudes in me, then it seems there is a real experiential meeting of persons in which each of us is changed. I think sometimes the client is changed more than I am, but I think both of us are changed in that kind of experience. (Rogers in Buber, 1988c, pp. 159-160)

It is not surprising that Buber characterized what Rogers had said as a very good example for a certain moment of dialogic existence. Present here are all the elements that Buber himself emphasizes: meeting the other as a partner and not an object, experiencing the client's side of the relationship without losing one's own, bringing oneself as a whole person, accepting the other as the person he or she is in their otherness. It is important to note that in this description Rogers does not claim total mutuality. Rogers as therapist sees the client from within, whereas the client's inclusion is limited to something of the therapist's attitude toward the client. It does not touch upon the therapist as a person with problems of his or her own.

At first glance it appears as if Rogers is talking about total mutuality. He never is. He never suggested that the client is concerned with Carl Rogers's problem, however much the client may help Rogers. Buber stressed that in this situation, which therapist and client have in common, the person comes to the therapist for help and insisted that this makes an essential difference in the role of therapist and client.

He comes for help to you, you don't come for help to him. And not only this, you are *able*, more or less, to help him. He can do different things to you, but not help you. You see him, just as you said, as he is. He cannot, by far, cannot *see* you. Not only in the degree but even in the kind of seeing. You are, of course, a very important person for him. But not a person whom he wants to see, and to know, and is able to. He is floundering around, and comes to you. He is, if I may say, entangled in your life, in your thoughts, in your being, your communication and so on. But he is not interested in you as you. It cannot be. You are interested in him as this person, this kind of detached presence he cannot have and give. (Buber, 1988c, p. 161)

In Buber's philosophical anthropology are two movements: distancing and relating. Buber is saying that this person, because of his or her problems, has lost that capacity for distancing that enables one to appreciate the other from where he or she is. This does not mean that it is difficult for a therapist and client to have an I-Thou relationship. I-Thou is mistakenly thought of as total mutuality. It is mutual in friendship and love, but certain relationships still are I-Thou yet have what Buber calls the "normative limitation of mutuality." The therapy relationship is one of them. Putting it another way, you have mutuality of contact, mutuality of trust, and from my own experience I would add a third, mutuality of the sense that you have a common problem. Every problem brought in is part of the whole communal reality. It may be focused in you, but you and I are both concerned with this at the moment. That is another sort of mutuality. But mutuality in the sense of inclusion, of experiencing the other side, cannot be demanded.

Years ago I sent Erich Fromm a copy of an article on Buber and psychotherapy entitled "Healing Through Meeting." When I saw him some time later, Fromm said, "I like that title very much; in fact, my patients heal *me*." I'm sure that every therapist is in some way healed by his or her clients, and every good teacher is to some extent taught by his or her students. But you do not set it as a goal, you do not make that a demand and say, "This has been a bad session because you have not healed Dr. Fromm, or taught Dr. Friedman." That is what I see as the difference. It is still an I-Thou relationship, not an I-It. It is an I-It only when the other becomes just an object that you know and use and manipulate. The relation between parent and child is I-Thou even though parent and child are not fully mutual and fully equal. When the child grows up to really experience the other side of the relationship, he or she is no longer a child.

Buber went on to say that, in the therapy situation, Rogers was able to observe and know and help the client from both his own side and that of the client. The therapist can experience bodily the client's side of the situation, feel touched by the client, whereas the situation itself makes it impossible for the client to experience the therapist's side of the relationship. "You are not equals and cannot be. You have the great . . . self-imposed task to supplement this need of his and do rather more than in the normal situation. I see you mean being on the same plane, but you cannot. These are the sometimes tragic limitations of simple humanity" (Buber, 1988c, p. 172). Rogers agreed that if the client could really experience fully the therapist's side of the situation, the therapy would be about over, but he also insisted that the client's "way of looking at his experience, distorted though it might be, is something I can look upon as having equal authority, equal validity with the way I feel life and experience it. It seems to me that really is the basis of helping" (Buber, 1988c, p. 162).

What Rogers said here is the essence of what I call the "dialogue of touchstones" (Friedman, 1985, chap. 18). But that does not change the fact that the situation is not equal, however much Rogers feels the equality. "Neither you nor he look on *your* experience," Buber said to Rogers. "The subject is exclusively him and his experience." In response, Rogers suggested that what Buber said applies to the situation looked at from the outside; this has nothing to do with the actual therapy relationship that is "something immediate, equal, a meeting of two persons on an equal basis even though in the world of I-It it could be seen as a very unequal relationship." Buber replied that effective human dialogue must be concerned with limits and that these limits transcend Rogers's method, especially in the case of the schizophrenic and the paranoid.

I can talk to the schizophrenic, as far as he is willing to let me into his particular world that is his own. But in the moment when he shuts himself, I cannot go on. And the same, only in a terrible, terrifyingly strong manner, is the case with the paranoiac. He does not open himself, he does not shut himself, he *is* shut. And I feel this terrible fate very strongly. Because in the world of normal men there are just analogous cases. When a sane man behaves not to everyone but behaves to some people just so, being shut. And the problem is if he could be open, if he could open himself, this is a problem for the human in general. (Buber, 1988c, pp. 165f.)

In my own role as moderator of this dialogue between Buber and Rogers, I suggested that the real difference was that Buber stressed the client's inability to experience Rogers's side of the relationship, whereas Rogers stressed the meeting, the change that takes place in the meeting, and his own feeling that the client is an equal person whom he respects. Rogers replied that in the most real moments of therapy the desire to help is only a substratum. Although he would not say that the relationship is reciprocal in the sense that the client wants to understand and help him, he did assert that when real change takes place it is reciprocal in the sense that the therapist sees this individual as he or she is in that moment, and the client really senses this understanding and acceptance. To this Buber replied that Rogers gives the client something in order to make him equal for that moment. This is a situation of minutes, not of an hour, and these minutes are made possible by Rogers, who out of a certain fullness gives the client what the client wants in order to be able to be, just for this moment, on the same plane with the client.

Acceptance and Confirmation

Rogers uses Buber's phrase "confirming the other," accepting the person not as something fixed and finished, but as a process of becoming. Through this acceptance, Rogers says, "I am doing what I can to confirm or make real his potentialities." If, on the contrary, writes Rogers, one sees the relationship as only an opportunity to reinforce certain types of words or opinions in the other, as Verplanck, Lindsley, and Skinner do in their therapy of operant conditioning, then one confirms him or her as a basically mechanical, manipulatable object and then tends to act in ways that support this hypothesis. Only a relationship that "reinforces" *all* that one is, "the person that he is with all his existent potentialities" Rogers concludes, is one that, to use Buber's terms, *confirms* him "as a living person, capable of creative inner development" (Rogers, 1961, pp. 55-56).

Rogers, however, tended to equate acceptance and confirmation, while Buber said no, I have to distinguish between the two. I begin with acceptance, but then sometimes to confirm this person I have to wrestle with, against, and for him or her. Although one part of you has direction, the other part of you is an aimless whirl. I have to help you in taking a direction rather just remaining with the aimless whirl.

In the course of his 1957 seminars at the Washington School of Psychiatry, Martin Buber threw out some hints concerning confirmation in therapy and its relation to healing through meeting. The therapist's openness and willingness to receive whatever comes is necessary in order that the patient may trust existentially, Buber said. A certain very important kind of healing—existential healing—takes place through meeting rather than through insight and analysis. This healing is not just of a certain part of the patient, but also of the very roots of the patient's being. The existential trust of one whole person in another has a particular representation in the domain of healing. So long as it is not there, the patient will not be able to disclose to the therapist what is repressed. Without such trust, even masters of method cannot effect existential healing.

The existential trust between therapist and patient that makes the relationship a healing one in the fullest sense of that term implies confirmation, but of a very special sort. Everything is changed in real meeting. Confirmation may be misunderstood as *static*. I meet another—I accept and confirm the other as he or she now is. But confirming a person *as he or she is*, is only the first step. Confirmation does not mean that I take the person's appearance at this moment as representative of the person I want to confirm. I must take the other person in his or her dynamic existence and specific potentiality. In the present lies hidden what can *become*.

This potentiality, this sense of the person's unique direction, can make itself felt to me within our relationship, and it is *that* I most want to confirm, said Buber. In therapy, this personal direction becomes perceptible to the therapist in a very special way. In a person's worst illness, the highest potentiality of this person may be manifesting itself in negative form. The therapist can influence directly the development of those potentialities. Healing does not mean bringing up the old, but rather shaping the new: It is not confirming the negative, but rather counterbalancing with the positive (Buber, 1990, pp. 169-173; Friedman, 1988, pp. 28-29).

Buber's insistence that confirmation is not static, but rather is a confirmation of the potentialities hidden in the worst illness of the patient, touches upon the issue that arose in the dialogue between Buber and Rogers concerning the difference between *accepting* and *confirming*. True acceptance, Rogers holds, means acceptance of this person's potentialities, as well as what the person is at the moment. If we were not able to recognize the person's potentiality, Rogers says, it is a real question whether we could accept him or her. If I am accepted exactly as I am, he adds, I cannot help but change. When the need for defensive barriers no longer exists, the forward-moving processes of life take over. Rogers holds that we tend to be split between our "should" part in the mind and a feeling part in the stomach. We do not accept ourselves, so if the therapist accepts us, we can somehow overcome that split. If we overcome it, we will become the person we are meant to be. In his stress on an unqualified acceptance of the person being helped, Rogers says that if the therapist is willing for the other person to *be what he is*—to possess the feelings he possesses, to hold the attitudes he holds—it will help him realize what is deepest in the individual, that is, the very aspect that can most be trusted to be constructive or to tend toward socialization or toward the development of better interpersonal relationships. Human nature, for Rogers, is something that can be trusted because the motivation toward the positive or constructive already exists in the individual and will come forward if we can release what is most basic in the individual. What is deepest in the individual can be released and trusted to unfold in socially constructive ways (Rogers in Buber, 1988c, pp. 169-170).

Buber replied that he was not so sure about that, for what Rogers saw as most to be trusted, Buber saw as least to be trusted. This does not mean that Buber saw man as evil while Rogers saw man as good, but that Buber saw man as polar. It is precisely Rogers's assumption that the processes of life will always be forward-moving that Buber (1988c) questions:

> What you say may be trusted, I would say this stands in polar relation to what can be least trusted in this man. . . . When I grasp him more broadly and more deeply than before, I see his whole polarity and then I see how the worst in him and the best in him are dependent on one another, attached to one another. (pp. 170-171)

This doctrine of polarity leads inevitably to Buber's distinction between acceptance and confirmation, for confirmation means wrestling with the other against his or her self in order to strengthen the one pole and diminish the power of the other:

> I may be able to help him just by helping him to change the relation between the poles. Not just by choice, but by a certain strength that he gives to the one pole in relation to the other. The poles being qualitatively very alike to one another. There is not as we generally think in the soul of a man good and evil opposed. There is again and again in different manners a polarity, and the poles are not good and evil, but rather yes and no, rather acceptance and refusal. And we can strengthen, or we can help him strengthen, the one positive pole. And perhaps we can even strengthen the force of direction in him because this polarity is very often directionless. It is a chaotic state. We could bring a cosmic note into it. We can help put order, put a shape into this. Because I think the good, what we may call the good, is always only direction. Not a substance. (Buber, 1988c, pp. 170-171)

Rogers speaks of acceptance as a warm regard for the other and a respect for the other as a person of unconditional worth, and that means an acceptance of and regard for a person's attitudes of the moment, no matter how much they may contradict other attitudes he or she has held in the past. In response to my (as moderator) question whether he would not distinguish confirmation from acceptance of this sort, Buber said:

> Every true existential relationship between two persons begins with acceptance. . . . I take you just as you. . . . But it is not yet what I mean by confirming the other. Because accepting, this is just accepting how he is in this moment, in this actuality of his. Confirming means first of all, accepting the whole potentiality of the other and even making a decisive difference in his potentiality, and of course we can be mistaken again and again in this, but it's just a chance between human beings. . . . And now I not only accept the other as he is, but I confirm him, in myself, and then in him in relation to this potentiality that is meant by him and it can now be developed, it can evolve, it can answer the reality of life. . . . Let's take, for example, a man and a woman, man and wife. He says, not expressly, but just by his whole relation to her, "I accept you as you are." But this does *not* mean, "I don't want you to change." Rather it says, "Just by my accepting love, I discover in you what you are meant to become." . . . it may be that it grows and grows with the years of common life. (Buber, 1988c, pp. 171-172)

Rogers, in his reply, recognizes that we could not accept the individual as is because often he or she is in pretty sad shape, if it were not for the fact that we also in some sense realize and recognize the individual's potentiality. But he went on to stress the acceptance that makes for the realization of potentiality: "Acceptance of the most complete sort, acceptance of this person as he is, is the strongest factor making for change that I know" (Rogers in Buber, 1988c, pp. 172-173). To this, Buber (1988c) replied:

> There are cases when I must help him against himself. He wants my help against himself. . . . The first thing of all is that he trusts me. . . . What he wants is a being not only whom he can trust as a man trusts another, but a being that gives him now the certitude that "there *is* a soil, there *is* an existence. . . . The world *can* be redeemed. I can be redeemed because there is this trust." And if this is reached, now I can help this man even in his struggle against himself. And this I can do only if I distinguish between accepting and confirming. (pp. 172-173)

Rogers says, in effect, "I will come to you and I will be concerned about you, I'll have unconditional positive regard for you, I'll have empathic understanding of you, but I can do so only if I do it authentically as the person I am." That is what Rogers calls congruence. But confirmation, as distinct from congruence, has to do with the other person. People do not just naturally develop so that all I have to do is accept them—in this I agree with Buber. They are in a struggle themselves about their own direction. Although I cannot impose upon them what their direction should be, I can help them in their struggle.

I do not confirm you by being a blank slate or blank check. I can confirm you only by being the person I am. You never will be confirmed by my simply putting myself aside and being nothing but a mirror reflecting you. Confirming the other may mean that I do not confirm him in some things, precisely because he is not taking a direction. It is not just that he is wrestling with himself; I am wrestling with him. An added factor here is not what one calls being empathic. It is not just that I am watching him wrestle with himself, but I also am entering into the wrestling. It means I wrestle with you, not just that I provide a ground for your wrestling, even though I may not impose myself on you, and say "I know better than you." It is only insofar as you share with me and we struggle together that I glimpse the person you are called to become (Friedman, 1983, chap. 6 and 7).

Empathy and Inclusion

Rogers's "deep empathic understanding," which enables him to see his clients' private world through their eyes, is close to Buber's "experiencing the other side," or "inclusion." Rogers states that "when I hold in myself the kind of attitudes I have described, and when the other person can to some degree experience these attitudes, then I believe that change and constructive personal development will *invariably* occur" (1961, p. 35). This faith in the latent potentialities that will become actual "in a suitable psychological climate," seems to expect of "healing through meeting" an effectiveness that goes beyond the concrete situation with its often tragic limitations. If the parent creates such a psychological climate, "the child will become more self-directing, socialized, and mature," says Rogers (1961, p. 37). Through relationship, the other individual will experience and understand the repressed aspects of himself, will become better integrated and more effective in functioning, closer to the person he would like to be, "more of a person, more unique and more self-expressive," and "will be able to cope with the problems of life more adequately and more comfortably" (Rogers, 1961, p. 38).

Empathy, in the strict sense of the term, means to feel oneself in the client by giving up the ground of one's own concreteness. One experiences the other side of the relationship through an imaginative aesthetic leap. In making this leap, one ceases for the time being to experience one's own side. One brackets or suspends one's awareness of oneself, as it were, in order to understand the other better. Carl Rogers's earlier uses of empathic understanding often suggest this with their emphases upon client- or person-centered therapy, upon the becoming of the client, upon acceptance of the client by the therapist, and upon unconditional positive regard. Empathy was never, to be sure, an aesthetic category for Rogers, but it seemed to be one in which one tended to lose sight of oneself and one's own side of the relationship.

In contrast with empathy, *inclusion* means a bold, imaginative swinging "with the intensest stirring of one's being" (Buber, 1988c, p. 71) into the life of the other so that one can to some extent concretely imagine what the other person is thinking, willing, and feeling, so that one adds something of one's own will to what is thus apprehended. It means grasping the other in his or her uniqueness and concreteness. A person finds himself or herself as person through going out to meet the other, by responding to the address of the other. One does not lose one's center, one's personal core, in an amorphous meeting with the other. If one sees through the eyes of the other, experiences the other side, one does not cease to experience the relationship from one's own side. We do not experience the other through empathy or analogy. We do not know another's anger because of our anger; the other might be angry in an entirely different way from us. But we can glimpse something of the other's side of the relationship because real persons do not remain shut in themselves or use their relations with others merely as a means to their own self-realization. Inclusion or "imagining the real" does not mean at any point that one gives up the ground of one's own concreteness, ceases to see through one's own eyes, or loses one's own touchstone of reality. In this respect it is the complete opposite of empathy in the narrower and stricter sense of the term.

It is striking that in his later formulations of empathic understanding Rogers stressed this very point. Rogers said to Buber, in describing his own therapy, "I am able to sense with a good deal of clarity the way his experience seems to him, really viewing it from within him, yet without losing my own personhood or separateness in that" (Rogers in Buber, 1988c, p. 160). In his later essays Rogers stresses accurately seeing into the client's world *as if* it were his own without ever losing that "as if" quality. This too is very close to Buber's definition of inclusion as the bipolar experiencing of the other side of the relationship without leaving one's own ground. The therapist runs the risk of being changed by the client but never loses his or her own separateness or identity in the process. Rogers's placing of congruence before both empathic understanding and unconditional positive regard in these later essays also represents a swing in this direction.

Carl Rogers's more recent statements on empathy belie our attempts to point to a clear chronological progression. In his 1980 essay "Empathic: An Unappreciated Way of Being," Rogers quotes his own 1959 definition of *empathy* as sensing the other's inner feelings as if they were one's own without losing sight of the "as if" and falling into identification. In this same essay, however, he updates his view on empathy in a way that sometimes resembles inclusion and sometimes empathy in a narrower sense.

An empathic way of being with another person means entering the private perceptual world of the other and becoming thoroughly at home in it, as well as being sensitive moment by moment to the changing felt meanings that flow in this other person—his fear or rage or tenderness or confusion or whatever he or she is experiencing. It means temporarily living the other's life, moving about in it delicately without making judgments. (Rogers, 1980, pp. 142-143)

Entering the private, perceptual world of the other and temporarily living in the other's life suggest empathy in the narrower sense of losing one's own ground, whereas communicating one's sensings of the person's world with fresh and unfrightened eyes and checking the accuracy of one's sensing suggest inclusion.

Those who are used to using "empathy" in the customary way may well ask what practical difference is made by the fine distinctions between empathy in the stricter sense and inclusion. A first answer would be that empathy (in the narrower sense) is a very limited means of understanding, within therapy and outside of it; it relies on only one side of the relationship. A second, deeper answer is that empathy, in the strict sense, cannot really confirm another person, because true confirmation means precisely that *I* confirm *you* in your uniqueness and that I do it from the ground of my uniqueness as a real other person. Only inclusion, or imagining the real, can confirm another; for only it really grasps the other in his or her otherness and brings that other into relationship with oneself.

Charles Brice (1984) provides us with an excellent summary of the difference between empathy and inclusion. Speaking of the psychoanalytic literature on empathy, he writes:

The patient as the other that he or she is, does not appear in these accounts. The analyst: (a) incorporates an image of the patient, in which case the patient's experience becomes the analyst's own and the exclusivity of the patient's experience is lost; (b) fuses with his image of the patient and theoretically disappears, making a true meeting with the patient impossible; or (c) searches his "repertoire" of emotional experiences for one similar to that of the patient's, thus empathizing with himself, not with the patient. To paraphrase Friedman (1967, p. 200), in order to empathize with my patient, the patient must become a function of myself or I must become a function of my patient. (Brice, 1984, p. 120)

Of inclusion, in contrast, Brice writes:

> When the patient's experience corresponds to the therapist's current
> or past experience, inclusion becomes an imperative. The therapist
> must "make present" the patient's experience in order to separate that
> which belongs to the patient from the idiosyncratic and exclusive
> character of the therapist's analogous circumstances. Unless these
> experiences are kept separate, real interhuman life will become im-
> possible, and the patient will be "reduced" to a stimulus for "em-
> pathic" incorporation, fusion, or projective identification. The
> uniqueness of the two positions must be preserved if an authentic
> "coming together" is to be achieved. (Brice, 1984, p. 120)

Congruence and Unconditional Positive Regard

The three chapters that Rogers (1967a) contributed to *Person
to Person*, chapters he wrote in 1962 and 1963, have in common
the assertion that the traits in the therapist that most facilitate
effective therapy are congruence, unconditional positive regard, and empathic understanding. Of these three, the most indispensable, says Rogers, with an emphasis that was relatively
late in his thinking, is *congruence*:

> Personal growth is facilitated when the counselor is what he *is*, when
> in the relationship with his client he is genuine and without "front"
> or facade, openly being the feelings and attitudes which at that
> moment are flowing in him. . . . It means that he comes into a direct
> personal encounter with his client, meeting him on a person-to-
> person basis. It means that he is *being* himself, not denying himself.
> (Rogers, 1967a, p. 90)

For Rogers, even when the therapist is annoyed with, bored
by, or dislikes his or her client, it is preferable for the therapist
to be real than to assume a facade of interest and concern and
liking that is not felt. What the therapist can do is recognize
that it is his or her feelings of being bored that are being expressed and not the supposed fact that the client is a boring
person. When the therapist expresses this feeling, which has
been a barrier between the therapist and the client, the client

will express himself or herself more genuinely in turn because the therapist has dared to be a real, imperfect person in the relationship. Although the qualities of unconditional positive regard and empathic understanding may be easier to achieve, it is better for the therapist to be what he or she is than to pretend to possess these qualities (Rogers, 1967a, pp. 90-92).

The client will pick up what the therapist actually feels and will experience dissonance between how the therapist appears and the way the therapist wants to appear. One of the questions often raised concerning Rogers's approach to psychotherapy is how his emphasis upon congruence in the therapist is to be reconciled with the importance he places upon unconditional positive regard. This latter emphasis is an older one in Rogers's thought, and means a warm, positive, and accepting attitude toward the client. The therapist meets the client in a totally nonpossessive way, rather than placing conditions upon his or her acceptance, thereby making constructive change more likely to occur. One possible answer to this question is that the therapist cares what the client is as a person and not just what the client does. Another is that, if the two principles conflict, then the therapist must be genuine (congruent) but need not turn his or her feelings toward the client into a judgment of the client.

In his essay "Learning To Be Free," Rogers (1967a) makes unconditional positive regard the second essential condition of good therapy. In "The Interpersonal Relationship" (Rogers, 1967a), he places it third after empathic understanding, as he calls it in the earlier essay. Rogers's stress upon seeing accurately the client's private world *as if* it were the therapist's own, without ever losing that *as if* quality, is very close, as we have seen, to Buber's definition of *inclusion* as the bipolar experiencing of the other side of the relationship without leaving one's own ground. In marked contrast with his earlier statement about "complete unity," Rogers (1967a) writes: "When the counselor can grasp the moment-to-moment experience occurring in the inner world of the client as the client sees and feels it, *without losing the separateness of his own identity* in this empathic process, then change is likely to occur" (p. 6) At the same time, Rogers warns that when therapists are truly open to the way life is experienced by their clients—making the clients' world their own and seeing life as they do—then therapists run the risk of being changed themselves. But therapists also must succeed in communicating the fact that they have or are trying to have empathic understanding of their clients if meaningful change is to occur (Rogers, 1967a, pp. 92-93).

In his discussion of empathy, Rogers adds a caution that was largely absent from his earlier work and that serves as a corrective to his assertions that change is *bound* to occur:

> I have learned, especially in working with more disturbed persons, that empathy can be perceived as lack of involvement; that an unconditional regard on my part can be perceived as indifference; that warmth can be perceived as a threatening closeness, that real feelings of mine can be perceived as false. (Rogers, 1967a, p. 96)

Rogers would *like* to behave so that what he is experiencing in relation to the client would be perceived unambiguously by the client. But Rogers recognizes that this is complex, and hard to achieve. In the case of a severely disturbed person, even this would seem to be an understatement! Yet, at the end of "The Interpersonal Relationship" Rogers (1967a) asserts that congruence, empathy, and unconditional positive regard "will have a high probability of being an effective, growth-promoting relationship" not only for maladjusted individuals who come on their own initiative seeking help, but also for "chronically schizophrenic persons with no conscious desire for help" (p. 101).

Rogers concludes by expressing his great personal satisfaction "that we have been able to help withdrawn, bizarre, hopeless individuals become human beings" (1967b, p. 191) and to Rogers this means persons, whether they are labeled schizophrenics or not:

> Behind the curtains of silence, and hallucination, and strange talk and hostility and indifference, there is in each case a person . . . if we are skillful and fortunate we can *reach* that person, and can live, often for brief moments only, in a direct person-to-person relationship with

him. To me that fact seems to say something about the nature of schizophrenia. It says something too about the nature of man and his craving for and fear of a deep human relationship. (Rogers, 1967b, pp. 191-192)

Here is no suggestion of full mutuality between therapist and client. Also, here is a realism about the fact that the person-to-person meeting is often a matter of moments only. This realism is very close to Buber's position in his dialogue with Rogers ten years earlier.

Conclusion

Rogers's emphases upon the I-Thou relationship in therapy, healing through meeting, acceptance, empathy, unconditional positive regard, and congruence are not only compatible with Buber's philosophy of dialogue but could be strengthened, clarified, and made more consistent by being seen within that framework—recognizing the origin of the person in a person-to-person relationship and recognizing that persons become themselves and reach self-actualization not by aiming directly at these goals but as a by-product of dialogue.

PART THREE

Dialogue

5

Therapists of Dialogue:
Straus, Goldstein, Boss, Binswanger, Jourard, the Polsters, Laing, von Weizsäcker, May, Bugental, and Yalom

In human life together, it is the fact that we set the other at a distance and make the other independent that enables us to enter into relation, as an individual self, with those like ourselves. Through this "interhuman" relation we confirm each other, becoming a self with the other. The inmost growth of the self is not induced by one's relation to oneself but by the confirmation in which one person knows himself or herself to be "made present" in his or her uniqueness by the other. Self-realization and self-actualization are not the *goal* but the *by-product*. The goal is completing distance by relation, and *relation* here means "cooperation, genuine dialogue, and mutual confirmation."

We have in common with everything the ability to become an object of observation, writes Buber in *The Knowledge of Man* (1988c), but it is the privilege of the human being, through the hidden action of our being, to be able to impose an insurmountable limit to our objectification. Only as a partner can a person be perceived as an existing wholeness. To become aware of a person means to perceive his or her wholeness as person defined by spirit: to perceive the dynamic center that stamps on all his or her utterances, actions, and attitudes the recognizable sign of uniqueness. Such an awareness is impossible if, and so long as, the other is, for me, the detached object of my observation; for he or she will not thus yield his or her wholeness and its center. It is possible only when the person becomes present for me.

Psychotherapists often give others technical aid without entering into relationship with them. Help without mutuality is presumptuousness, writes Buber; it is an attempt to practice magic. "As soon as the helper is touched by the desire, in however subtle a form, to dominate or enjoy his patient, or to treat the latter's wish to be dominated or enjoyed by him as other than a wrong condition needing to be cured, the danger of falsification arises, beside which all quackery appears peripheral" (Buber, 1985, p. 95).

For the therapists the distinction between arbitrary and true will rests upon a quite real and concrete experiencing of the client's side of the relationship. Only if they discover the "otherness" of clients will therapists discover their own real limits and what is needed to help the persons with whom they are working. They must see the position of the other in his or her concrete actuality yet not lose sight of their own. Only this discovery will remove the danger that their will to heal will degenerate into arbitrariness.

Arbitrariness is a form of decisionlessness, of failure to make a decision with one's whole person. Decisionlessness makes a person divided and unfree, conditioned and acted upon. It is failure to direct one's inner power. Decision, in contrast, means transforming one's passion so that it enters with its whole power into the single deed. It is not a psychological event that takes place within the person but the turning of the whole being through which one enters once again into dialogue. Such decision means the transformation of the urges, of the "alien thoughts," of fantasy. We must not reject the abundance of this fantasy but transform it in our imaginative faculty and turn it into actuality. "We must convert the element that seeks to take possession of us into the substance of real life" (Friedman,

1976b, p. 134). The contradictions that distress us exist only that we may discover their intrinsic significance. There can be no wholeness "where down-trodden appetites lurk in the corners" or where the soul's highest forces watch the action, "pressed back and powerless, but shining in the protest of the spirit."

True decision can be made only with the whole being, and it is decision in turn that brings the person to wholeness. Yet, this wholeness is never a goal in itself but only the indispensable base for going out to meet the Thou. Decision is made *with* the whole being, but it takes place *in* dialogue. The person who decides continually leaves the world of It for the world of dialogue in which I and Thou freely confront each other in mutual effect, unconnected with causality. It is in dialogue, therefore, that true decision takes place. Decision within dialogue is a corollary of personal unification, for it means giving direction to one's passion.

This approach to will and decision is like psychoanalytic "sublimation" in that it makes creative use of basic energies rather than suppressing them. But it differs from sublimation, as conceived by Freud, in that this channeling of the urges takes place as a by-product of the I-Thou relationship rather than as an essentially individual event in which individuals use their relationship with other beings for their own self-realization. Freud's sublimation takes place *within* the person, Buber's direction *between* person and person. In therapy itself, to Buber, it is will and decision within dialogue that is decisive. Therapy should not proceed from the investigation of individual psychological complications but from the whole person, for it is only the understanding of wholeness as wholeness that can lead to the real transformation and healing of the person and of one's relations with one's fellow humans. No phenomenon of the soul is to be placed in the center of observation as if all the rest were derived from it. Persons ought not be treated as objects of investigation and encouraged to see themselves as "It"s. They should be summoned to set themselves to rights, to bring their inner being to unity so that they may respond to the address of being that faces them.

In their dialogue with others and in their life with the community, it is possible for persons to divert fear, anger, love, and sexual desires from the casual to the essential by responding to what comes to meet them, to what they become aware of as addressing them and demanding from them an answer.

In order to be responsible, it is essential that we make use of that "disciplined fantasy" that enables us to experience the other person's side of the relationship. Only through a quite concrete imagining of what the other is thinking, feeling, and willing can I make the other present to myself in his or her wholeness, unity, and uniqueness.

Buber distinguishes the "interhuman" from the "social" in general and from the "interpersonal." The "social" includes the I-It relation, as well as the I-Thou: Many interpersonal relations really are characterized by one person's treating the other as an object to be known and used. Most interpersonal relations are a mixture of I-Thou and I-It, and some are almost purely I-It. Buber calls the unfolding of the sphere of the between the "dialogical." The psychological, that which happens within the soul of each, is only the secret accompaniment to the dialogue. This distinction between the dialogical and the psychological constitutes a radical attack upon the psychologism of our age that tends to remove the events that happen between persons into feelings or occurrences within the psyche. It also makes manifest and fundamental ambiguity of those modern psychologists, like Carl Rogers and Erich Fromm, who affirm the dialogue between person and person but who are unclear about whether this dialogue is of value in itself or is merely a function of the individual's self-realization. By pointing to dialogue as the intrinsic value and self-realization as only the corollary and by-product, Buber also separates himself from those existential analysts and psychotherapists like Ludwig Binswanger and Rollo May who tend to make the I-Thou relationship just another dimension of the self, along with one's relation to oneself and to one's environment.

Dialogue, or the I-Thou relationship of openness and mutuality between person and person, is not to be confused with interpersonal relations in general. Dialogue includes a reality of over-againstness and separateness quite foreign to Sullivan's definition of the self as entirely interpersonal. Moreover, neither Sullivan nor Mead makes any basic, clear distinction between indirect interpersonal relations in which people know and use each other as subject and object—the I-It relation in Buber's terms—and direct, really mutual interpersonal relations in which the relationship itself is of value and not just a means to some individual satisfaction or goal. This latter relationship Buber calls "the interhuman." In interhuman relationships, the partners are neither two nor one. Rather, they stand in an inter-action in which each becomes more deeply his or her self as he or she moves more fully to respond to the other.

Dialogue should also not be confused with the internalized relations of Object Relations Psychology and Self Psychology, even though they have many striking points of convergence (see Friedman, 1985, chap. 6). The term *object-relations* "begins to date," confessed Harry Guntrip, who stood in direct line with Winnicott and Fairbairn as one of the chief object-relations psychologists, because it has as yet no adequate way of under-standing the mutual relationship between two persons:

> Object-relations theory . . . [provides] an important view of what happens to the individual psyche under the impact of personal relations in real life. But the theory has not yet properly conceptual-ized Buber's I-Thou relation, two persons being both ego and object to each other at the same time, and in such a way that their reality as persons becomes, as it develops in the relationship, what neither of them would have become apart from the relationship. This is what happens in good marriages and friendships. (Guntrip, 1969, p. 389)

This distinction is made even clearer by Charles Brice in his excellent article on Buber's existential relations theory and object-relations theory:

> In self-object relations, I appropriate others not in their otherness but in conformance with my desire of how I wish them to be. Typically, such appropriations are neurotically driven; hence the others are seen as I *must* see them. (Brice, 1984, pp. 111f.)
>
> Psychoanalytic theory . . . allows little room for a description of what goes on "between man and man," little room for the reality of the other. As long as the theory can account for human relation-ships only in terms of the image of the self placed in the other or

the image of the other placed in the self, it cannot grasp an entire sphere of human reality—the interhuman. (Brice, 1984, pp. 119f.)

In this chapter I wish to present what I consider to be the *quintessential* contributions of a number of therapeutic writers to the understanding of dialogical psychotherapy, or healing through meeting,[4] leaving to the next chapter a fuller discussion of Leslie Farber, Hans Trüb, and Richard Hycner, the three therapists who come closest to developing a truly dialogical psychotherapy.

Erwin Straus and Kurt Goldstein

In his central theoretical work, *The Primary World of Senses*, Straus (1963) goes beyond any merely descriptive phenomenology of temporality and spatiality to an anthropological grounding of the whole world of senses, time, and place in a primary movement and a primary distancing. Both the Here and the Now are particular delimitations of the totality of my self-world relation. "In the Now, I experience my self-world relation and my self as that which becomes" (Straus, 1963, p. 250). Distancing arises out of this becoming, out of reaching and desiring. The articulation of distances depends upon my Here and Now, and direction depends upon distance. The unity of time and space "would not be possible without openness into the future," and this implies both sensing and moving. Distance is the spatiotemporal form of sensing, "the form of a process of becoming which is open to the future and which itself is not yet fully determined." Psychosis, by the same token, is a deformity of distance and movement. It may take the form of the passivity of depersonalized individuals whose hallucinations are the result of the world pressing in on them and of all sympathetic communication being suspended or of the groundlessness of those who have no firm stance, no hold on themselves that enables them to limit themselves, as over against their world. Depressed persons are alienated both in time and space. "Frozen in unmoving time," they look at the world as if from above, unable to enter relation with it.

The combination of primal distancing and primal relation that is central to Martin Buber's philosophical anthropology is present also in Straus's "The Primary World of Senses" (1963), as well as in Viktor von Weizsäcker's untranslated *Der Gestaltkreis* ("The Unity of Perception and Movement") (Friedman, 1991, p. 404f.), both of which thinkers Buber refers to in "Distance and Relation" (*The Knowledge of Man* [Buber, 1988c]). Individual sensations of touch and vision do not produce communication, Straus points out. "Because I *am* in communication, a particular given here and now can determine me." To exist is to exist in the world but also opposite it, directed toward it, and meeting it in its counterdirection. Every sensing subject has a Here that is of equal dignity with the There and that enables it to move toward the There in communication with the *other*.

> Community, mutual understanding, and communication and connections between living beings founded on the relations of the together-with and towards-each-other, which do not eliminate the monadic autonomy of the partners, their duality or plurality.... Community demands distance which continues even during the most perfect forms of togetherness, of nearness, of the "we." ... The encompassing *other* which becomes visible to us in seeing, makes possible the communion between us; it mediates between Me and You.... All communication, lingual included, is based in the being-with-another of mobility, of meeting and fleeing in a common surrounding world.... In primal and basic communication I am not a knower and the other is not the object of my knowledge. He is not a thing singled out from a neutral background as an object of special interest. I discover the other, my fellow man or fellow creature, as a partner in my waking motor intentions, as a being which can come near me or withdraw from me. (Strauss, 1963, pp. 178-289)

The distinguished neuropsychiatrist Kurt Goldstein, although emphasizing the unity of togetherness rather than the distance, makes a statement similar to that of Straus in his discussion of "the sphere of immediacy," which represents the deepest character of the world, as opposed to the subject-object world in which "we experience only isolated parts of ourselves and the world." By surrendering ourselves to the world with which we come in contact, we achieve the immediacy that "makes unity possible between the world and ourselves, particularly in our relationship to other human beings." These experiences of immediacy disturb the stability of the ordered world, particularly when our expectations of a response are disappointed. "Our well-being and possibilities for self-realization are endangered, our very existence and that of the world," for they all are based upon the sphere of immediacy. Although order is necessary for the attainment of knowledge, "the impulse to *seek* for knowledge originated fundamentally in the sphere of immediacy."

> Through it, human life acquires its dynamic character. In this sphere is not only the source of all creativity, the development of friendship, love and religion, but also those possibilities for failure, sorrow and anxiety which are part of our life. While being in the sphere of immediacy may involve danger, we deliberately take this risk, since only thus can we realize ourselves fully. (Goldstein, 1963, pp. xiif.)

Medard Boss

The fact that the world is one's world does not stand in the way of one's existing with others and of one becoming immediately aware of them as what they are, writes the German existential analyst Medard Boss. It is the essence of existence to be with others, and my world is necessarily one that I share with others.

> We never exist primarily as different subjects who only secondarily enter into interpersonal relations with one another and exchange ideas about the objects all of us perceive. Instead, as any direct observation shows, we are all out there in the world together, primarily and from the beginning, with the same things shining forth in the common light of all our existences. (Boss, 1963, pp. 55f.)

The implication of this approach to psychiatry is that "no psychopathological symptom will ever be fully and adequately understood unless it is conceived of as a disturbance in the texture of the social relationships of which a given human existence fundamentally consists" (Boss, 1963, p. 56).

Respecting everything as a direct conveyor of meaning, the Daseinsanalyst "has no need to destroy what he actually sees and hears from the analysand and to replace it with assumed forces supposedly underlying the patient's behavior and perception." The analyst "will not try to persuade patients that much of what they feel and mean is only a cloak for opposite wishes and tendencies," thus avoiding giving the impression of devaluating their experiences (Boss, 1963, pp. 234f.). The Daseinsanalyst must relate to others on the level where they are, and that means in most cases on the level of adults who have remained small children at the very core of their existence and who must be met on that same childlike level (Boss, 1963, p. 242).

Ludwig Binswanger

The Swiss existential analyst Ludwig Binswanger describes meeting, or the I-Thou relationship, as a dual mode of love and friendship, in contrast with Heidegger's authentic existence for oneself. Binswanger speaks of the dual role as "we-ness" and as "communal love." It is the lack of the *communio* of love and the *communicatio* of friendship, says Binswanger, that leads to *extravagance*—that basic element of schizophrenia that sets up an impossible ideal and progressively narrows the ground of its own existence in relation to this ideal. Only where mere intercourse and traffic with "others" and with one's self has taken over the exclusive direction of one's existence, "only there can height and depth, nearness and distance, present and future, have so much importance that human existence can go *too far*, can attain to an *end* and a *now* from which there is neither retreat nor progress." "Detached from loving *communio* and authentic *communicatio*, all too far and hastily *driven forward* and *carried upward*, the manic hovers in fraudulent heights in which he cannot take a stand or make a 'self-sufficient' decision" (Binswanger, 1963, pp. 166, 169f., 212-214, 218-220, 284-286, 288, 290-292, 294f., 300, 343-349).

Like Buber, Binswanger sees the self as coming to be in the I-Thou relationship. "It is out of the undivided fullness of being of the Each-Other that I and Thou first emerge to attain their 'selfhood' *in* each other" (Binswanger in Friedman, 1991, p. 419). When people *take* the other *at* the other's weak point or at the other's word, this is a fall from the being-together of meeting into the mere being-with of the self-sufficient ego. Psychology, in our time, proceeds from this absolutized individual ego and its powers, dispositions, events, processes, activities, tendencies, functions, or acts. In contrast with such purely objectifying psychology, based upon the isolated ego, Binswanger sees existential knowledge as having its authentic ground and basis in the loving being-together of I and Thou.

In opposition to those who see the meeting of I and Thou as a means to the end of self-realization, Binswanger recognizes a genuine We of relationship that is more than the sum of two separate psychic or personal entities. He sets this dual selfhood of love in explicit opposition to the disclosure of the world as *mine* that Heidegger posits, and Boss accepts, as the true way of authenticating the self. "Only if Dasein already has the character of meeting, only when 'I and Thou' are already part of its ontological structure, is love between Me and You at all possible." "Here self-hood issues only from the We." Taking-part, participation, does not bring the I-Thou relationship; it is rather the relationship that is the ground of taking-part. Like Buber, Binswanger sees this mutual participation not as a "one-sided" act of "empathy," putting oneself in the other's place, or of fellow-feeling, but as "a 'two-sided' receiving and giving based on a 'mutual' readiness for what the future has to offer" (Binswanger in Friedman, 1991, pp. 416-420).[5]

Sidney Jourard

Sidney Jourard was influenced both by Carl Rogers and by Martin Buber and found no conflict between the two in his own approach to mutuality. Jourard (1968, 1971) places Buber's I-Thou relationship, or "dialogue," at the center of therapy, which implied to him that he must share himself as he is with his patient: "I can come closest to eliciting and reinforcing authentic behavior in my patient by manifesting it myself." Jourard counsels the therapist to hear out his patient but at the same time to maintain his separate identity. The therapist's spontaneity and honesty invite those of the patient: "Self-disclosure begets self-disclosure." The heart of the I-Thou relationship, to Jourard, is abandoning all attempts to shape his patient's behavior according to some predetermined scheme. Therapy is not a setting in which the therapist *does* things to a patient, but rather "an honest relationship gradually developing into one of I and Thou; a dialogue, in which growth of both parties is an outcome." Jourard agrees with Rogers that good listening reinforces further self-disclosure by the patient, but he also testifies that over the years he has come more and more to supplement such listening by "giving advice, lecturing, laughing, becoming angry, interpreting, telling my fantasies, asking questions—in short, doing whatever occurs to me *during* the therapeutic session in response to the other person" (Jourard, 1971, pp. 141-151). As the therapist grows in the capacity for dialogue, he becomes more wholehearted in his "invitation to terrified, self-concealing people to disclose themselves as they are." Jourard not only makes the I-Thou relationship the center of healing but also sees it as the *sine qua non* for any good interpersonal relationship between therapist and patient, "where the influencer is as vulnerable and open as the one to be influenced." "No technique will work when I and thou are not thus open" (Jourard, 1968, pp. 23, 61-65).

Erving and Miriam Polster

According to the Gestalt therapists Erving and Miriam Polster, in the moment of meeting a between comes into existence that is more than the sum of me and thee. They recognize the danger of engulfment: "In contacting you, I wager my independent existence," but they also recognize the necessity of taking this risk: "Only through the contact function can the realization of our identities fully develop." If I am experienced in full contact, then I can meet you "full-eyed, full bodied, and full-minded" and retain the sense of separateness at the boundary without the threat of overwhelming or being overwhelmed (Polster & Polster, 1974, pp. 98f., 102f.).

Contact may lead to dialogue, but is not in itself dialogue. Some part of contact, as the Polsters use it, touched upon that mutuality within the ebb and flow of distancing and relating that characterize dialogue at its most authentic. But precisely because we so desperately lack and need contact, the initial movement toward it is likely to be more an affair of the individual than of the interhuman, more I-It than I-Thou. Yet, if this movement expresses itself in a genuine openness and reaching toward the other and meets with a response, it may flower into that mutual contact that stands at the heart of dialogue (Hycner, 1985).

Ronald Laing

"The science of persons is the study of human beings that begins from a relationship with the other person and proceeds to an account of the other still as person," writes the British psychiatrist R. D. Laing (1969, p. 21). Laing postulates as fundamental that separateness and relatedness are mutually necessary. "Personal relatedness can exist only between beings who are separate but not isolate" (Laing, 1969, p. 26). Both our relatedness to others and our separateness are essential aspects of our *being*. Psychotherapy, accordingly, is an activity in which the patient's relatedness to others is used for therapeutic ends. Since relatedness potentially is present in everyone, the therapist "may not be wasting his time in sitting for hours with a silent catatonic who gives every evidence that he does not recognize his existence" (Laing, 1969, p. 26). *Inclusion*, in Buber's sense of the term, is an absolute and obvious prerequisite in working with psychotics. One can have a thorough knowledge of ego defects, disorders of thought, and hereditary incidence of manic-depressive psychosis without being able to understand one single schizophrenic. In fact, such data are all ways of *not* understanding the person, for seeing the "signs" of schizophrenia as a "disease" and looking and listening to a person simply as a human being are radically different and incompatible ways of knowing. If we do the latter, however, we must have the plasticity to transpose ourselves into another strange and even alien view of the world without forgoing our own sanity. Only thus can we arrive at an understanding of the patient's existential position (Laing, 1969, pp. 33f). None of this means that we see the schizophrenic as really just the same as ourselves. "We have to recognize all the time his distinctiveness and differentness, his separateness and loneliness and despair" (Laing, 1969, p. 38).

In order that one may be related as one human being to another, Laing points out, a firm sense of one's own autonomous identity is required. But this sense is just what the schizophrenic lacks. Any and every relationship threatens the schizophrenic with the loss of identity, or engulfment. The schizophrenic substitutes for the polarities of separateness and relatedness of the autonomous individual "the antithesis between complete loss of being by absorption into another person (engulfment) and complete aloneness (isolation)." The schizophrenic does not have the option of a third alternative—a dialogical relationship between two persons each sure of his or her own ground and for this very reason able to "lose himself" in the other (Laing, 1969, p. 44).

Viktor von Weizsäcker

Twenty years before R. D. Laing, the German psychiatrist Viktor von Weizsäcker also applied this dialogical approach to psychotics. What makes us mistrustful of many psychotics, he wrote, is that their self-deification and self-degradation lack all moderation. The cause of this overvaluation of the self is the isolation of the psychotic, the fact that he has no Thou for his I. The result of the absence of a Thou is an inner double. This illusion of the double is unavoidable after a man has lost his connection with a Thou, von Weizsäcker wrote, for the state of aloneness that he has reached then is unbearable. "The cleavage of the I represents—for a moment—the relationship of the

I to the Thou which has become unattainable" (Weizsäcker, 1991, pp. 407, 409).

Rollo May

The distinguished American psychologist Rollo May suggests that the way out of the dilemma of isolation and loneliness is directing and channeling that daimonic energy, which, undirected, acts as an *impersonal* force driving us toward blind assertion in rage or sex. Consciousness can integrate the daimonic, make it personal, and this is the purpose of psychotherapy. But psychotherapy cannot accomplish this integration without the support of community. "The community gives a humanly trustworthy, interpersonal world in which one can struggle against the negative forces." Only within such a community of support can we identify with the negative that haunts us, not in order to fight it off, but rather to take this previously rejected element in us into ourselves (May, 1969, pp. 126, 133).

When the daimonic is admitted in the course of therapy through the expression of anger, animosity, and even hatred for a spouse, the result is often a totally surprising feeling of love toward this partner. Correspondingly, when aggression toward a partner is suppressed, love also is suppressed. "To be able to experience and live out capacities for tender love requires the confronting of the daimonic." "The most important criterion which saves the daimonic from anarchy is *dialogue*," writes May.

> For dialogue implies that man exists in relationship. The fact that dialogue is possible at all—that it is possible, in favorable circumstances, for us to understand each other, stand where the other is standing—is, in itself, a remarkable point. Communication presupposes community, which, in turn, means a communion between the consciousness of the persons in the community. This is a meaningful interchange which is . . . a built-in aspect of the structure of human intercourse. (May, 1969, pp. 155f.)

Intentionality is central to May's approach to healing through meeting, for "intentionality is based upon a meaning-matrix which patient and therapist share" (May, 1969, pp. 266f). For this sharing to be therapeutically helpful, the therapist must practice that imagining of the real side of the other without losing his or her own that Buber calls inclusion:

> I must be able to participate in my patient's meanings but preserve my own meaning-matrix at the same time, and thus unavoidably, and rightfully, interpret for him what he is doing—and often doing to me. The same thing holds true in all other human relationships as well: friendship and love require that we participate in the meaning-matrix of the other but without surrendering our own. This is the only way human consciousness understands, grows, changes, becomes clarified and meaningful. (May, 1969, p. 262)

James Bugental and Irvin Yalom

Although James F. T. Bugental (1976) subtitles his *Search for Existential Identity* "Patient-Therapist Dialogues in Humanistic Psychology," Bugental's emphasis is not at all dialogical, focusing wholly upon subjectivity and awareness of one's own being. It was only subsequently that the dialogue between therapist and client entered Bugental's awareness as a central element of therapy (Hycner, 1989, 1991). It is in his discussion of presence and intimacy in *The Art of the Psychotherapist* (Bugental, 1987) that Bugental reaches what properly may be termed dialogical psychotherapy. "Psychotherapy which does not involve intervals of genuine intimacy may be helpful," Bugental writes, "but will never lead to the depth of confrontation necessary for major life change" (Bugental, 1987, p. 43). A mutuality of intimacy exists but one that does not take the same form, because the therapist is less verbally open yet allows his or her human responsiveness to be played upon by the client's experiencing and often allows that impact to be evident to the client.

> In such engagements, I have wept, laughed, felt deep dread, experienced exaltation, ached with knowledge of loneliness and despair,

grown tense with anger or sexual excitement, and fallen silent in appreciation of my client's courage and latent wisdom. (Bugental, 1987, p. 43)

At his keynote speech at the First Annual Conference of the Institute of Dialogical Psychotherapy in San Diego in 1985, Bugental called *presence* "the one essential ingredient of therapy." Bugental emphasizes that presence is not the same as rapport: It is an existential involvement of the whole being of the therapist that cannot be turned on through any technique. Bugental freely admits that his "view is in marked contrast to the traditional notion of the therapist as a skilled but objective director of therapeutic processes" and comments, "The fear of involvement that such doctrines convey makes one wonder what motivated their exponents to undertake careers in a field whose core is relationship" (Bugental, 1987, pp. 47, 49).

The therapist's own presence is needed continually to develop an effective therapeutic alliance . . . the powerful joining of forces which energizes and supports the long, difficult, and frequently painful work of life-changing psychotherapy. The conception of the therapist here is . . . of a fully alive human companion for the client. (Bugental, 1987, p. 49)

In the prologue to his book *Love's Executioner: And Other Tales of Psychotherapy* (Yalom, 1989), Irvin Yalom carries over from his earlier book *Existential Psychotherapy* (Yalom, 1980) the four "givens" that "are particularly relevant to psychotherapy: the inevitability of death for each of us and for those we love; the freedom to make our lives as we will; our ultimate aloneness; and, finally, the absence of any obvious meaning or sense to life." Yalom sees in these givens "the seeds of wisdom and redemption" and hopes "to demonstrate, in these ten tales of psychotherapy, that it is possible to confront the truths of existence and harness their power in the service of personal change and growth" (Yalom, 1989, pp. 4f.). In my opinion he does much more, and that places him squarely among the ranks of therapists of dialogue.

That Yalom is not unaware of the central place of healing through meeting in his approach to psychotherapy is shown by his own statement in the prologue:

> The powerful temptation to achieve certainty through embracing an ideological school and a tight therapeutic system is treacherous: Such belief may block the uncertain and spontaneous encounter necessary for effective therapy.
>
> This encounter, the very heart of psychotherapy, is a caring, deeply human meeting between two people, one (generally, but not always, the patient) more troubled than the other. Therapists have a dual role: they must both observe and participate in the lives of their patients. As observer, one must be sufficiently objective to provide necessary rudimentary guidance to the patient. As participant, one enters into the life of the patient and is affected and sometimes changed by the encounter.
>
> In choosing to enter fully into each patient's life, I, the therapist, not only am exposed to the same existential issues as are my patients but must be prepared to examine them by the same rules of inquiry. (Yalom, 1989, p. 13)

This dialogical emphasis is carried forward both in the tales and in his comments on them. In the title tale Yalom stresses again that the more the therapist is able to tolerate the anxiety of not knowing, the less need for the therapist to embrace orthodoxy. In this story of a 70-year-old woman in love with her former therapist, Yalom recognizes that his best chance to help his patient is not to focus upon the *content* of their discourse (e.g., the flight from freedom and the isolation of separateness) but "in the development of a meaningful relationship with her." "I hoped that the establishment of an intimate bond with me might sufficiently attenuate her bond with Matthew so that she could pry herself loose from him" (Yalom, 1989, p. 41). This is just what Yalom does.

The most impressively dialogical of all the tales of therapy is "If Rape Were Legal"—the one that Yalom presented when he was keynote speaker at the annual conference of our Institute for Dialogical Psychotherapy in 1989 before *Love's Executioner* was published. In this tale Yalom makes himself present to a man who would have discouraged any lesser therapist both by his totally antisocial behavior and his condition as a terminal cancer patient. Yet, when Yalom visits him in the hospital when he is dying and is so weak he can barely move, he raises his head, squeezes Yalom's hand, and whispers, "Thank you. Thank you for saving my life" (Yalom, 1989, p. 86). What is stunning about this expression of gratitude is how different it is from our ordinary conception of saving someone's life—prolonging their biological existence. In marked contrast, this man, who knows he is dying, thanks Yalom for making his life meaningful through the meeting that has occurred between them!

The tale of the "Fat Lady" is almost equally impressive because in it Yalom accepts the challenge of working with a person whose overweight body is so repugnant to him that for the first months he can barely bear to look at her. In the midst of his painful struggle to help her, he confesses that his "professional rosary," which he often says to his students, is, "It's the relationship that heals" (Yalom, 1989, p. 91).

In the tale entitled "Two Smiles" Yalom joins other therapists of dialogue in stressing the centrality of the wholeness and uniqueness of the person whom he treats and the inadequacy of all attempts at diagnosis:

> Others, and among them I include myself, marvel that anyone can take diagnosis seriously, that is can ever be considered more than a simple cluster of symptoms and behavioral traits. Nonetheless, we find ourselves under ever-increasing pressure (from hospitals, insurance companies, governmental agencies) to sum up a person with a diagnostic phrase and a numerical category.
>
> Even the most liberal system of psychiatric nomenclature does violence to the being of another. If we relate to people believing that we can categorize them, we will neither identify nor nurture the parts, the vital parts, of the other that transcend category. The enabling relationship always assumes that the other is never fully knowable. (Yalom, 1989, p. 185)

Yalom twice makes specific use of Buber's terminology, even if the second time he seems to do so grudgingly (as if Buber were not really up to Yalom's own standard of aesthetic writing!):

The overactive therapist often infantilizes the patient: He does not, in Martin Buber's term, guide or help the other to "unfold" but instead imposes himself upon the other (Yalom, 1989, p. 197).

It seemed to me that the important consideration was my relationship with my patient—the betweenness (one of Buber's endless store of awkward phrases) of Marge and me. Unless I could protect and remain faithful to that relationship, any hope of therapy was lost. It was necessary to modify my basic rule, "Treat the patient as an equal," to "Be faithful to the patient." (Yalom, 1989, p. 224)

In this same tale of Marge ("Therapeutic Monogamy"), Yalom sums up with all possible force the centrality of healing through meeting in his actual approach to psychotherapy:

The drama of age regression and incest recapitulation (or, for that matter, any therapeutic cathartic or intellectual project) is healing only because it provides therapist and patient with some interesting shared activity while the real therapeutic force—the relationship—is ripening on the tree. (Yalom, 1989, p. 227)

6

Dialogical Psychotherapists:
Leslie H. Farber, Hans Trüb, Richard Hycner

Leslie H. Farber

The American psychoanalyst Leslie Farber distinguishes between a first and a second realm of the will, both of which are necessary in themselves and in their interdependence. The first realm of will moves in a direction rather than toward a particular object. Farber sees will of the first realm as unconscious in Buber's sense of the wholeness of the person underlying the split into physical and psychic. It exists in the hope of I-Thou, and I-Thou increasingly requires this first realm of will for its realization. Will stands in reciprocity with relation through life, but when will tries to do the work of relation or relation that of will, both will and relation are infringed. Memory and imagination within the first realm of will share in that realm's dialogical potentiality. "In fact, even in solitude these capacities seem to move in the direction of another human being." Will of the second realm moves consciously toward a specific, utilitarian object. Our day-to-day existence could not be got through without this will, and our burgeoning technology owes everything to it. Farber stresses the interdependence of the two realms of will, even as Buber stresses the necessary dialectical alternation of I-Thou and I-It. The first without the second would result in a mysticism that betrays the appropriate objectifications the will is capable of; the second without the first would result in a rationalism that betrays the realities of the wholeness that makes existence possible (Farber, 1976, pp. 4-6).

As I-It becomes evil only when it seeks to dominate exclusively and prevents the ever-new transmuting of It into Thou, so Farber's will of the second realm becomes "willfulness" only at the point where it seeks to do the work of the will of the first realm. We fall into willfulness, says Farber, when we succumb to the recurring temptation to apply the will of the second realm to those portions of life that not only will not comply, but also will become distorted under such coercion:

> I can will knowledge, but not wisdom; going to bed, but not sleeping; eating, but not hunger; meekness, but not humility; scrupulosity, but not virtue; self-assertion or bravado, but not courage; lust, but not love; commiseration, but not sympathy; congratulations, but not admiration; religiosity, but not faith; reading, but not understanding. (Farber, 1966, p. 15)

In willfulness, the will tries to do the work of the imagination. This applies to the therapist, as well as the client. The therapist, because he knows that genuine listening is essential to true therapy, may try, in vain, to make himself listen. But listening is the work of the will of the first realm and becomes willfulness when it is taken over by the will of the second:

> In "Martin Buber and Psychoanalysis," I have suggested that listening requires something more than remaining mute while looking attentive—namely, it requires the ability to attend imaginatively to another's language. Actually, in listening we speak the other's words. It is not merely that listening does not respond to the constraints we impose, but that it withers as human possibility under will's dominion, as all of us realize who have tried to force our attention to an event, while our inclination struggled to look elsewhere. (Farber, 1976, p. 7)

As Farber develops his contrast between genuine will and arbitrary willfulness, the former emerges as an expression of real dialogue, the latter as a hysterical produce of the absence of dialogue. In contrast with Freud, who sees hysteria as a product of repression, which can be cured by bringing the repressed material to consciousness, Farber defines hysteria as a disorder of the will that expresses itself in willfulness. "In willfulness the life of the will becomes distended, overweening, and obtrusive at the same time that its movements become increasingly separate, sovereign, and distinct from other aspects of spirit" (Farber, 1966, p. 103). This leads to that very failure of discretion and judgment, as well as imagination and humor, that Farber points to as the inadequacy of the schizophrenic in the world of It, as well as in the relationship with the Thou.

Farber sees the origin of willfulness as the desperate need for wholeness. The proper setting of wholeness is dialogue. When this setting eludes us, "we turn wildly to will, ready to grasp at any illusion of wholeness (however mindless or grotesque) the will conjures up for our reassurance." This is a vicious circle, for the more dependent a person becomes upon the illusion of wholeness, the less he is able to experience true wholeness in dialogue. "At the point where he is no longer capable of dialogue he can be said to be *addicted* to his will" (Farber, 1966, p. 50). Willfulness, then, is nothing other than the attempt of will to make up for the absence of dialogue by handling both sides of the no longer mutual situation. No longer in an encounter with another self, he fills the emptiness with his own self, and even that self is only a partial one, its wholeness having disappeared with the disappearance of meeting. "This feverish figure, endlessly assaulting the company, seeking to wrench the moment to some pretense of dialogue, is the image of the eternal stranger: that condition of man in which he is forever separated from his fellows, unknown and unaddressed—it is the figure of man's separated will posing as his total self" (Farber, 1966, p. 57).

In his essay "Martin Buber and Psychoanalysis," Farber (1966, chap. 7) affirms that without meeting, no successful treatment is possible. The "compulsive," "schizoid," or "hysterical" traits that therapist and patient have in common indicate only that both have an incapacity that hinders the meeting. Many of the disturbances that are seen as arising from "transference" are more correctly described as the striving for or retreating from the hope for a reciprocal relationship. Usually, what we mean by transference is the very opposite of meeting, with its warmth, contact, and spontaneity. What is important, however, is to combine reciprocity or trust with truthfulness and proportion. These two can combine in a unique immediacy: Meeting becomes truth. Such moments are lacking entirely in utility for ordinary goals of knowledge.

At the same time, Farber emphasizes that Buber's philosophy is based as much upon the necessary structures and categories of the world of It as upon the bringing of those structures and categories into the meeting with the Thou.

> The mistake is often made, especially with the schizophrenic, of overvaluing his lonely gropings toward the *Thou* and of underestimating his actual incompetence in the world of *It*, so that he becomes a tragic saint or poet of the *Thou*, martyred by the world of *It*.
>
> Once it is realized, however, that the *Thou* relation depends upon the world of *It* for its conceptual forms or meanings, then psychosis can be seen as not only a failure of the *Thou*—of so-called personal relations. It is an equal failure of knowledge, judgment, and experience in the world of *It*. Whatever class the disorder falls into—whether it is marked by a recoil from relations, as in schizophrenia, or by a grasping at relation, as in hysteria or mania—underlying its manifestations one can always find much ineptitude with people, much early failure to acquire the elementary tools of knowledge. . . . Without sufficient knowledge, memory, or judgment, every *Thou* invoked is apt to be a perilously shy and fleeting one. It recedes very quickly into its impoverished world of *It*, where there is little promise of return. And with each loss of the *Thou*, the schizophrenic is in special danger of retreating more permanently or deeply toward his far pole of alienation: into that *loneliness* of which both Sullivan and Fromm-Reichmann have written. (Farber, 1966, pp. 148f.)

Farber describes this loneliness as a hopeless longing for the *Thou*, a despair that afflicts everyone at times "and overwhelms the more desperate ones we call psychotic." In this sense, the

chatter by which we detain even an unwelcome guest at parting is no less a confession of the total failure of the wedding of
minds than that even madder chattering by which the "manic"
patient detains all humanity as his parting guest. "We strive
wildly on the doorstep for one departing *Thou*" (Farber, 1966,
p. 149). For the schizophrenic this often means that the longing
for the Thou is accompanied by a fear of his loneliness being
momentarily entered by a Thou and then leaving him all the
more desolate and empty-handed when he returns to the vacant world of *It*. Unable to endure this possibility, he "exiles
himself from both earth and heaven, and, with a surprising dignity, takes up his residence in limbo" (Farber, 1966, p. 149f.).
The sickness arising from lack of dialogue thus makes itself
worse by striving in desperate or inadequate ways for the Thou
or by fearing the loneliness that will follow the fleeting appearance of the Thou.

If patient and therapist alike are to have any hope of reaching
real dialogue, they must be willing to face the despair that occupies so central a place even in the attempt at healing through
meeting:

> It is when we stand stripped of every artifice and prop, every techni-
> cal support of our profession, that we are closest to reality. And if it
> is only then, in the moment of extremity, that we approach genuine
> dialogue, genuine confirmation—the lack of which has driven us to
> this despair—so we may find the remedy concealed in the disease. It
> may be that only in such moments do we approach reality at all. It
> may be that at such moments the patient, too, is obeying such deep
> and elementary needs that it would be gratuitous to speak of pity and
> despair. (Farber, 1966, p. 182)

Hans Trüb

I have placed next to last a figure who chronologically is
much earlier than most of those dealt with in this chapter and
the one before because he remains the most important expo-
nent of healing through meeting. In his theory and practice of
therapy, the Swiss psychiatrist Hans Trüb made real the fusion

of C. G. Jung's analytical psychology with Martin Buber's philosophy of dialogue. According to Trüb, making conscious images by which the patient is passively assaulted enables the patient to meet the reality of the world steadily. Introspective analysis, for Trüb, in marked contrast to Jung, does not open up for us an inner world in which one can live, a world that has to compete with reality. "Rather it puts us in possession of the *world of images* with which alone we are truly enabled to meet the one and only real world" (Trüb in Friedman, 1991, p. 504). The neurotic person reacts to reality, but he no longer opens himself to it. The result of this flight from reality is a profound, uncanny, and inexplicable dread out of which the patient constructs within himself a system of barely penetrable protections and defenses. Conversely, the uncovering of these inner psychic defense mechanisms by means of depth psychology can truly succeed only if it recognizes that they are based in the self's *personally* executed flight from meeting (Trüb in Friedman, 1991, pp. 500-503).

Only mutual personal trust assures the positive treatment of such a neurosis. The therapist's recognition of a presence of another provides him with a yardstick for psychoanalytic work. "How far I must and may follow my psychological work with this person confronting me is always to be decided on the basis of personal relationship." When the patient does execute an authentic about-face toward the world, this is experience by both partners in the relationship "as an autonomous act, bursting forth out of freedom, startling."

> The patient is lost to us at a blow as an object of treatment, and that which remains to be done proceeds from a fundamentally new point of departure. For now the problem lies *between* us. The situation from now on is an obviously dialogical one. (Trüb in Friedman, 1991, p. 504)

Trüb describes how in his work with his patients he became aware of the invariable tendency of the primary consciousness to become monological and self-defeating. He also tells how this closed circle of the self was forced again and again outward toward relationship through those times when, despite his will, he found himself confronting his patient not as an analyst, but rather as a human being. From these experiences he came to understand the full meaning of the analyst's responsibility. The analyst takes responsibility for lost and forgotten things, and with the aid of his psychology he helps bring them to light. But he knows in the depths of his self that the secret meaning of these things that have been brought to consciousness first reveals itself *in the outgoing to the other* (Trüb in Friedman, 1991, p. 497).

> *Psychology* as science and *psychology* as function know about the soul of man as about something in the third person. . . . They look down from above into the world of inner things, into the inner world of the individual. And they deal with its contents as with their "objects." They give names and they create classifications while carefully investigating the manifold connections and presenting them vividly in meaningful systems.
>
> But the psychotherapist in his work with the ill is *essentially a human being*. . . . Therefore he seeks and loves the human being in his patients and allows it . . . to come to him ever again. (Trüb in Friedman, 1991, p. 497)

The personal experience that moved Trüb from the dialectical psychology of Jung to the dialogical anthropology of Buber was, he tells us, an overwhelming sense of guilt. This guilt could no longer be explained away or removed, for it was subjectively experienced as the guilt of a person who had stepped out of a real relationship to the world and tried to live in a spiritual world above reality. Trüb, like Buber, holds that guilt is an essential factor in the person's relations to others and that it performs the necessary function of leading him to desire to set these relations right.

Real guilt is the beginning of *ethos*, or responsibility, writes Trüb in his essay "From Self to World" (Trüb in Friedman, 1991, pp. 497-499), but before the patient can become aware of it, he must be helped by the analyst to become aware of himself in general. This the analyst does through playing the part of both confidante and big brother. The neurotic is given the understanding the world has denied him, which makes it more and more possible for him to step out of his self-imprisonment and into a genuine relation with the analyst. In doing this, Trüb says, the analyst must avoid the intimacy of a private I-Thou relationship with the patient *and* the temptation of dealing with the patient as an object. This means, in effect, that he must have just that dialogical relationship of concrete, but one-sided inclusion upon which Buber insists in his Postscript to *I and Thou* (1958). It cannot become the mutual inclusion of friendship without destroying the therapeutic possibilities of the relationship. But neither can it make the patient an It. The analyst must be able to risk himself and to participate in the process of individuation.

The analyst must see the illness of the patient as an illness of relations with the world, Trüb writes. The roots of the neurosis lie both in the patient's closing himself off from the world and in the pattern of society itself and its rejection and non-confirmation of the patient. Consequently, the analyst must change at some point from the consoler who takes the part of the patient against the world to the person who puts before the patient the claim of the world. This change is necessary to complete the second part of the cure—the establishment of real relationship with the world that can take place only in the world itself. On the analyst falls the task of preparing the way for the resumption in direct meeting of the interrupted dialogical relationship between the individual and the community. The psychotherapist must test the patient's finding of himself by the criterion of whether his self-realization can be the starting point for a new personal meeting with the world. The patient must go forth whole in himself, but he must also recognize that it is not his own self, but rather the world with which he must be concerned. This does not mean, however, that the patient is simply integrated with or adjusted to the world. He does not cease to be a real person, responsible for himself; but at the same time he enters into responsible relationship with his community (Trüb in Friedman, 1991, pp. 497-499).

By viewing the isolated patient from the beginning as one who has sacrificed his capacity for dialogue in withdrawing his self from meeting with the world, and by addressing him immediately, dialogical psychotherapy sets him up as a fellow human being, a Thou, the original partner in a fully human meeting. It seeks out this stubborn self, this introvert captive of the psyche, and will not release it. It summons this self by name as the one called upon to answer, the one personally responsible. And by addressing it in this manner, it challenges the self to disclose itself in its self and to individuate itself in the new dialogue with the physician-partner and beyond him in intercourse—and not merely the introverted kind—with the world. (Trüb in Friedman, 1991, pp. 500f.)

For Trüb, the dialogical meeting is both the starting point and the goal of therapy. The success or failure of the cure focuses upon the risk of this meeting. The tension of psychic conflict that derives from the contradiction of the conscious and unconscious arrives at a psychotherapeutic resolution in the framework of this basic partnership. "The healing process takes place between *this* physician and *this* patient, in the totality of their personal confrontation" (Trüb in Friedman, 1991, p. 502). The therapist embodies for the patient a loving inclination of the world that seeks to restore the patient's dispirited and mistrustful self to a new dialogical meeting with the forces of nature and history. Thus, the therapist quiets and harmonizes the psychic tension of the patient not only according to the latter's wish, but also as a partner penetrating the personal basis of his being, the actual origin of that elemental introversion that nourishes all neuroses. The unconscious is precisely the personal element that is lost in the course of development, the element that escapes consciousness. In dealing with this lost element, the psychotherapist cannot point to a truth he *has*, but only to a truth to be sought *between* him and the patient. Only thus can he equalize again the enormous advantage given him by the fact that the other one seeks him out and asks him for help. Thus, the equality of respect for which the humanistic psychologist seeks is attained, according to Trüb, not by the insistence upon a complete mutuality of situation, but rather by the recognition of the *betweenness* itself as the place where real meeting, real healing, and real finding occur.

It is very important, of course, that the therapist not demand responsibility in dialogue before the patient is ready for it. That is why the reconstruction of the capacity for dialogue must go hand in hand with the methodical attempt to loosen and dismantle the complex defense mechanisms in the psychic realm of expression as fast as the recuperating self permits. "Without this supplemental assistance of depth psychology, what is dialogically expected of the patient's self in the meeting situation with the world would place too great a demand on it and expose it to the danger of regression" (Trüb in Friedman, 1991, p. 502).

But Trüb does *not* hold, like Jung and his followers, that one must become individuated first and only then enter into a dialogue with others. The therapist, Trüb says, must keep in view "the one true goal of healing, the unlocking of the locked up person for the meeting with the world" (Trüb in Friedman, 1991, p. 503). Only this enables the therapist to answer *both* for the patient *and* for the world. Only by so doing can the therapist risk personal commitment, even to the neurotic self-entanglement of the patient. Only by starting from the meeting as partner can physician and patient hold their ground with a positive attitude in the face of the cure's completion, which generally occurs unexpectedly and which may be compared, Trüb suggests, to a leap over the abyss. All this implies no choice between the inner personal wholeness and the social self, such as Jung makes in his repeated valuing of the inner personal wholeness over the social self. On the contrary, "the willingness of the self to meet the world, the situation of a living dialogue, that is between within and without, should be striven for and furthered *simultaneously* with the effort to attain a psychic integration of the self" (Trüb in Friedman, 1991, p. 503). When the psychological cooperation and dialectical interaction of patient and therapist are conducted dialogically, with mutual personal trust between therapist and patient, then there gradually awakens and grows in the patient at one and the same time, and as corollaries of the same happening, a new confidence in himself *and* in the other (Trüb in Friedman, 1991, pp. 504f.).[6]

It is to Hans Trüb that Buber points, in "Healing Through Meeting," as the man who broke the trail as a practicing psychotherapist in the recognition and realization of the therapeutic possibilities of dialogue. Speaking of this crisis through which the psychotherapist passes when he discovers the paradox of his vocation, Buber writes:

In a decisive hour, together with the patient entrusted to and trusting in him, he has left the closed room of psychological treatment in which the analyst rules by means of his systematic and methodological superiority and has stepped forth with him into the air of the world where self is exposed to self. There, in the closed room where one probed and treated the isolated psyche according to the inclination of the self-encapsulated patient, the patient was referred to ever-deeper levels of his inwardness as to his proper world; here outside, in the immediacy of one human standing over against another, the encapsulation must and can be broken through, and a transformed, healed relationship must and can be opened to the person who is sick in his relationship to otherness—to the world of the other which he cannot remove into his soul. . . .

This way of frightened pause, of unfrightened reflection, of personal involvement, of rejection of security, of unreserved stepping into relationship, of the bursting of psychologism, this way of vision and of risk is that which Hans Trüb trod. . . . Surely there will not be wanting persons like him—awake and daring, hazarding the economics of the vocation, not sparing and not withholding themselves—persons who will find his path and extend it farther. (Buber, 1990, pp. 142f.)

This chapter offers evidence that the persons Buber called for do exist.

Richard Hycner

One such person who is a dialogical psychotherapist in the fullest sense of the term is Richard Hycner, Co-Director of our Institute for Dialogical Psychotherapy in San Diego. Hycner's book *Between Person and Person: Toward a Dialogical Psychotherapy* (1991) offers more insight into the actual process of dialogical psychotherapy than any other writing since that of Hans Trüb.

Hycner is well aware of "The Problematic of Mutuality" in therapy (Friedman, 1985, chap. 16). Certainly the "wounded healer" heals, writes Hycner, echoing the famous saying of Jung, "yet if that woundedness is paramount in the therapy the focus then becomes the healing of the therapist, not the client, and that is never the purpose of therapy." (Hycner, 1991, p. 12) The therapist's healing is always the by-product of the interaction between therapist and client. The therapist struggles to bring his or her woundedness into play and develops his or her self in the process. Yet the therapist never makes the healing of his or her self the focus. What makes this struggle so central is that, ultimately, the therapist's self is the "instrument" that will be utilized in therapy.

> It is not the therapist's theoretical orientation that is as crucial in the healing process, as is the wholeness and availability of the self of the therapist—such that there can be a meeting of self and self, and in that meeting a wholeness is engendered in the client which was absent before this meeting. (Hycner, 1991, pp. 12-13)

Hycner is particularly insightful in his understanding of the tension between the therapist's conscious awareness of what is occurring, coupled with his or her recognition that the conscious always is permeated by the unconscious:

> An overly "conscious" therapist fails to partake of the nether world that surrounds us and resides at the edge of consciousness, whereas a therapist participating too much in his unconscious processes may connect with the client at that collective unconscious level where there is the "presence" of archetypes but not the meeting of persons. (Hycner, 1991, pp. 13-14)

Similarly, the therapeutic relationship will be enhanced by the therapist's counterbalancing the intellectual or the feeling orientation of the patient and the patient struggling to ferret out which is the "real" therapist. Like Buber, Hycner asserts that the "unfettered elementalness of human meeting demands that the therapist *first* be a person available to others as a human being, and *secondarily* be a professional trained in the appropriate methods of practicing psychotherapy." Above all "these methods must never keep the therapist from confronting the abyss that always hovers threateningly at the threshold of a genuine human meeting." (Hycner, 1991, p. 21)

Whereas Buber seems to make it a blanket rule that the patient can never practice "inclusion" with the therapist, Hycner quite rightly recognizes that one of the indications that a person is ready to end therapy is that frequently the client begins to experience the situation from the therapist's side: "The self of the client recognizes and appreciates the uniqueness of the self of the therapist, and by extrapolation, the self of others. This is the basis for any genuine dialogue, the client's availability for genuine relatedness to others". (Hycner, 1991, p. 42)

At a panel for the American Psychiatric Association in which I took part, a psychiatrist in the audience who identified himself as first and foremost a psychopharmacologist declared that as a therapist he used only the I-Thou relationship and never the I-It. This is an illusion. Neither in human life in general nor in therapy in particular can we do without the swinging alternation between both. By the same token, Hycner recognizes that dialogical psychotherapy must make use of techniques yet stresses equally that the technique always must be secondary to the dialogue and never an end in itself:

> *Techniques need to arise out of the context of the relationship.* . . . There is nothing wrong with techniques as such, so long as they are not *arbitrarily* imposed on the situation. This always requires that there is a trusting relationship which gives "permission" to the therapist to use certain techniques. So-called techniques need to arise out of the "between." (Hycner, 1991, p. 45)

A similar awareness of the necessary dialectic between I-Thou and I-It informs Hycner's discussion of "presence":

> Presence "demands" that the therapist stay in the "pregnant moment," and allow the encounter to develop out of that. The natural flow of human experience will tend to take the therapist from one moment to the present situation to the next. However, our cognitive training will often take us out of this present-centeredness. . . . Such present-centeredness is what keeps the process of the therapy fully alive . . . respond[ing] moment by moment to the ongoing changes. (Hycner, 1991, p. 98)

Hycner understands "psychopathology" as an aborted dialogue—the residue of an attempted dialogue that was not responded to, a desperate calling to the world to respond and to recognize the face of human need behind the face of human hurt. By the same token, the healing of the psychopathological means an entrance into dialogue with others:

> As we open up to those parts of us we've disowned, that allows us to recognize our human frailty and to be more compassionate with the frailty and vulnerability of others. Correspondingly, it allows us to withdraw our "projections" from others, and truly meet them, *not* "projection to projection," but person to person. (Hycner, 1991, pp. 123-124)

In his conclusion on "The Wisdom of Resistance" Hycner carries forward Gestalt therapy's valuation of the creativity of resistance into deeper and more concrete understanding of the relation of resistance to the "between" than any of his psychotherapeutic forebears has ever done. "In the therapeutic context, resistance is inextricably a phenomenon of the 'between.'" (Hycner, 1991, p. 135) Although relationship is central in all of therapy, in dealing with resistance it must call upon all of the "credits" built up in the dialogue with the client, for it is, ultimately, the trust in the therapist and the relationship that establishes a bridge across the chasm of resistance and gets both therapist and clients through the moments of mismeeting. The greatest challenge the therapist faces is that of genuinely being with someone who is experienced as oppositional, recognizing that the resistance is part and parcel of the whole person, and creatively finding a means to establish a dialogue with this person and her resistance.

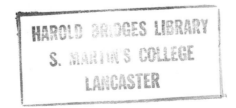

7

Martin Buber and Ivan Boszormenyi-Nagy: The Role of Dialogue in Contextual (Intergenerational Family) Therapy

The most remarkable breakthrough to healing through meeting beyond the intrapsychic has been the work of Ivan Boszormenyi-Nagy. In *Between Give and Take: A Clinical Guide to Contextual Therapy (1986), Ivan Boszormenyi-Nagy* and Barbara Krasner write: "Martin Buber contributed more to building the foundations of accountable human relating than any other thinker of our time." Buber's "dialogic notion of responsible responding," they add, "was an important underpinning of the first formulation of the intergenerational dialectic" (p. 28). The centrality of Buber's philosophy of dialogue to contextual therapy is also made explicit in many passages in *Foundations of Contextual Therapy*. Boszormenyi-Nagy speaks of "the relational humanism of Martin Buber" which "introduces the dialectic view of man as being unthinkable without his being party to a dialogue with another" (Boszormenyi-Nagy, 1987, p. 140).

> Buber's concept of the dialogue came closest to a requisite framework which can describe two or more individuals in a personally engaged

relationship. Actually there is no psychological theory capable of
considering the dynamics of two selves simultaneously from the
multiple subjective vantage points. (Boszormenyi-Nagy, 1987, p. 241)

What emerges as an ideal model of relational psychology is the
dialogue. A capacity for *responding* and being open to the other's
response is the core of the genuine Dialogue. It serves as a model
of "healthy" functioning, aimed at developing those humanistic
potentials of man that transcend a mere absence of illness. Dialogue is a means of growth and maturation in the social sense; it
encompasses the processes of active assertion as well as interpersonal responsiveness and reactivity. It is a means of developing
and maintaining selfhood through meeting the other, as well as
having one's own needs met. (p. 72)

Dialogue can serve as a shaper of autonomous identity as
long as a meaningful self-other confirmation keeps the process
in motion. The family therapist, correspondingly, has both
partners in mind when addressing either of the two—a clear
link with Boszormenyi-Nagy's basic postulate of multidirec-
tional partiality (see Boszormenyi-Nagy, 1987, pp. 72-74, 76ff.).

Boszormenyi-Nagy suggests that the concept of health in
family therapy should be fashioned according to modes of relating rather than the values of reality, genitality, effectiveness,
and self-actualization that are current in the individual-based
writings on psychopathology. The intergenerational family
therapist has to face what Boszormenyi-Nagy holds to be the
most difficult aspect of a genuine dialogue: "our responsibility
for our actions and our responsibility for also holding the others
responsible in their dealings with each other and ourselves."

The relating partners' shared need for trust bridges dialecti-
cally the apparent contradiction between self-interest and consideration of others. This "capacity to acquire and retain at
least a few trustworthy relationships in the face of increasing
dehumanization and alienation in the public world cannot be
equated with either altruism or with guilt-laden compliance fu-
eled by superego demands" (Boszormenyi-Nagy, 1987, p. 155).

The Common Order and Existential Guilt

In "What Is Common to All" Buber (1988c) unfolds the implications of Heraclitus's statement, "One should follow the common." Using the terms of Heraclitus, Buber calls that building together first the *logos*—the common speech-with-meaning—and then the *cosmos*—the world that humanity builds in concert over a thousand generations. From this common world comes the idea of the just human order that is central to the thought of Boszormenyi-Nagy. The just human order is nothing other than this world we build together. That we build it together does not mean that we have to conform. On the contrary, one must stand one's ground and make one's unique contribution. This is not a matter of the individual versus society, for we are all part of the common order together.

Given this understanding of the common order, it is also possible to understand how we injure it. We all stand, says Buber, in an objective world of relatedness, and this objective relatedness can rise then to an actual existential relation to other people. It is this existential relation that we can injure. "Man," Buber asserts in "Guilt and Guilt Feelings" (Buber, 1988c), "is the creature who can become guilty." The originators of primitive taboos did not invent guilt; they used it and manipulated it. To understand this, we must follow Buber in distinguishing between guilt feelings born of neurotic guilt and real, or existential, guilt. Guilt feelings may be the result of the social climate, taboos, neurosis, your internalized superego, or the like. But such a thing as real or existential guilt also exists.

Existential guilt is guilt that you have taken upon yourself as a person in a personal situation. Freud's guilt is repressed; you do not know it. But existential guilt you do know. Only you may no longer identify yourself with the person who committed the injury. Existential guilt comes of injuring the common order of existence, the foundation of which you know—at some level—to be the foundation of your own and of all human existence.

Buber puts forward three steps that may be taken toward overcoming existential guilt. The first is that we illuminate this guilt: We who are so different are nonetheless the persons who did this. Second, we have to persevere in that illumination—not in an anguished self-torment but in a strong, broad light.

If we were guilty only in relation to ourselves, the process might stop there. But we are always also guilty in relation to others. Therefore, we must take the third step of repairing the injured order of existence, restoring the broken dialogue through an active devotion to the world. If we have injured it, only we can restore it. But we may not be able to find the person we injured: That person may be dead or the situation may be radically changed. Yet, in a thousand places we can, in fact, restore the injured order of existence, not just the one in which we injured it.

The Place of Existential Guilt in Contextual Therapy

Buber's just order of human existence and the existential guilt that arises from injuring that order are central to *Invisible Loyalties: Reciprocity in Intergenerational Family Therapy* (Boszormenyi-Nagy & Spark, 1973/1984). Boszormenyi-Nagy (1987) himself points to that centrality:

> Contextual therapists had to rely on a concept borrowed from Buber, "the justice of the human order," as a quasi-objective criterion of interpersonal fairness. . . . The objectivity of relational justice is not an independent entity. It really is a dialectical criterion derived from the simultaneous consideration of the balance between two (or more) relating persons' subjective, self-serving rights and entitlements. (p. 306)

You may go to the other end of the world to escape your family and be paralyzed by interhuman existential guilt. *Invisible Loyalties* goes beyond psychology with its emphasis on the intrapsychic by bringing in the notion of the interpersonal fabric, the merit ledger that is passed on from generation to generation. Some people will never face or recognize the injuries that they have done to the common order except perhaps through their grandchildren. But even for those who do not face it, there will be consequences:

The party who fails to earn merit vis-à-vis his relational partners or lastingly ignores his factual accountability for damaging consequences to posterity may become depressed, insomniac, anorectic, addicted, ruined by success, sexually malfunctional, relationally stagnant, accident-prone, or psychosomatically ill. As a psychological consequence, conscious or unconscious feelings of guilt may or may not accompany the person's disentitlement, i.e., the accumulation of existential guilt on his or her side. (Boszormenyi-Nagy, 1987, p. 311)

Boszormenyi-Nagy points out that what Buber defined as the genuine "I-Thou dialogue" is implicit in the systemic notion of the ledger of merits and the balance of give and take. "Only through the dialectic of the genuine mutuality of needs . . . can we arrive at the concept of the ethical existential ledger, according to which no concerned relative can gain by the 'success' of exploitative mastery over the other members of the family" (Boszormenyi-Nagy, 1987, p. 160).

Like Buber, Boszormenyi-Nagy does not stop with insight but goes on to action. Insight alone cannot overcome existential guilt. "Rejunction" must occur, an actual repairing of the injured order of the world. Rejunction in no way cancels out the necessary movement of the child toward autonomy:

Rejunction should not be confused with a thrust toward clinging togetherness. On the contrary, anything that undermines the trustworthy credibility of individual integrity drives people away from each other. Exploitative clinging to one's children, for example, has to be examined in the light of multilateral interests. Reasonable steps have to be made toward the autonomous development of the child. The "permission" for individuation represents an important trust-generating or rejunctive measure. (Boszormenyi-Nagy, 1987, p. 261)

In *Between Give and Take* Boszormenyi-Nagy and Krasner (1986) say that "the fundamental premise of the dialogical process is that people can still hope to bridge the chasm that exists between them and their legacies without having to relinquish their personal integrity and their capacity to be fair" (p. 329). They also speak at length of "entitlement" in which through caring and concern for others you will become entitled yourself. Rejunction and entitlement are clearly their ways of repairing the injured order of existence, of overcoming existential guilt. Existential guilt is the rupture of the dialogue that stands at the heart of human existence, and the restoration of the injured order is the renewal of the dialogue through trustworthiness, merited trust built in a relationship, which Boszormenyi-Nagy (1987) calls the fundamental resource of family therapy:

> The goal of contextual therapy is re-junction, rejoining that which has come apart. That is (1) an acknowledgement of the principle of equitable multilaterality [for example, the therapist uses multi-directed partiality to get every person to bring in his or her subjective accounts and their understandings of the others]. (2) an ethically definable process of re-engagement in living mutuality, and (3) a commitment to fair balances of give-and-take. In other words, family members explore their capacity for reworking stagnant imbalance in how each of them uses the other and in how they are available to each other. The courage they invest in the review and repair of inadvertent relational corruption and exploitation yields returns in therapeutic resources, the chief among them being: earned trustworthiness. (Boszormenyi-Nagy, 1987, p. 200)

Meeting Others and Holding One's Ground

In *I and Thou* Buber (1958) says of the "I-Thou" relationship, "By the graciousness of its coming and the solemn sadness of its going it teaches you to meet others and to hold your ground when you meet them" (p. 330). It takes a lifetime to learn to meet others and to hold your ground when you meet them. Again and again in what Ivan Boszormenyi-Nagy has written, alone or with Geraldine Spark earlier and Barbara Krasner later, one finds a dual emphasis on meeting others and holding one's ground when one does so.

Therapists cannot function indefinitely as the primary source of trustworthiness, to take one example, for their own resources become depleted as they become captive of their patients' expectations. Liberation from the revolving cycle of destructive action, to take another example, takes place only through discovery of sources of trustworthiness. Contextual therapy helps in such discovery not only through bringing family members into genuine dialogue with one another but also through teaching them to stand up against guilt and for their own entitlements. The enhancement of the family's dormant resources through trustworthiness requires mutuality of effort among family member through which they become more multilaterally fair and in so doing change and improve the nature of their own entitlement. "This is a different and a deeper way of standing up for oneself" (Boszormenyi-Nagy & Ulrich, 1981). In *Between Give and Take* Boszormenyi-Nagy and Krasner (1986) speak about developing courage "to take the risk of investing trust in new relationships; to hear people on their own terms (centrifugal concern) without abandoning one's own position (centripetal concern); to claim one's own side and, in the process, to gain autonomy" (p. 105).

Distancing and Relating and Family Therapy

Boszormenyi-Nagy's goals of family therapy are best understood in terms of Buber's philosophical anthropology of *distancing* and *relating* as the two ontological movements fundamental to human existence. To Boszormenyi-Nagy, therapy can never stop with getting out the buried hostility toward parents, because that would lead inevitably to a violation of the universal legacy of filial loyalty, a rejection of the therapist, or a building of guilt: "In our clinical experience, no one ends up a winner through a conclusion which predicates a hopelessly incorrigible resentment and contempt towards one's parent" (Boszormenyi-Nagy & Spark, 1973/1984, p. 20).

"In contrast with individual psychotherapy, family or relationship-based therapy proceeds step by step to remove deeper and deeper layers of *inauthentic loyalty definitions*" (Boszormenyi-Nagy & Spark, 1973/1984, p. 134). The family therapist can encourage a mutual dialogue so that the aged parents (the grandparents) can reveal their own past, as well as current longings. When each generation is helped to face the nature of the current relationships, exploring the real nature of the commitments and responsibility that flow from such involvements, an increased reciprocal understanding and mutual compassion between the generations results. The grandchildren, in particular, benefit from this reconciliation between the generations; they are helped to be freed of scapegoated or parentified roles, and they have a hope for age-appropriate gratifications plus a model for reconciling their conflicts with their parents (Boszormenyi-Nagy & Spark, 1973/1984).

Distancing and relating, give and take apply to parent and child, including the grown-up "child":

> Our concept of relational autonomy pictures the individual as retaining a modified yet fully responsible and sensitively concerned dialogue with the original family members. In this sense the individual can be liberated to engage in full, wholly personal relationships only to the extent that he has become capable of responding to parental devotion with concern on his part and with the realization that receiving is intrinsically connected with owing in return. (Boszormenyi-Nagy & Spark, 1973/1984, p. 105)

In *Invisible Loyalties* (1973/1984) Boszormenyi-Nagy calls for reciprocal justice and fair acknowledgment to rebalance the merit ledger between the generations. This can be done only through listening to each member's subjective construction of his or her accountability to the rest of the family in order to discover the intrinsic balances between hidden loyalty ties and exploitations. This discovery leads in turn to acknowledgment and exoneration in which each person's point of view is confirmed precisely through coming into dialogue with the opposing views of others. "Personal exploitation is measurable only on a subjective scale which has been built into the person's sense of the meaning of his entire existence" (Boszormenyi-Nagy & Spark, 1973/1984, p. 81). Being confirmed is not a matter of the quantity of the world's goods that one gets, but rather of "a reality-based or action dialogue, which is more than the sum total of two persons' subjective experiences" (p. 82).

The Task of the Family Therapist

The therapist guides the family members to the multilaterality of fairness in which one person's being heard or being held accountable makes it easier to hear others or to let oneself be called to account. Thus, the therapist helps them take the first steps toward engagement in a mutuality of trust and trustworthiness. "The lack of trustworthiness in one's relational world is the primary pathogenic condition of human life" (Boszormenyi-Nagy, 1987, p. 230). The therapist can address this problem of eroding trust by eliciting each family member's own responsible review of his or her side of mutual entitlements and indebtedness. Trust resources among family members are identified, elicited, mobilized, and used. Above all, the family therapist looks for that atmosphere of trustworthiness and availability of basic trust that enables children to acquire the building material for the fundamental stage of personality development (Boszormenyi-Nagy, 1987).

Building trust makes possible the recognition and reworking of long-standing balances of unfairness in the legacies of parents, thus freeing them from defensive and retributive behavior and freeing their offspring from being overburdened by them and condemned to a similar fate. Building trust includes a respect for equitability on every member's own terms, an integrity of give and take in relationship, a mutuality of consideration, and a capacity for redistributing the returns that reside in joint accounts of trust investments. Trust does not develop exclusively between client and therapist, as in much traditional therapy, but is rechanneled into strengthening relationships between family members. Through multidirected trust-building efforts, the contextual therapist can help family members reveal one another's unacknowledged consideration and contributions and elicit responsible attitudes that may lead to a more genuine dialogue among them (Boszormenyi-Nagy, 1987). Above all, the family therapist must have that "inclusion" of which Buber speaks, by which the therapist "imagines the real," that is, experiences the patient's side of the relationship without losing his or her own.

Between Give and Take

Like *Invisible Loyalties, Between Give and Take* is grounded solidly in Martin Buber's philosophy of dialogue: "A mutually responsible relationship benefits the self at the same time as it benefits others. Contextual therapy is based on the healing evoked through due concern, a refinement of 'healing through meeting' " (Boszormenyi-Nagy & Krasner, 1986, p. 20). Talking about interpersonal balances of the relational context, Boszormenyi-Nagy and Krasner (1986) say, "What is called for here is an integration of individual modes of psychic restoration with a supraindividual regulatory force that is what Buber termed 'the justice of the human order'." The justice of the human order, as we shall recall, is the common cosmos that we build together through speech with meaning. It is that life together that may be injured and that we have to repair. "Genuine dialogue depends on the reciprocity of responsible caring. . . . It is the core of that relational reality that becomes the context of mature *individuation*" (p. 73). Contextual therapy is concerned also with individuation, as are Jung and many other schools of therapy. But it cannot imagine individuation taking place outside of the context of responsible and caring relating. "Disregard of these basic, functional principles of relatedness underlies much of what is considered pathology. For example, both hostile distance and fused enmeshment reflect failure of genuine dialogue" (p. 73). Thus, Buber's basic principles of distancing and relating are taken up here and with them the recognition that if you do not have the proper back and forth between them, either one can be pathology: too much distancing or too much enmeshment. "Mutual delineation leads to a creative use of otherness" (p. 73).

Boszormenyi-Nagy and Krasner (1986) identify two major options for genuine dialogue. The first is self-delineation, the use of relationships for defining oneself vis-à-vis the other as ground. The self comes to be in the give and take, even in the struggle, the tug of war, between selves. The other major option is self-validation, "the validation of self-worth through entitlement earned by offering due care." That is the spiral of merit.

"Contextually, individuation is a relational process." From the side of family members, contextual therapy requires

> . . . the capacity of each family member to define their claim of subjective fairness, and to develop courage to assert their respective sides of entitlement.
>
> The capacity of each family member to hear each other and to care about each other's subjective vantage points on entitlements and interests.
>
> The capacity of each family member to strive toward a trust-worthy balance of positions in the family as well as to move toward their own idiosyncratic goals.
>
> The capacity of each family member to acknowledge their personal accountability for the outcome of changed attitudes and behaviors and their impact on more vulnerable members of the family, such as young children.
>
> The capacity of each family member to support and gain from a mutual regard for everyone's attempts at fulfilling legacy obligations.
>
> The willingness and ability of each member to discriminate between expediency and integrity in personal relationships.
>
> The capacity of each family member to claim and grant tolerance and privacy for needed moratoria; that is, the time required for change to occur. The time required for equitable reworking and correcting displacements, projections, and denials is an example of the need for moratoria in interrelationships. (Boszormenyi-Nagy, 1987, pp. 263ff.)

In a clearly ontological and not just psychological statement Boszormenyi-Nagy and Krasner (1986) assert: "Intergenerational dialogue with its will to mutual responsibility is an interhuman absolute assumed by contextual therapy"(p. 306). This is a ground that cannot be overlooked, they are saying. To claim that you do not feel yourself a part of your family or of your group leaves out an important part of your existence. Boszormenyi-Nagy explains that he is not just moralizing, and he is not. Indeed, "the broad humanistic base of a genuinely relational ethic will inevitably challenge and test the priority schemes of particular relational codes" (Boszormenyi-Nagy, 1987, p. 143).

Existential guilt depends on the factuality of consequences of the injury we do to the justice of the order of being. In other words, the extent of injury suffered by the victim rather than the extent of the perpetrator's capacity for guilt feelings constitutes the criteria of existential guilt, therefore of the intrinsic transgenerational tribunal, too. . . . Consequences for another relating partner imply a factual reality rather than a psychological process. Relational ethics stresses the factual reality of both inflicting of injury and earning of merit. (p. 309)

Martin Buber repeatedly stressed that the mutuality of contact and trust in the therapist-patient relationship did not imply mutuality of inclusion, or imagining the real. The therapist is a very important person to the client, but the client cannot have a detached interest in the therapist for his or her own sake or see the therapist's problems from within. Without the I-Thou relationship between therapist and patient, you can do a little repair work, writes Buber (1958). But if you want to get to the real core of the therapy—the healing of the atrophied personal center—you must have the great glance of the doctor, the contact of I and Thou. This glance is bipolar, on this side and on that side, too. But the doctor cannot demand of the client that the client also practice inclusion.

In their conception of the therapist's role as one of a "concerned caretaker," Boszormenyi-Nagy and Krasner (1986) recognize precisely this combination of mutuality between therapist and client with a normative limitation that cannot and should not be set aside:

The therapist invests genuine care, competence, skill and confidentiality in return for the client's implicit investment of trust in the person of the therapist. Reciprocity stands at the very core of their contract and is ample but never symmetrical. The therapist meets his client and reveals himself as a fellow human being. But he neither reveals his own wounds to the same degree as the client nor depends on him for a cure. . . . Therapy may provide moments of genuine meeting between two people. Still the degree of investment and the level of expectations between them are always uneven. (p. 395)

The person who has been treated badly early on carries this over and tends to treat others badly in the present. The abused child, for example, often becomes an abusing parent in turn. This "destructive entitlement" is related closely to what Boszormenyi-Nagy and Spark (1973/1984) call the "revolving slate":

> Characteristically, the person who unjustly lays blame on another person in order to protect his parents tends to be immune to guilt toward the innocent victim of the revolving slate. A lack of merit transferred from an invisible filial account to a third party results in a person's false capacity to claim entitlement, at the tragic cost of new unfairness done to another aspect of the human context. (Boszormenyi-Nagy, 1987, p. 272)

Boszormenyi-Nagy holds that the contextual model of therapy as a self-delineating and self-validating dialogue builds safeguards against a multigenerational escalation of destructive entitlement. This is a distinct note of hope in what might otherwise seem like a fateful visitation of the sins of the parents upon the children from one generation to the next:

> By extending partiality to the destructive entitlement of the currently victimizing parent, the therapist helps extinguish the motivating strength of the heretofore unrecognized consequence of past damages. Having acknowledged the parent's past victimization, the therapist can then expect a more accountable behavior toward the next generation. (Boszormenyi-Nagy, 1987, p. 315)

Caring about posterity's fair chances represents transgenerational solidarity and safeguards what Buber calls the "justice of the human order." "Consistent with the good of posterity, reciprocal trustability becomes the 'golden rule' of 'relational negentropy.' " The earning of entitlement through fair give and take becomes a determinative, self-sustaining dynamic of relating (Boszormenyi-Nagy, 1987, p. 304).

"Multidirected partiality" has long been a central insight and concern of Boszormenyi-Nagy. It means that the therapist is able to practice Buber's inclusion, or imagining the real, first with one member of the family and then with another. Techniques fail to provide a basis for trust. "Only multidirected partiality can establish the kind of structure that provides the safety for exploring, identifying, mobilizing, and earning residual trust" (Boszormenyi-Nagy & Krasner, 1986, p. 400). A therapist can achieve this therapeutic attitude only if he or she has personal freedom, conviction, courage, knowledge, skills, a capacity for inclusion, and an ability to claim his or her own private existence.

> Like other therapists, the contextual therapist may well feel sympathy with the victim in a situation: Deep sympathy for other people's suffering probably connects the professional therapist with her own moments of helpless pain, despair and shame. Her alliance with a suffering person is thus likely to be real and honest. It would seem to follow, then, that an alliance *with* the victim implies an alliance *against* the victimizer. (p. 405)

Actually such an alliance could only destroy the contextual therapy: "Unlike individually oriented therapists, family therapists view *any fixed* unidirectional partiality as essentially irrational and destructive to the process of building trust." If the contextual therapist favors a given child, this in itself can undermine the therapeutic process if the youngster feels that the therapist is prejudging either one of the parents. The contextual family therapist cannot turn away from the other family members who are affected by an individual client's treatment or "delude himself with tunnel vision, i.e., the hope that the treatment of one person can effectively address his or her entire reality" (pp. 405ff.).

Contextual Therapy and the Confirmation of Otherness

"Invisible loyalties" often represent the pathology of the family, as well as its potential health. The emphasis upon the vertical, multigenerational dimension of relationship is necessary, in part, because the partners in marriage bring their family of origin into their new relationships. Without realizing it, they tend to place their mates within the old family system or, what amounts to the same thing, to see them as the magic helpers who will save them from their family system. Marriage, as Buber has said, means "the acknowledgement of vital, many-faced otherness." Otherwise, it is not a true marriage. Each marriage ideally means bringing not only the individual partners but also their families, their family systems, and their multigenerational merit-ledgers into genuine dialogue. When this is *not* done, the new family becomes stagnant and the progress of the children toward their rightful autonomy becomes impossible. Thus, the healthy ongoingness of the generations not only is not impeded by the dialogue with otherness for which Martin Buber calls, but is made possible by it.

Boszormenyi-Nagy's touchstone of reality is not functional efficiency but rather the intrinsic balances between hidden loyalty ties and exploitations. This leads in turn to what I call the "dialogue of touchstones," acknowledgment and exoneration in which each person's point of view is confirmed precisely through coming into dialogue with the opposing view of others. The goal of Boszormenyi-Nagy's family therapy is not the community of affinity, or like-mindedness, but what I call the "community of otherness" (Friedman, 1983).

In marriage, it is not just two individuals who join, but rather two quite different family systems of merit. If one does not intuitively perceive this, one marries the other only in fantasy, as the wishfully improved re-creation of one's own family of origin. Each mate may struggle then to coerce the other to be accountable for those of his or her felt injustices and accrued merits that come from his or her family of origin. By improving their reciprocal loyalty exchanges with their families of origin, Boszormenyi-Nagy's contextual therapy helps husband and wife relate to each other and to their children.

Thus, confirmation in the dialogue of touchstones leading to the community of otherness is both the way and the goal of Boszormenyi-Nagy's contextual therapy. He has rejected explicitly the old formula of "reality testing" in favor of a dialogue of touchstones. He appeals to parallel subjective reactions to validate consensually the relative objectivity of the suffered injustice of a partner in relationship. "While the concept of reality testing in psychology is a comparatively monothetical notion (one is either reality bound or subject to distortion), the concept of the just order of the human world is a dialectical [I would say dialogical] one." A person's betrayal of a friend involves not only the repressed childhood wishes of the betrayer but also the friend's vantage point (Boszormenyi-Nagy & Spark, 1973/1984, p. 82).

8

Dialogical Psychotherapy

Healing Through Meeting

One of the most important issues the approach of healing through meeting addresses is the extent to which healing proceeds from specific healer and the extent to which it takes place in the "between"—in the relationship between therapist and client, among the members of a group or family, or even within a community. When it is the latter, does a special role exist, nonetheless, for the therapist as facilitator, midwife, enabler, or partner in a "dialogue of touchstones"? We must ask also whether such healing takes place through an "existential grace" that cannot be planned and counted on, however much it can be helped along. To what extent does healing through meeting imply that meeting must be the *goal*, as well as the means to that goal? And to what extent are we talking about a two-sided event that is not susceptible to techniques in the sense of willing and manipulating to bring about a certain result?[7]

What is crucial is not only the skill of the therapist, but what takes place *between* the therapist and the client *and* between the client and other people. The one *between* cannot totally make up for or take the place of the other. No amount of therapy can be of decisive help if a person is too enmeshed in a family, community, or culture in which the seedlings of healing are choked off constantly and the attempts to restore personal wholeness are thwarted by the destructive elements of the system. If this fact underlines the importance of supplementing one-to-one therapy with family therapy and even intergenerational (three or more generations) family therapy, as Ivan Boszormenyi-Nagy advocates, it also underlines the importance of creating that climate of trust, that confirmation of otherness (Friedman, 1983), in which healing through meeting can flourish on every level. That such healing has tragic limitations is obvious, but it is not equally obvious that we should accept the present state of "community" as a given and restrict ourselves to the intrapsychic and the intrafamilial.

In moving into the realm of healing through meeting, we must face the radical question of whether true healing, in the first instance, is not only *psycho*therapy, but also family, social, economic, and political therapy. The readjustment and integration of the intrapsychic sphere is the by-product, but the locus of true healing is the interhuman, the interpersonal, the communal, the social, the cultural, and even the political. To embark seriously upon healing through meeting is to leave the safe shores of the intrapsychic as *the* touchstone of reality and to venture onto the high seas in which healing is no longer seen as something taking place *in* the patient. Although one hopes that the client becomes wholer in the process, and although the therapist has a special role as initiator, facilitator, confidant, big brother or big sister, and representative of the dialogical claim of the world, the healing itself takes place in that sphere Buber calls the "between." This healing cannot be limited to the client alone or even to the relationship between therapist and client. To be real healing, it eventually must burst the bounds of *psycho*therapy and enter in all seriousness into the interhuman, the family, the group, the community, and even the relations between communities and nations. In his address to the Jungian Psychological Club of Zurich in 1923, "The Psychologizing of the World," Buber explicitly pointed to the problematic limits of the province of psychotherapy and the need that healing transcend that sphere:

The sicknesses of the soul are sicknesses of relationship. They can only be treated completely if I transcend the realm of the patient and add to it the world as well. If the doctor possessed superhuman power, he would have to try to heal the relationship itself, to heal in the "between." The doctor must know that really he ought to do that and that only his boundedness limits him to the one side. (Buber, 1990, p. 150)

The patient cannot experience equally well the relationship from the side of the therapist or the pupil from the side of the teacher, as we have seen, without destroying or fundamentally altering the relationship. This does not mean that the therapist is reduced to treating the patient as an object, an It. The one-sided inclusion of therapy is still an I-Thou relationship founded on mutuality, trust, and partnership in a common situation, and it is only in this relationship that real healing can take place. A common situation, however, does not mean one that each enters from the same or even a similar position. In psychotherapy the difference in position is not only that of personal stance but also of role and function, a difference determined by the very difference of purpose that led each to enter the relationship. If the goal is a common one—the healing of the patient—the relationship to that goal differs radically as between therapist and patient, and the healing that takes place depends as much upon the therapist's recognition of that difference as upon the mutuality of meeting and trust.

The Unconscious and Dreams

Martin Buber has suggested that the unconscious really may be the ground of personal wholeness before its elaboration into the physical and the psychic. Freud, he holds, and after him, Jung, have made the simple logical error of assuming that the unconscious is psychic because they wished to deny that it was physical. They did not, Buber holds, see this third alternative and with it the possibility of bursting the grounds of psychologism by recognizing that the division of inner and outer that applies to the psyche and the physical need not apply to the unconscious. As a result, direct meeting and direct communication might occur between one unconscious and another. The unconscious, by this reading, is our being itself in its wholeness. Out of it the physical and the psychical evolve again and again and at every moment. Therefore, the exploration of psychology is not of the unconscious itself but rather of the phenomena that have been dissociated from it. The radical mistake that Freud made was to think that he could posit a region of the mind as unconscious and at the same time deal with it as if its "contents" were simply repressed conscious material that could be brought back, without any essential change, into the conscious. Dissociation is the process in which the unconscious "lump" manifests itself in inner and outer perceptions and may be, in fact, the origin of our whole sense of inner and outer.

Freud, holding that the unconscious must be simply psychical, places the unconscious *within* the person, and so do most of the schools that have come after Freud. (At some point both Freud and Jung spoke of the meeting between one unconscious and another. The Jungian therapist Marvin Spiegelman has stressed the creation of a third reality *between* one unconscious and another as an important transference phenomenon [Spiegelman, 1965].) As a result, *the basis of human reality itself comes to be seen as psychical rather than interhuman, and the relations between person and person are psychologized.* Freud held that the therapist can induce the patient to bring out into the open the materials that he had repressed into the unconscious. Buber, in contrast, holds that we do not have a deep freeze to keep fragments that can be raised as they were. The dissociation into physical and psychic phenomena means a radical change of the substance. The therapist helps in this process and has an influence upon it. This means that the responsibility of the therapist is greater than has usually been supposed. Buber calls for a more "musical," floating relationship of therapist to patient, for *the deciding reality is the therapist, not the methods.* Although no therapist can do without a typology, at a certain moment the therapist throws away as much of his typology as he can and accepts the unforeseeable happening in which the unique person of the patient stands before the unique person of the therapist. The usual therapist imposes himself on his patient without being aware of it. What is necessary is the conscious liberation of the patient from this unconscious imposition and from the general ideas of the therapist's school of psychology. "It is much easier to impose oneself on the patient," says Buber, "than it is to use the whole force of one's soul to leave the patient to himself and not to touch him. *The real master responds to uniqueness*" (Buber, 1990, p. 168).

Buber sees the dominating importance of repression as arising from the disintegration of the organic community from within so that mistrust becomes life's basic note: "Agreement between one's own and the other's desire ceases, and the dulled wishes creep hopelessly into the recesses of the soul. . . . Now there is no longer a human wholeness with the force and the courage to manifest itself. . . . *The divorce between spirit and instincts is here* [italics added], as often, *the consequence of the divorce between man and man* [italics added]" (Buber, 1985, pp. 196f.).

Hans Trüb, similarly, sees the unconscious as precisely the personal element that is lost in the course of development. Repression, instead of being a basic aspect of human nature or an inescapable manifestation of civilization and its discontents, becomes the early denial of meeting, and its overcoming means the reestablishment of meeting, the breakthrough to dialogue:

> The unconscious touched by us has and takes its origin from that absolute "no" of the rejected meeting behind whose mighty barrier a person's psychic necessity for true meeting with the world secretly dams itself up, falls back upon itself, and thus, as it were, coagulates into the "unconscious." (Trüb in Friedman, 1991, p. 504)

In the relatively whole person, the unconscious would have a direct impact, not only on the conscious life, but also on others, precisely because it represents the wholeness of the person. In the relatively divided person, on the contrary, the unconscious itself has suffered a cleavage so that not only can some repressed materials not come up into consciousness but what does come up does not represent the wholeness of the person but only one of the fragments. As the unconscious of the relatively whole person is the very ground of meeting and an integral part of the interhuman, the unconscious of the relatively divided person is the product of the absence or denial of meeting. From this we can infer that the overcoming of the split between the repressed unconscious and the conscious of the divided person depends upon healing through meeting, including such confirmation as the therapist can summon from the relationship with the client to counterbalance the "absolute no" of the meeting rejected or withheld in childhood.

Healing through meeting means the concrete unfolding in therapy of the "ontology of the between." That means, among other things, the discovery of the implications of our understanding of the unconscious for the dream-work that the client carries out in dialogue with the therapist. Martin Buber questions whether we know or *have* dreams at all. What we possess, rather, is the work of the shaping memory that tells us of the dreamer's relation to the "dream," but nothing of the dream in itself. The dreamer, so long as he is dreaming, has no share in the common world and nothing, therefore, to which we can have access. Dreams are the residues of our waking dialogues. Not only do we have no real meeting with otherness in our dreams, but even the traces of otherness are diminished greatly. This does not mean, as Jung and Fritz Perls hold, that every person in the dream is really ourselves. But we cannot speak of dream relations as if they were identical with relations to persons in waking life. What we can say is that having set the dream over against us, thus isolated, shaped, elaborated, and given form as an independent opposite, we enter into dialogue with it. From now on it becomes one of the realities that addresses us in the world, just as surely and as concretely as any so-called external happening. From this it follows that the therapist cannot know what method of dream interpretation he will use beforehand but must place himself in the hands of the patient and, practicing what Buber calls "obedient listening," let himself be guided by what the patient brings him (Buber, 1990, pp. 167f.).

Neurotic and Existential Guilt

Although not denying the existence of repressed neurotic guilt, Buber went beyond Freud in positing the existence of an "existential guilt" attached to events that are accessible to the conscious mind but that have lost their character of guilt because of our attitude toward them. Healing through meeting necessarily implies the existence of a real, existential guilt, usually confusedly intermingled with neurotic and/or merely social guilt. Existential guilt is an ontic, interhuman reality in which the person dwells, in the truest sense of the term, an illness of one's relations with the world. True guilt does not reside *in* the human person but rather in one's failure to respond to the legitimate claim and address of the world, and the sickness that results from the denial of such guilt is not merely a psychological phenomenon but an event between persons (Buber, 1988c, pp. 94-132). Existential guilt, as we have seen, is "guilt that a person has taken on himself as a person and in a personal situation." Real guilt is neither subjective nor objective. It is dialogical—the inseparable corollary of one's personal responsibility, one's answerability for authenticating one's own existence, and by the same token, for responding to the partners of one's existence, the other persons with whom one lives. Where there is personal responsibility, there must also be the possibility of real guilt—for failing to respond, for responding inadequately or too late, or for responding without the whole self.

Such guilt is neither inner nor outer. We are not answerable for it either to ourselves alone or to society apart from ourselves but to that very bond between ourselves through which we again and again discover the direction through which we can authenticate our existence. If a relation with another cannot be reduced to what goes on within each of the two persons, then the guilt one person has toward a partner in a relationship cannot be reduced to the subjective guilt he or she feels. The order of the human world that one injures is the sphere of the "interhuman" itself, precisely those We's that we have built in common in family, group, and community and to which our own existence belongs in the most literal sense of the term.

Everyone knows quite well how, through attacking or withholding oneself, one may injure one's family, friends, community, colleagues, or fellow employees.

Guilt is an essential factor in the person's relations to others: It performs the necessary function of leading one to desire to set these relations to rights. It is actually here, in the real guilt of the person who has not responded to the legitimate claim and address of the world, that the possibility of transformation and healing lies. The therapist may lead the person who suffers from existential guilt to the place where that person can walk the road of illuminating that guilt, persevering in his or her identification of oneself as the person who, no matter how different from what one is now, took on that guilt, and, insofar as one's situation makes possible, restoring and repairing "the order of being injured by one through the relation of an active devotion to the world" (Buber, 1988c, chap. 6), that is, reentering the dialogue with the community.

Buber's and Boszormenyi-Nagy's concept of "the just order of the human world" is a dialogical one. However pathological it may be, the unique experience of each of the persons in the family is itself of value: It enters into the balance of merit and into the dialogical reality-testing—the "dialogue of touchstones," as I call it. The scapegoater in the family may be looked upon as needing help and the scapegoat as a potential helper, for the former is taking an ever heavier load of guilt upon himself and the latter is accumulating merit through being loaded upon by others.

The injustice of the parentification of children by their parents can be redressed only if one first goes back to the relationship of the parents to their family of origin and does something about constructive repayment of indebtedness there. The family therapist must help the children obtain release from their captive victimization. To accomplish this, however, it is first necessary that the adults' own unmet dependency needs and unresolved negative loyalty ties, based upon unjust treatment and exploitation by their families of origin, be recognized and worked through—whenever possible with the families of origin themselves.

In the end the therapeutic application of the distinction between neurotic and existential guilt must be understood in the broader context of confirmation and the "dialogue of touchstones" that can, more than anything, lead to healing through meeting.

Confirmation

No one can confirm us through *empathy* in the strict sense of the term—because they do not give of themselves thereby—or through identification—because they miss us in our uniqueness and filter through only what is like themselves. They can confirm us only if they bring themselves in their uniqueness into dialogue with us in ours and confirm us while holding in tension the "overagainstness," and, if necessary, even the opposition and conflict that come out of this unique relationship between two unique persons. Only inclusion, or imagining the real, really grasps the other in his or her otherness and brings that other into relationship to oneself.

If confirmation is central to human and interhuman existence, then it follows that disconfirmation, especially in the earliest stages of life, must be a major factor in psychopathology. Instead of finding the genesis of neurosis and psychosis in frustrated gratification of drives à la Freud, we shall find it more basically and more frequently in disconfirming situations in the family that impair the child's basic trust. "One can hypothetically assume that if the parent is prematurely lost as a component of the child's identity delineating ground," writes Ivan Boszormenyi-Nagy, "a fixated bottomless craving for trust becomes his permanent character trait"(Boszormenyi-Nagy, 1965, p. 120). Boszormenyi-Nagy's hypothesis is confirmed at length by the theories and clinical practice of Heinz Kohut, Harold Searles, Ronald Laing, Helm Stierlin, and Carl Rogers (see Friedman, 1985, chap. 11).

If disconfirmation or the absence of confirmation lies at the root of much psychopathology, then confirmation lies at the core of healing through meeting. Healing through meeting, as we have seen, goes beyond the repair work that helps a soul that is diffused and poor in structure to collect and order itself to the essential task—the regeneration of an atrophied personal center. This means the healing not just of a certain part of the patient but also of the very roots of the patient's being. Without the existential trust of one whole person to another, there will be no realization on the part of the patient of the need to give up into the hands of the therapist what is repressed. Without such trust even masters of method cannot effect existential healing.

The therapist has to realize that the person before him or her is someone who has been rejected and disconfirmed by the community, someone who stands in need of the understanding and confirmation that a confidant can give. Only later, after the therapist has succeeded in giving the patient the confirmation he or she has been denied, does the therapist enter the second stage and place upon the patient the demand of the community to help the patient renew the dialogue with the community that has been injured or destroyed. Placing the demand of the community does not mean any moralizing from above. It means connecting the hour of therapy with real life so that the client can recognize in the therapist a really other person who has real ties to the community and stands within it. Without that second stage—not replacing but combined with the first—no real healing can come about. It is not enough for the therapist to help call people to account in terms of their self-betrayal or even their guilt toward their family. It must, at the same time, be a calling back into the dialogue with the community. Both stages probably must be there at every moment, but the right proportion between the two at any one time is a matter of real listening and of the "grace" that allows one to discover what is called for in each situation through openness and response. Some persons could be injured severely by a premature placing upon them of the demand of the community, just as some persons could be injured severely if the therapist never reached that stage. True confirmation is an event that happens *between* the therapist and patient, one that helps the patient go back into the world to give and receive confirmation in the mutual interaction with others.

The "Dialogue of Touchstones"

An important link between Trüb's two stages, as between confirmation and healing through meeting, is what I call the "dialogue of touchstones." In touching we do make contact, even if it is only a partial one, and that contact itself is a reality and a form of direct knowing, however illusory the inferences from the contact may be. It is not just that we have the *experience* of touching. On the contrary, to touch is to go through *and beyond* subjective experiencing: If I touch, if we touch, then the communication is neither merely objective nor merely subjective, nor both together. The very act of touching is already a transcending of the self in openness to the impact of something other than the self. When two people really touch each other as persons—whether physically or not—the touching is not merely a one-sided impact: It is a mutual revelation of life stances.

Real communication means that each of us has some real contact with the otherness of the other. But this is possible only if each of us has related to the other's touchstones in his or her unique way. We really can listen only if we are willing to be open and to respond personally. The product of such communication will be something different from what either you or I intend. But it will be real communication, in contrast to that habitual misunderstanding in which we all are too often imprisoned—closed circuits in which we make a little voyage toward the other and then come back. The real "dialogue of touchstones" means that we respond from where we are, that we bring ourselves into the dialogue. The other person needs to know that he or she really is coming up against us as persons with touchstones and witnesses of our own.

We help one another along the road when we share our touchstones *and* the confusion that sometimes accompanies them. We evolve our touchstones in relation with one another; we witness to one another. We have an impact on one another through which we grow in our own touchstones. Growing in this way, we come to recognize that the "dialogue of touchstones" is itself a touchstone of reality.

When I wrote my book *Touchstones of Reality* (Friedman, 1972) I thought of the "dialogue of touchstones" as fully mutual.

Shortly afterward it struck me that a dialogue of touchstones could occur within therapy with that normative limitation of mutuality that characterizes therapy. The so-called psychotic, the schizophrenic, or the paranoid live facing the impossible choice of retreating within and pretending to go along with socially approved ways of speaking and acting or of "expressing" themselves and alienating everyone else in so doing. If they too have their touchstones of reality, such an impossible choice represents a sort of death for them.

The schizophrenic's touchstones of reality are not just "real for him." They represent a genuine dialogue with "reality" that can enrich deeply our own relation to reality. Put in the language of Buber's "What Is Common to All" (Buber, 1988c), schizophrenics, even in their desire to have a world of their own apart from the common world, help build up the common world of speech-with-meaning. Their voices cannot be excluded without impoverishing us all.

From the standpoint of the dialogue of touchstones, much of what we call "mental illness" may be seen as something that has happened to distort, objectify, or make merely cultural our touchstones of reality. Touchstones of reality and the dialogue of touchstones begin in and are renewed by immediacy. Sickness is what prevents the return to immediacy. From this standpoint, "health" is not "adjustment," becoming rational or emotional, but rather coming to a firmer grasp of one's own touchstones of reality in dialogue with the touchstones of others. In this sense, the dialogue of touchstones may be the goal of therapy, as well as the means. This goal helps the therapist avoid three equally bad alternatives—adjusting the client to the culture, imposing the therapist's own values upon the client, and accepting whatever the patient says and does as healthy and romantically celebrating it.

Clients fear that in entering into therapy they will have to sacrifice their own touchstones of reality, that they will have to subordinate themselves to an external authority and join in invalidating their own touchstones as "sick." What makes this fear all too real is not only the psychotherapist who sets up his or her own "reality" as the sole standard of health, but also the "responsible" and "helpful" person who tends to handle both sides of the dialogue and thus *disenables* the other person to bring his or her own touchstones into the dialogue.

The therapist in the dialogue of touchstones cannot be someone who merely analyzes or reflects what the client says. The therapist also must be someone who brings his or her own touchstones into the dialogue. The normative limitation to mutuality in the therapeutic dialogue of touchstones lies not only in the structure—who comes to see whom for help—but also in the fact that the therapist brings something to the dialogue that the severely neurotic and psychotic patient cannot bring. It is not that the therapist's experience is more real, deeper, and, certainly not by a long shot, more intense. It is only that he or she has more experience in inclusion, in imagining the real, in experiencing the other side of the relationship, in seeing through the other's eyes, as well as through his or her own.

If we begin by honoring each person's unique relation to reality, then to say of a person that he or she is "sick" does not imply that this person is outside reality, but only that he or she needs help in being brought into the dialogue of touchstones. The terrible dilemma of the "sick" person, we have seen, is having to choose between giving up one's touchstones to communicate or giving up communication. But a touchstone that is not brought into the dialogue ceases to be a touchstone. Instead, the person is divided into an outer "social" mask and an inner hidden reality, and both are less than real. It does not matter whether the outer mask is social conformity or the defenses and postures of the schizophrenic who regards others and/or himself or herself as unreal; it is still far less than human reality. It also does not matter whether the inner "reality" is repressed from consciousness or is cherished eagerly as the most precious "inward" possession, the "real self," as Horney, Rogers, and many others like to say. It too is vestigial, atrophied, less than a fully human or even fully personal reality.

Such a person needs the help of someone who can glimpse and share the unique reality that has come from this person's life experience and can help this person find a way of bringing it into the common order of existence to raise what he or she has experienced as "I" into the communal reality of "We." Such a person needs the help of a therapist who can imagine the real and practice inclusion to help the patient enter into a dialogue of touchstones.

The help of the therapist is not, in the first instance, a matter of finding the right words, still less techniques of communication. It is a matter of the dialogue of touchstones coming into being between one who cannot reach out and one who can. "When one person is singing and cannot lift his voice," said a Hasidic rabbi, "and another comes and sings with him, another who can lift his voice, then the first will be able to lift his voice. That," said the rabbi, "is the secret of the bond between spirit and spirit." The title that Martin Buber gave this Hasidic story was not "The Healer" or "The Helper," but "When Two Sing." In the language of this book it might be called "Healing Through Meeting" or even "A Dialogue of Touchstones." For that *is* the secret of the bond between spirit and spirit.

The helpfulness of the therapist does not lie, as we have seen, in the fact that he or she is a better Socratic dialectician or that he or she articulates or analyzes better, but rather that he or she can help the patient out of the unfruitful either/or of choosing between faithfulness to one's own emergent touchstones and relation with the community. Yet, this is possible only in a situation of mutual trust. To the extent that patients are afraid to expose themselves for fear that the therapist or family or friends will invalidate what they have to contribute as worthless, they will not be able to enter into the venture of the dialogue of touchstones. The goal of healing through meeting, of confirmation, and of the dialogue of touchstones is, therefore, the same—to establish a dialogue on the basis of trust.

The "confirmation of otherness" (Friedman, 1983) that the dialogue of touchstones assumes and brings into existence means that no voice is without value, no witness without reality. Every voice needs to be heard precisely because it represents a unique relationship to reality. Even though that voice may be distorted, "sick," and miserable, it still contains the nucleus of a unique touchstone that its very negativity both bears and conceals. Confirming the other, in the end, cannot mean just healing in the limited sense of making a single person whole. It must mean also a movement in the direction of a climate of trust, a caring community, a community that confirms otherness. Such a community gives each person a ground of his or her own, a ground from which they can touch the other's touching, a ground in which mutual confirming and healing through meeting can take place in spiraling circles that bring more and more of each person's touchstones—whether born of trauma or of ecstasy—into the reality of life together. This is the secret of the bond between person and person.

PART FOUR

The Image of the Human

9

Philosophical Anthropology
and the Image of the Human

Contemporary Philosophy and Psychology:
"Human Nature" Reconsidered

If the divergent schools of contemporary philosophy are united in little else, they do at least join rejecting the notion that man has some fixed, identifiable, universal essence. We look to contemporary philosophy, therefore, not so much for new definitions of human nature as for a new critical awareness of the issues that surround this term. This critical awareness is of particular significance for psychology and psychoanalytic theory because both have often taken over quite uncritically many of the formulations of classical philosophy.

One of the classic problems of "human nature" is that of "free will" versus "determinism." Transposed into the realm of psychology, it becomes the much more fruitful problem of personal freedom and psychological compulsion. The reality of unconscious compulsion makes it impossible to assert the existence of full, conscious freedom. But it is equally impossible to reduce man to a purely deterministic system. Human existence—in the well person as in the ill—is a complex intermixture of personal freedom and psychological compulsion, a paradoxical phenomenon that can be understood only from within. As I have written in *Problematic Rebel*:

> The problem of the relation of personal freedom to psychological compulsion cannot be solved by the attempt to reduce man to a bundle of instinctual drives, unconscious complexes, the need for security or any other single factor. . . . Motivation is inextricably bound up with the wholeness of the person, with his direction of movement, with his struggles to authenticate himself. . . . No general theory of psychogenesis and no general knowledge of a person will tell us in advance what will be his actual mixture of spontaneity and compulsion in any particular situation. (Friedman, 1970, pp. 470, 472)

Another problem of human nature that psychoanalytic theory has inherited from classical philosophy is that of mind-body dualism. At first glance, most psychoanalysis would seem to be a denial of this dualism. In fact, however, the problem has only been transposed into the complex interrelationship between biological instinct and consciousness or, on a subtler plane, between the pleasure principle and the reality principle. Even the division between the conscious and the unconscious that is so central to psychoanalysis is in a certain sense a variant of the Cartesian mind-body dualism. Freud's "censor," Sartre points out, is in "bad faith" with itself; for it must know what it censors and then pretend not to know it. Thus Freud's psychoanalysis introduces into subjectivity the deepest structure of intersubjectivity. It leaves a dualism between the unconscious and consciousness, a dualism that is bridged only by an autonomous consciousness, which knows the drive to be repressed precisely *in order not to be* conscious of it.

Commenting on my statement about Freud's Cartesian dualism in the above passage, Charles Brice writes:

> What you have here are dualisms, but not of mind and body. The real Cartesian split will be found in Freud's theory of the drives—when a drive per se is chemical (body) and all that can appear in the mind is a "representation" of the drive. Same for affects—since an affect is an *ex*pression of a feeling (*res extensia*), an affect cannot be unconscious—only the "idea" of an affect can. This gets Freud into the

impossible question of how an affect "attaches" to its corresponding idea in the unconscious—which leads to the problem of repression proper. See Freud, "Instinct and Their Vicissitudes," "The Unconscious," and "Repression" in the Standard Edition. (C. W. Brice, personal communication, 1990)

Philosophical Anthropology

According to Martin Buber's philosophical anthropology, what gives man a world and an existence as a self over against other selves is the ability, unique to man, of executing two primary ontological movements—that of setting at a distance and that of entering into relation. If, as Buber holds, only these constitute man as man, then the attempt of some psychological and psychoanalytical theories to deal with man in fundamentally biological terms, as if he were continuous with all other animals except for the modifications forced by civilization, is fundamentally in error. In error, too, is the individualism of the isolated consciousness that both Freud and Jung inherited from Descartes. Starting with "I think, therefore I am," Descartes was left with the insoluble problem of the knowledge of other minds. Edmund Husserl's phenomenology, Heidegger's ontology, and Sartre's existentialism have all transposed (but not necessarily solved) this problem by seeing the self as existing only in its transcendence toward a field of consciousness, or a world. The classic subject-object relation of knower and known is replaced here by the self and its world.

Immanuel Kant was the first philosopher explicitly to stake out philosophical anthropology as a branch of philosophy. Not only is the question, "What is man?" a part of the question, "What can I know?" but it is a very special part of this question, with problems unique to itself. At the same time, as the view of man the knower changed, the view of what man is inevitably changed with it. Kant's great successor, Friedrich Hegel, removed Kant's dualism of the noumenal and the phenomenal into the concrete universal of the world-historical spirit. Among some of the radical neo-Hegelians, the continued cultivation of the philosophical soil they inherited was coupled with a rebellion against the idealist subject in favor of the whole human person (Kierkegaard and Nietzsche), against the historical spirit in favor of the concrete realities of social, economic, and political life (Feuerbach, Marx, and Nietzsche), against the isolated thinker in favor of the recognition of the origin of all thought and all philosophy in the dialogue of I and Thou (Feuerbach), or against metaphysics in favor of philosophical anthropology (Feuerbach and Nietzsche) (cf. Löwith, 1964).

An important advance in philosophical anthropology was the development of "phenomenology" by the German philosophers Wilhelm Dilthey and Edmund Husserl. Dilthey based his thought upon the radical difference between the way of knowing proper to the *"Geisteswissenchaften"* (the human studies, such as philosophy, the social sciences, and psychology) and that proper to *"Naturwissenschaften"* (the natural sciences). In the former, the knowers cannot be merely detached scientific observers but must also participate themselves; for it is through their participation that they discover both the typical and the unique in the aspects of human life that they are studying. At the same time, they must suspend the foregone conclusions and the search for causality that mark the natural scientist in favor of an open attempt to discover what offers itself. Only through this open understanding (*das Verstehen*) can one value the unique that reveals itself in every human phenomenon.

Husserl elaborated phenomenology into a full-fledged systematic philosophy. He went decisively beyond Descartes's *cogito* in his recognition that one cannot divorce the "I think" from what is thought, consciousness from intentionality. By the method of "parenthesizing," or phenomenological reduction, Husserl replaced the detached subject and independent object of older philosophy by a field of knowing in which the phenomena are accepted as pure phenomena without questioning their independent existence. From this he also obtained a "transcendental ego" which, as the subject of knowing, transcended all contents of knowing, including the psychophysical me. The exploration of the field of transcendental experience thus becomes equivalent to the phenomenological knowledge of the world.

Husserl's existential successors either emphasized the direct experiential quality of his thought as opposed to the idealist, as did Maurice Merleau-Ponty, or broke with the transcendental ego altogether while retaining the method of phenomenology, as did Jean-Paul Sartre, or transformed phenomenology from a method of knowledge into "fundamental ontology," as did Martin Heidegger. Both Sartre and Heidegger accept Husserl's motto "To the things themselves" as an obstacle to scientism's attempt to posit a substratum of independent but nonperceivable "matter" behind the phenomena. Only an existential analysis of the existent will yield any knowledge of being. For Heidegger this analysis is posited on his special use of *Dasein*— the person's "being there" in the world, thrown into a situation apart from which neither subject nor consciousness has any meaning. Heidegger and Sartre see the self as existing only in its transcendence toward a field of consciousness or a world. To exist is to be there, in the situation, and the situation includes, of course, the world of intersubjectivity in which we have to do with other persons. Yet Heidegger and Sartre still basically see the ontological as essentially discovered in the self, with the relations to others as an "ontic" dimension of the existence of the self or an "intersubjectivity" in which each makes the other an object or is made object by the other.

Martin Buber, who stems from Feuerbach and Dilthey rather than from Husserl, sees the ontological as found in the *meeting* between person and person and between person and world, with the realization of the self the indispensable accompaniment and corollary of the dialogue. Buber has sharpened the social theory of the self to a distinction between direct, mutual interpersonal relations—"I-Thou"or "the interhuman"—and indirect, nonmutual interpersonal relations—"I-It." The American social psychologist and philosopher George Herbert Mead, the American psychiatrist Harry Stack Sullivan, and Erich Fromm all share with Buber what Paul Pfuetze (1973) calls "the social self." But, as we have seen, they have not made the distinction Buber has made between direct and indirect, mutual and nonmutual interpersonal relations. And this distinction is not grasped adequately by Heidegger's *Mitsein* or Sartre's "world of intersubjectivity." Heidegger's "being-with" undoubtedly includes the I-Thou relationship in principle, but it gives very little attention to anything that could be recognized as such, and the ultimate relationship for him is explicitly with oneself. Sartre's intersubjectivity excludes free mutuality in principle in favor of a tormented interaction of subjectivity and objectivity in which one recognizes the other's freedom either as a threat and a limitation to one's own or as something to be possessed and dominated for a time through sexual love.

Buber's view of man leads him to assert, as we have seen, that the chasm between spirit and instincts is not an inherent structure of human nature, as Freud holds, but is a product of the sickness of Modern Man—the destruction of organic confidence and of organic community and the divorce between person and person (Buber, 1985, pp. 196f.). It also has led Buber, and myself following him, to a more dialogical understanding of the task of the philosophical anthropologist than even Feuerbach and Dilthey. Philosophical anthropology goes beyond cultural anthropology in that it asks the question not just about human beings but about the human: about our wholeness and uniqueness, about what makes us human. As such, it necessarily transcends, even while making full use of, those sciences that deliberately deal with the human being only as a part and not as a whole—whether it be Economic Man, Political Man, Sociological Man, Psychological Man, or Biological Man. It can only touch upon the problem of the human, however, insofar as it recognizes that the philosophical anthropologist himself or herself is a human being and as such is *as subject* and not just as object a part of what he or she seeks to know. One must share in and not merely observe the problematic of Modern Man. One must reject all attempts to reduce this problematic to any single motive or complex of motives or to comprehend the human simply on the analogy of biology or the behavior of animals. Only if as philosophical anthropologist one is a problem to oneself can one understand the human as a problem to itself.

Only if one knows from within one's own situation and in dialogue with the others with whom one has to do can one begin to approach that wholeness and uniqueness of the human that slips through the net of every concept of man as object. To understand the human, one must be a participant who only afterward gains the distance from one's subject matter that will enable one to formulate the insights one has attained. Otherwise, one inevitably sees man as a sum of parts, some of which are labeled "objective" and, hence, oriented around the thing known, and some "subjective" and, hence, oriented around the knower.

Philosophical anthropology today begins on the far side of earlier notions of understanding the human in terms of a universal and timeless "human nature." It looks away from essences of the human in order to grasp human beings in their particularity and their complexity, their dynamic interrelatedness with others, and the interplay within them of possibility, freedom, and personal direction. Existentialism similarly replaces the concept of "human nature" by the concept of the "human condition." Man is without a predetermined essence because man is free, but his freedom is a finite one, as Tillich points out. It must operate within the general human condition—the need to work, one's existence as a self in relation to other selves and to the nonhuman world, the awareness of solitude, of possibility, and of death. These approaches represent radical changes in our view of man and have far-reaching implications that have only begun to be spelled out. Yet the critical task of modern philosophy in relation to the concept of human nature cannot stop here.

The Image of the Human

If we wish to make a decisive break with the universal and essential "human nature" of earlier philosophy and attain a picture of the human in its uniqueness and wholeness, we must move from *concepts* about the human, no matter how profound, to the *image* of the human. It is this I have tried to do in my trilogy of books on the human image: *Problematic Rebel, To Deny Our Nothingness*, and *The Hidden Human Image*. The human image, as I use the term, is not only an image of what we are but also an image of authentic personal and social existence that helps us discover, in each age anew, what we may and can become, an image that helps us rediscover our humanity. "Image" in this context means not a static picture but a meaningful, personal direction, a response from within to what one meets in each new situation, standing one's ground and meeting the world with the attitude that is rooted in this ground. The human image embodies a way of responding. Because it is faithful response and not objective content that is central to the human image, each individual stands in a unique personal relation to his or her image of the human, even when it happens to be shared by a society as a whole. One becomes oneself in dialogue with other selves and in response to one's image, one's images of the human. Yet, the more genuine the dialogue, the more unique the relationship and the more truly is the one who is becoming, becoming oneself. The fruit of such response is not that bolstering of the ego that comes from comparing oneself favorably with another or modeling oneself on an ideal, but the confirmation of one's unique personal existence, of the ground upon which one stands.

The human image does not mean some fully formed, conscious model of what one should become—certainly not anything simply imposed upon us by the culture or any mere conformity with society through identification with its goals. The paradox of the human image is that it is at once unique and universal, but universal only through the unique. For each one of us, the human image is made up of many images and half-formed images, and it is itself constantly changing and evolving. In contrast to any static ideal whatsoever, it always has to do only with the unique response to the concrete moment, a response that cannot be foreseen and cannot be repeated, objectified, or imitated.

The human image is our becoming in the truest sense of the word, that is, our becoming as a person and as a human being. In this becoming, what we call the "is" is not a static given. It is a dynamic, constantly changing material that continually is being shaped and given form not merely by inner and outer conditioning but by the directions that one takes as a person. Similarly, what we call the "ought" is not some abstract ideal but a constantly changing, flowing direction of movement that is at one and the same time a response to the present, a choice between possibilities in a given situation, and a line of advance into the future.

In *The Hidden Human Image* (Friedman, 1974), I pointed to the human image as the hidden ground underlying many disciplines that are usually seen as quite separate—philosophy, literature, religious studies, psychology, social sciences, intellectual and cultural history. I also pointed to the fact that the human image stands in continual need of being revealed—in each new situation—but, like a face or a myth, can never be revealed fully. It is like a river of eternity running beneath the depths of time. In addition, I pointed to the truly terrible way in which the human image has been obscured and all but eclipsed in our day by the Holocaust, atomic bombings, mass starvation, and a thousand gross and subtle ways in which we deny our common humanity and demonstrate "man's inhumanity to man." I pointed, too, to the tragic irony that much that in our day seeks to bring the human image out of its hiddenness only deepens its eclipse.

Psychotherapy and the Human Image

An important aspect of my three books on the image of the human has been exploring the meeting between the image of the human and psychotherapy. No field is perhaps of more interest for the hidden human image than psychotherapy. On the one hand, "depth psychology," or "depth analysis," undertakes to reveal, to bring to the light of day, much that is hidden, including for some persons their hidden humanity. On the other hand, psychotherapy in its various schools of theory and practice has contributed its share to the eclipse of man, to the further hiding of the human image. This is in part because of the mechanistic approach that was taken toward science and even toward the human. Psychiatry in the nineteenth century was a specific matter of curing symptoms. It had little to do with the wholeness of the human. Psychoanalysis represented an important step in the direction of a concern for the whole person, but only a step. It arose under the aegis of "Science" and even of scientism. In many branches of psychotherapy today, however, the movement is away from seeing it as an exact science toward seeing it as a humanistic task and a humanistic discipline.

Each school of psychotherapy has, with various degrees of clarity, its own image of the human. That image stands in fruitful dialectic with the therapeutic practice of the members of the school, but it is not, for all that, a scientific product of that school. On the contrary, the far-reaching differences between the many schools of psychotherapy derive in part from the fact that implied in the positive goals they enunciate are different images of the human. Such central therapeutic terms as *health, integration, maturity, creativity,* and *self-realization* imply not only an image of the human but also usually essentially different ones for different schools and even different members of the same school. "The critical battles between approaches to psychology and psychoanalysis in our culture in the next decades, as always," writes Rollo May, "will be on the battleground of the image of man" (Friedman, 1991, p. 447).

Human nature is often taken by schools of psychotherapy to be itself the norm. The human being should live according to his or her "nature," according to his or her "real self," and the like. It is also part of human nature to become ill. The very meaning of *health,* therefore, implies some sense of what is authentic direction for the human being, for this particular person—in short, an image of the human. As Helen Merrell Lynd points out, the "real" or "spontaneous" self is not a given that need only be freed from its social encrustations. It is the product of a lifelong dialogue with our image of the human.

Horney, Fromm, and even Sullivan at times, seem to assume that there is an already existent real or true or spontaneous self which can be evoked into active existence almost at will. There is a tacit assumption that somehow we know the dictates of the real self, and that we should live in terms of these rather than of a romanticized self-image or of the pseudo-self of others' expectations. But . . . such *a real self is something to be discovered and created, not a given, but a lifelong endeavor* [italics added]. (Lynd, 1958, p. 203)

Psychology and Literature

"Through considering together both literary and nonliterary works," I suggest in my book *To Deny Our Nothingness*, "we can gain a deeper understanding of the image of man as the hidden ground in which literature, philosophy, psychotherapy, religion, and social thought all meet" (Friedman, 1978, p. 27). The human image might well be called the matrix from which each of these fields emerges, which they continue to embody within them, and which continues to bind them together in essential ways no matter how stringently the disciplines pertaining to each particular field make it necessary to hold them apart. This ground or matrix must necessarily remain hidden. It can be pointed to through one or the other field or through the meeting between them, but it cannot be disclosed or made manifest because this would always mean translating one discipline or field into another and thereby destroying its integrity. We cannot translate literature into psychology and thereby get the image of the human; for literature and psychology are *both* rooted in the human image. Realizing this, we can at one and the same time take seriously the need for the human image to be revealed, the need for remaining faithful to each of these various ways of knowing the human, and yet the need not to take seriously the ultimate overclaim that it alone contains all the important knowledge about its own field. For each field is simply a human and ultimately arbitrary marking off that shades into another field. These fields of knowledge are so many partial ways of trying to get a purchase on the multidimensional reality of the wholeness and concreteness of the human.

Contemporary psychology obscures the human by its implicit claim that it alone possesses the "real" way of looking at guilt, anxiety, and motivation. Literature usually is taken as at best an illustration of psychological concepts, at worst a luxury, an ornament of the superstructure that does not get down to the foundations. Actually literature gives us a *deeper* understanding of most of these phenomena because it is concrete and because it sees persons from within and not just from the outside. Isidor Chein writes of the clinician: "He gains more from reading Dostoevsky, Mann, Proust, and Shakespeare than all of the pages of the *Journal of Experimental Psychology*." For literature, as Chein observes, can give us an example of the particular in all its complexity, as opposed to "statistically significant generalizations about highly circumscribed behaviors occurring under laboratory conditions" (Chein, 1972, p. 313).

Leslie Farber goes even farther than Chein. He opts for literature, not only instead of experimental psychology, but also instead of the statements of the psychoanalysts themselves, none of whose competing systems "is—to my present way of thinking—fit for human habitation." Freud took pains, to be sure, to dissociate his theories from those of metaphysics or religion. "Yet, for lack of any other definitions of the fully human, it is virtually impossible nowadays for the psychiatrist *not* to derive his norms and standards from his own psychopathology" (Farber, 1966, p. 132). Then, after citing quotations from Karl Abraham, W. Ronald D. Fairbairn, Harry Stack Sullivan, and C. G. Jung, Farber comments:

> Though the creatures described above may bear some resemblance to animals or to steam engines or robots or electronic brains, they do not sound like people. They are, in fact, constructs of theory, more humanoid than human; and, whether they are based on the libido theory or on one of the new interpersonal theories of relationships, it is just those qualities most distinctively human that seem to have been omitted. It is a matter of some irony, if one turns from psychology to one of Dostoyevsky's novels, to find that, no matter how wretched, how puerile, or how dilapidated his characters may be, they all possess more humanity than the ideal man who lives in the pages of psychiatry. (Farber, 1966, p. 133)

Freud, to be sure, recognized the genius of Shakespeare and Dostoievsky. Yet his followers, in the ranks both of psychoanalysts and of literary critics, have often contented themselves with Freudian analyses of Shakespeare's *Hamlet*, Dostoievsky's *Crime and Punishment*, or Kafka's *Trial*. Then they have turned around and used these analyses as evidence of the way in which literature illustrates the Oedipus complex! Despite their enormous interest in literature, myth, and fairy tales, the Jungians have done essentially the same. Whether in Melville's

Moby Dick, for example, one says that the harpoons are phallic symbols or falling into the whale's head a return to the womb or whether one sees the whole thing in Jungian terms as a descending into the archetypal unconscious and working through to the individuation of the self, what one tends to do is to reduce the actual novel to the set of meanings that one has brought to it and prevent *its* saying what it is. This also means reducing the dynamic moving event of what takes place between one and the book to something that can be put into a static category.

In some of the chapters that follow I shall draw on my interpretations presented in *Problematic Rebel* of Melville, Dostoievsky, Kafka, and, to a lesser extent, Camus to show how literature can give us a deeper insight than can psychological theory into a number of problems that stand at the heart of the human condition. These perennial human problems are still more intensified by the alienation of Modern Man, and they come to us, thus intensified, in peculiarly modern guise: anxiety, freedom and compulsion, the divided self, conflict of values, sex and love, guilt and shame. Precisely because such problems are regarded by most educated people today as the exclusive province of psychology, such a turning toward literature can contribute to our understanding of the image of the human.

10

Our Age of Anxiety

Rollo May tells of how, when he was laid up for a year with tuberculosis as a young man, he read both Freud and Kierkegaard on anxiety. Freud deals with anxiety objectively and from the outside. Kierkegaard deals with it subjectively and from within. Freud sees anxiety as a generalized attack resulting from the repression of specific unconscious fears. By bringing these fears into consciousness, psychoanalysis can overcome them and anxiety with them. Kierkegaard, in contrast, sees anxiety (*Angst*) as an inescapable part of the human condition that can never be cured. Indeed, it is part and parcel of what makes us human beings, as Kierkegaard spells it out in his book *The Concept of Anxiety* (1980), in which he shows man as propelled by the anxiety of potentiality from the stage of original innocence to some actual sin, a fall that is a relief, compared to the omnipossibility that before threatened man.

Whether we follow W. H. Auden in dubbing the present time "the age of anxiety," no one would deny that there are a great many evidences of anxiety in our culture, manifestations that are all the more striking given the fact that we have attained a level of technological advance and a standard of living never before know to humankind. The hydrogen bomb, the cold war, racial conflict, the growing pressure upon children to compete for grades so that they may have a chance to enter college, down to the anxiety of parents about toilet training and the right balance of discipline and permissiveness—all these are too well known to need elaboration.

Yet, these manifestations of anxiety raise the question of whether we should regard anxiety as a product of our culture or our culture as an elaborate mechanism for warding off basic human anxiety, or both. Here we shall part company according to our approach. If we are Freudians, we shall see anxiety as the repression of childhood fears, on the one hand, and as the individual's discontent with civilization, on the other; in either case, we shall see it as a product of guilt connected with the Oedipus complex or the too harsh repression of libidinal instincts. If we are Sullivanians, we shall see anxiety in terms of the dissociation between our images of ourselves and our actual interpersonal performance, necessitated by the fear of the disapproval of significant others. If we are Jungians, we shall see anxiety as the repression of the "shadow" self, those frightening elements of the self that turn negative and "evil" when we fail to integrate them with the rest of our personality. If we take a sociopsychological approach, we shall see anxiety in terms of competition, "keeping up with the Joneses," "what makes Sammy run." Or we shall talk of the anxiety created, as well as allayed, by the patterns of social conformity, such as the "Organization Man" and the "other-directed" person.

In contrast to these approaches are those that see anxiety as basically human and culture as either a manifestation or avoidance of this anxiety. For Kierkegaard anxiety begins with the leap from innocence to experience, the fear and trembling that the "single one" experiences in his unique relationship with God, the dread of the person who has fallen into demonic shut-in-ness, the despair of wishing to be or not to be oneself. For Martin Heidegger anxiety is the primordial phenomenon that the "They" of culture, ambiguity, gossip, idle talk, cover over and conceal, and by the same token it is that which calls one back to one's "thrownness" and with it one's authentic existence.

Paul Tillich also takes an ontological approach to anxiety and sees beneath the layers of individual neuroticism, on the one hand, and our specific culture, on the other hand, the general human anxiety before fate and death, before emptiness and meaninglessness, and before guilt and self-condemnation Tillich holds that to exist is to exist face-to-face with nonbeing, by which he means what is changing and passing away—all the negative in existence. The neurotic, according to Tillich, is not the one who is anxious but the one who is not anxious, that is, the one who through fear of facing the anxiety of nonbeing is cut off from being as well and cruelly curtails the possibilities of existence.

All of these approaches have enough truth in them to add to our understanding of anxiety, yet none of them can answer the question of whether anxiety is a product of our culture or whether culture is a means of warding off a basic human anxiety. To answer this question we need a new approach that does not choose between the psychological, sociological, and ontological but unites them within a larger framework, the historical. Anxiety in our culture at its basic level means the special role our culture plays in reflecting, concealing, and creating anxiety about authentic existence, an anxiety that derives in turn from the absence of a modern image of the human.

Martin Buber begins his little classic *The Way of Man* by recounting the story of a gendarme who asked a Hasidic rabbi why God, who presumably knows everything, said to Adam, "Where art thou?" "In every era, God calls to every man, 'Where are you in the world?' " replied the rabbi. " 'So many years and days of those allotted to you have passed, and how far have you gotten in the world?' God says something like this: 'You have lived forty-six years. How far along are you?' " Forty-six years was the age of the gendarme, and the effect of hearing his age mentioned thus was to awaken in him a heart-searching that destroyed his system of hideouts and led him to render accounts so that he might find the unique direction purposed for him in his creation (Buber, 1988b, Book IV).

When I was 46 years of age, I received from my Harvard class a printed book in which each of my classmates described "how far along" he was in his world, 25 years after graduation. When I read from my classmate Cabot that he is head of the million-dollar Cabot industries, that it helped to have the right grandfather, and that he is busy every night of the week on the board of one or another important organization or university, I did not envy classmate Cabot his millions. But I did have to ask myself just what I had done in the quarter of a century since I graduated from Harvard to justify that feeling of superiority to the Harvard "club man" that, as an undergraduate socialist, I took for granted.

I can remind myself, to be sure, that Buber is not talking about success and power. On the contrary, he writes: "Whatever success and enjoyment he may achieve, whatever power he may attain and whatever deeds he may do, life will remain way-less, so long as he does not face the voice" (Buber, 1988b, p. 134). I can remind myself, too, following Buber's philosophy of dialogue, that "heart-searching" does not mean anything comparative but is the unique demand that is made on me as the person I am in the unique situation in which I find myself. Yet I cannot so easily as that divorce my anxiety about whether my existence is authentic and whether I am answering the true call of my vocation, from the anxiety concerning my place in my culture, my age, my status, my social position, my accomplishments or lack of them. It is not just that both anxieties co-exist in me, as they must, I suppose, in a child of this culture, and most especially in the child of immigrants. They become confusedly intermingled through the very conception of being a certain age and of being so far along in the world.

In my book *Problematic Rebel*, I try to find the historical link that joins the basic anthropological, or ontological, reality of human existence, on the one hand, and the special alienation experienced by the persons of our culture, on the other hand. I call this historical link "the death of God and the alienation of modern man." The "death of God" is not just a question of the relativization of "values" and the absence of universally accepted mores. It is the absence of an image of meaningful human existence, the absence of the ground that enabled Greek, biblical, and Renaissance Man to move with some sureness even in the midst of tragedy. The "death of God" is an anthropological-historical anxiety that is still more basic than the *Angst*—or dread—with which Kierkegaard's "knight of faith" is tried and the anxiety that makes Heidegger's individual turn from the "They" to the possibilities of his or her own authentic existence toward death. Indeed, I should go so far as to say that the *Angst* of Kierkegaard and Heidegger are secondary products of this more basic anxiety. Both Kierkegaard and Heidegger reject society and culture for the lonely relation of the "single one" to God or the self to its own authentic existence. Both posit a dualism between the "crowd" or the "They" and the individual. Both reflect the loss of faith in the universal order and in the society that purports to be founded upon it.

The "death of God" means the alienation of Modern Man, as Albert Camus has tirelessly pointed out in his discussion of the "absurd." Similarly, the ultimate terror to Herman Melville in *Moby Dick* is the blank indifference of an absolute that excludes us: "Is it by its indefiniteness," Ishmael asks, that whiteness "shadows forth the heartless voids and immensities of the universe, and thus stabs us from behind with the thought of annihilation, when beholding the white depths of the milky way?" (chap. XLII). Although Ahab has a more terrible aloneness and isolation from other people than Ishmael, his exile is less profound than that of Ishmael, who cannot come up against, much less hate, the indifferent evil that oppresses him. An exactly analogous situation has occurred in our times with the scientific extermination of whole populations. Speaking of the Nazis who murdered six million Jews, Martin Buber said, "They have . . . so transposed themselves into a sphere of monstrous inhumanity inaccessible to my power of conception, that not even hatred, much less an overcoming of hatred, was able to rise in me" (Buber, 1990, p. 195).

Ishmael's impression as he stood at the helm of his ship "that whatever swift, rushing thing I stood on was not so much bound to any haven ahead as rushing from all havens astern" suggests Modern Man's sense of the earth hurtling through the empty space of the heavens on its meaningless progress to extinction. The "heartless immensity" forces us to realize our own limitedness, our own mortality. When one loses one's limits, one has lost that condition that makes human existence possible. But it is not the infinity of time and space alone that threatens Modern Man. It is one's increasing inability to stand before this infinite. One less and less sees oneself as a self with a ground upon which to stand, and at the same time one less and less trusts that existence outside oneself to which one must relate. As a result one cannot accept Pascal's dictum that one is neither all or nothing. One feels compelled, instead, to the Either/Or of what I call the "Modern Promethean," the rebel who believes that one must destroy the other that confronts one or one will be destroyed oneself.

In Dostoievsky's "Underground Man," the anxiety of the Modern Exile is manifested in a different constellation, that of isolation from others, inner emptiness, and inauthenticity. The Underground Man, Raskolnikov, Svidrigailov, Kirilov, Stavrogin, and Ivan Karamazov are all essentially isolated from others, and their attempts to break out of this isolation, such as Raskolnikov's murder of the pawnbroker woman and Stavrogin's debauchery, leave them more isolated still. It is interesting to compare the different kinds of anxiety that are manifested in Dostoievsky's suicides. The Underground Man has spoiled his life in his funk-hole because of his anxiety before any "real life," as he puts it—his desire to protect himself in his grandiloquent world of fantasy from the dirt and degradation that he considers his inevitable portion in reality. Svidrigailov kills himself out of inner emptiness, isolation, and guilt connected with a child he has raped, whose image he cannot get out of his mind. Kirilov kills himself in an effort to liberate humankind from the fear of death and to make his own will absolute in the place of God's. Yet, his actual suicide is a pure concentrate of fear and frozen horror, which transmutes him from a human being into a jerking, grotesque monster. It is his anxiety before his own fear of death, coupled with his terror before the infinite Other, that he can neither accept nor disregard that manifest themselves here. Stavrogin's suicide is the last act in an inauthentic existence. It is anxiety before boredom and inner emptiness, dissociation and vacuity, fixated guilt (he has committed the same crime as Svidrigailov), and the inability to bring himself wholly into any one act or relationship.

Even Dostoievsky's supposedly Christlike character Prince Myshkin ends in a suicide, or more literally "selficide," through his passive identification with the sufferings of the demonic and tormented. Myshkin's attraction to suffering is a desperate release of the inner tension that he cannot bear. Even the element of compassion in it touches one of the deepest sources of anxiety in our culture: It is the hopeless attempt of the one who is unconfirmed himself to supply an absolute confirmation to others. Myshkin's anxiety leads directly to a self-destruction beyond all mere self-denial, the portion of the one who walks the lonely path of fear and trembling without the grace received from others that enables one to be human.

Franz Kafka's whole work is a profound demonstration of anxiety in our culture. In it is reflected Kafka's own anxiety about his choice between the imprisonment of marriage, on the one hand, and the progressive exile of the bachelor, on the other hand. Kafka chooses the latter way for himself and his heroes, and they all end with only enough space to bury them. Kafka's heroes move from self-sufficiency to ever more anxious isolation and exile. From beneath their compulsive mastery of their surroundings ever fresh anxiety inevitably breaks forth. Their metamorphosis turns someone who stands upon a very narrow plot of ground into someone who has no ground at all. The self is torn out of the social role and the accustomed routine that it has built up for itself.

Absence of confirmation is also a central source of anxiety in Kafka. Had the "hunger artist" found some way open to a direct, meaningful existence, he would not have needed to seek the indirect confirmation of his art. In Kafka's novel *The Castle*, K. needs to be confirmed in his vocation as "land-surveyor" before he can practice it. To receive it, he must make contact with the Castle, which he cannot do; yet without this confirmation from the Castle, he cannot remain in the Village.

All of this leads to "the problematic of modern man": the complex intermixture of personal freedom and psychological compulsion that brings deep anxiety not only to the sick person but to any modern individual who is aware of the discontinuities of a personal existence in which one sometimes acts relatively wholly and spontaneously but very often more as a conditioned reflex or partial compulsion and not infrequently in such a way that one cannot tell which of these two is predominant and how they relate. The relationship between anxiety and compulsion that threatens the sense of being a person must be coupled with the equally important relationship between anxiety and will. The mental illness of Modern Man is not just individual neurosis but the result of one's uprooting from the community in which one formerly lived. It is only an aspect of one's existence as an exile, one's own exile and that of Modern Man.

This anxiety also applies to the modern individual who goes through that crisis of motives in which one can no longer take at face value either other people's motives or one's own. This means a mutual mistrust in which people cease to confirm one another, but it also means a mistrust and fragmentation of the self in which one is incapable of confirming oneself. In Camus's novel *The Fall* (1957), it is the anxiety before the shattered image of the "man of good-will" that leads Jean-Baptiste Clamence to abandon any attempt at real existence. An even deeper anxiety leads Joseph K. in *The Trial* (Kafka, 1957) to try to handle his case as a business deal, to forget it almost entirely, and then to abandon his position at the bank in favor of futile efforts to circumvent a judgment that he can never comprehend.

How can we live in the face of the anxiety in our culture? Must we choose between accepting those cultural forms that help us repress this anxiety—only to see it break out afresh in ever new areas—and being so aware of anxiety that it is reflexively intensified and reduplicated? Not necessarily. It is also possible to revolt against our modern exile rather than to deny or underscore it. But here, too, the way in which we revolt against it makes an enormous difference whether this revolt will result in new anxiety that is greater than we need to bear or in holding our own before anxiety in a way that allows us some margin for a human and even a meaningful existence. The all or nothing of the Modern Promethean represents a romantic revolt that can only in the end make one subject to the very anxiety one is trying to escape, whereas the Modern Job's trust and contending within the "Dialogue With the Absurd" represents a sober, unprogrammatic revolt that accepts the anxiety of our culture yet gains real ground in the face of it. By neither accepting nor cutting ourselves off from the anxiety of our culture but by fighting with it and receiving from it, we may attain the meaning it has to give us.

The answer to our original question then is "Both": Anxiety is a product of our culture and our culture is a means of warding off basic human anxiety. Just for this reason, the Modern Job's stance toward the anxiety of our culture—the stance of trust *and* contending—also means a stance toward the *Angst* of the human condition itself. This is an integral part of the meaning that the anxiety of our culture has to give us.

11

Sex and Love

The paradox of the human image is that it needs to be revealed yet must also remain, in its depth-dimension, concealed. This paradox is complemented and complicated by a second paradox—that many of the contemporary attempts to reveal it only serve to conceal it further, or sometimes reveal surface facets at the expense of causing the depth-image of the human to draw ever deeper into hiding. In no case is this more so than in the case of sex and love. One part of the natural hiddenness of the human that can and should be naturally revealed is sex—or more exactly, sexual relationship, love, and marriage. Yet, a large part of the obscuring of the human in our day comes through precisely this area of our existence.

In the 1920s T. S. Eliot expressed this dilemma with great forcefulness in his classic poem *The Waste Land.* The modern Waste Land is a sterile place. It has been violated because of the misuse of sex—because modern sex has nothing to do with real human emotions or depth and still less with genuine relationship between people. In his early poetry Eliot splits humankind,

---

AUTHOR'S NOTE:This chapter is reprinted from Maurice Friedman, *The Hidden Human Image* (New York: Delacorte Press and Delta Books, 1974), chapter 10, pp. 165-182.

in almost Freudian fashion, into Sweeney, an embodiment of pure "id," and Prufrock, a man entirely dominated by "super-ego." Sweeney is hardly human, while Prufrock has lost touch with his vital forces almost entirely. Prufrock cannot summon up passion, for in the moment of giving himself to another, he is afraid that a chilling response from the other suddenly will make his action seem inappropriate., leaving him ludicrous and exposed. Hence, he is cut off equally from the lust of Sweeney and from the personal relationship of which Sweeney is incapable. Together Prufrock and Sweeney make up the world of *The Waste Land*—consciousness without life and lust without love. Both preclude any relationship between persons. This absence of meeting between persons is distilled in the figure of "Gerontion," the old man finishing out his meaningless existence with "thoughts of a dry brain in a dry season."

> *I have lost my passion: why should I need to keep it*
> *Since what is kept must be adulterated?*
> *I have lost my sight, smell, hearing, taste and touch:*
> *How should I use them for your closer contact?*

I cannot use my passion in any pure way, says Gerontion, for my meaningless existence adulterates it as I use it. I have lost my five senses, the means whereby I came near your heart, but I could not have any real contact with you even if I had not lost them. All that is left to me is the decadence of pure sensation.

In *The Waste Land* Eliot uses the ancient myth of the land cursed by sterility because of the rape of the virgins at the shrine to portray the sterility of modern life, the rape of lust without love. The waste land is the world not only of the animal lust of Sweeney but also of the frustrated and trivialized passion of Prufrock. Above all, the modern violation of sex means isolation: "I have heard the key/Turn in the door once and turn once only/We think of the key, each in his prison/Thinking of the key, each confirms a prison." Only sympathy, Eliot implies, can begin to overcome the isolation of Modern Man, and with it control, discipline, direction, bringing oneself into the focus of a single intent. Yet, this possibility seems to be open only for the exceptional individual. At the end of the poem the waste land is as sterile as before.[8]

Sex, which should be the crown of human relationships, becomes the opposite—the mark of its inauthenticity. Sex touches upon the problematic of the hidden human image as few things do. One reason, as we have seen, is that people are inclined to distrust themselves, and they are inclined to mistrust each other. This mistrust arises in part because of the popular Freudian view of man as a two-layer being whose instincts are likely at any moment to take over control from the rational mind. That ancient dualism in which the body and sex are regarded as evil has been modernized in no less puritanical form by Freud, who tells us that our conscious thoughts *and* feelings are often rationalizations for the drive toward fulfillment of libidinal urges that we cannot admit directly to ourselves.[9] How this affects the relationship of men and women is vividly illustrated by Germaine Greer in her book *The Female Eunuch*:

> As long as man is at odds with his own sexuality and as long as he keeps woman as a solely sexual creature, he will hate her, at least some of the time. . . . Shakespeare was right in equating the strength of the lust drive and the intensity of the disgust that followed it. (Greer, 1971, p. 250)

This is not to imply that Freud has not revealed something of the hidden human image in his stress on the dominant role of sex in human motivation. If we cannot join Freud in making the conscious mind so much the superstructure determined by and reflecting our unconscious motivations, we can certainly assert that what Martin Buber called "the world of It" and "the world of Thou" are nowhere so completely intermingled as in sex and love. That would be no problem if the It were transformed by and taken up into the Thou. Often, in fact, we do not know which is in the service of which. Even if we could rid ourselves of the tenacious notion that sex is something innately evil, we still would have the problem of when it is a revealing of the human image and when an obscuring. More terrible still, how often does what seems to be a beautiful and gracious revealing turn out to be a hideous obscuring!

Although it may no longer be true to say that Freud dominates the psychiatric thought of our time, it certainly is true
that he dominates its approach to sex. Although many people
might quarrel with the central role that Freud ascribes to libidinal sexuality in the human psychic economy, few look at sex
itself in terms basically other than those of Freud—namely, as
an irrational, instinctual, and largely unconscious drive that
must be understood in the first instance in terms of the biological needs of the individual organism and only secondarily and
derivatively in terms of interpersonal relations. The significance of Jean-Paul Sartre's approach to sex lies in the fact that,
without any attempt to minimize its significance, he lifts it out
of the Freudian categories to which we are accustomed and
places it squarely within his own existentialist thought, with its
emphasis upon the relation of the subject to itself and to others.
This means, in the first instance, that Sartre rejects the Freudian
unconscious that magically acts as its own censor in such a way
that it knows what it must keep itself from knowing. Sartre
puts forward instead the self which, in the middle of all facticity, inescapably remains responsible for itself, for the person
whom it becomes through its own project, and for the image of
the human that it chooses for itself and for all human beings.

This approach of Sartre deals a death blow to the favorite
concept of romantic love—the passion that overwhelms one
and by which one has no choice but to let oneself be carried
along. Man, to Sartre, is responsible for his passion. Sartre's existentialist "will never agree that a sweeping passion is a rav-
aging torrent which fatally leads a man to certain acts and is,
therefore, an excuse" (Sartre in Friedman, 1991, p. 137). This
does not mean that Sartre has retrogressed to some naive rationalism that ignores the dark, swirling forces in man's being
that have been uncovered by the romantics and by depth psychology. It means, rather, that human existence can never be
reduced for him to a psychological state, a pure content of
feeling, minus the attitude that the subject has toward that state
or feeling. The pederast who admits that he has sexual relations
with young boys but denies that he is a pederast is in bad faith,
says Sartre; yet his friend, who hopes to liberate him by getting him to admit that he is a pederast, is equally in bad faith,

because he wants him to call himself a pederast as one calls this table a table.

To understand Sartre's approach to sex we must understand his approach to intersubjectivity—the relation between subject and subject. "The Other *looks* at me and as such he holds the secret of my being, he knows what I am. Thus the profound meaning of my being is outside of me, imprisoned in an absence" (Sartre in Friedman, 1991, pp. 193ff.). The Other steals my being from me, and I recover myself only through absorbing the other. Nonetheless, I exist by means of the Other's freedom; for I need the Other's look in order to be. Therefore, I have no security in making him or her into an object. I must instead try to get hold of his or her freedom and reduce it to being a freedom subject to my freedom, This, to Sartre, as to Proust before him, is the essence of love. "The lover does not desire to possess the beloved as one possesses a thing; he . . . wants to possess a freedom" (Sartre in Friedman, 1991, p. 194). I want to ensnare the Other's freedom within his or her facticity, to possess his or her body through his or her consciousness being identified with his or her body. But "desire is itself doomed to failure"! Pleasure is the death and failure of desire, says Sartre, for pleasure produces a reflective consciousness that destroys the immediacy of desire and makes one forget the Other's incarnation. The very attempt to seize the Other's body, pull it toward me, grab hold of it, bite it, makes me aware of my own body as no longer flesh but a synthetic instrument and, thus, destroys my incarnation as well.

What this approach to sex means in concrete situations of human life, Sartre has abundantly illustrated in his novels, plays, and stories. In *No Exit* it is the hopeless situation of a man and two women, one of them a lesbian, shut together in a room in which no one can possess another without interference by the third, which occasions, in part, the conclusion "Hell is other people." But even in less contrived situations, even when only two are present, as in the scenes in *The Age of Reason* in which Matthieu is alone with Marcelle, his mistress, or with Ivich, the self-centered young student, the sexual relations between two people are abundant illustration of the thesis "hell is other people." Not only sexual desire must inevitably fail but love as well. The plot of *The Age of Reason* turns on Matthieu's inability to experience Marcelle's side of the relationship, to imagine that she might want a child and not an abortion when she becomes pregnant after seven years in which he has spent four nights with her regularly every week.

Martin Buber would certainly agree with Sartre that sex is human and not animal and that it cannot be divorced from our relations to others. Sex is an "urge," or passion, that becomes evil only when we leave it undirected and allow an undirected possibility to turn into an undirected reality. What counts here is not the expression, repression, or sublimation of sexual desire but the response with one's whole being that diverts our powerful desires from the casual to the essential. We are not to turn away from what attracts our hearts but are to find mutual contact with it by making our relationship to it real. We are not necessarily torn between a cruel id and a cruel superego. Where some degree of trust and relationship exists, we may bring our passions into unification of a personal wholeness that is itself a by-product of the ever-renewed act of entering into dialogue. Buber calls this becoming a whole, this shaping of the chaos of matter into the cosmos of personal existence, "a cruelly hazardous enterprise." It is, nonetheless, an enterprise that one can and must undertake. Man is not for Buber what he is for Sartre—"a useless passion."

It would not be possible from Buber's standpoint to treat sexuality in abstraction from human relationships and, specifically, from the interplay and interaction between the I-Thou and the I-It. On the other hand, we must recognize, perhaps even more strongly than Buber himself did, that nowhere is the relationship between these two attitudes so intermingled and confused as precisely in this sphere. Although we need not define bad faith as essentially one's relation to oneself, as Sartre does, we must certainly agree that in this sphere of sexuality, deception, illusion, and bad faith of every kind appear. Here, more than anywhere else, monologue loves to mask itself as dialogue—not only because we are all of us "seeming" persons who seek confirmation from the other by trying to appear what we are not, but also because we do not wish to recognize the extent to which we are treating the other as an It and are letting the other do the same to us. Real love, as Buber has pointed out, is not *in* the person but *between* I and Thou. Yet, in all the much-discussed erotic philosophy of the age, it is not love between I and Thou that is represented but the precious experience of the I that enjoys the feelings that the other produces in him or her without giving himself or herself to the other. Love of this sort, love without dialogue, without genuine outgoing to the other, Buber calls Lucifer. "Lame-winged beneath the rule of the lame-winged" Eros, the souls of lovers "cower where they are, each in his den, instead of soaring out each to the beloved partner."

The kingdom of the lame-winged Eros is a world of mirrors and mirrorings.

> Many years I have wandered through the land of men, and have not yet reached an end of studying the varieties of the "erotic man" (as the vassal of the broken-winged one at times describes himself). There a lover stamps around and is in love only with his passion. There one is wearing his differentiated feelings like medal-ribbons. There one is enjoying the adventures of his own fascinating effect. There one is gazing enraptured at the spectacle of his own supposed surrender. There one is collecting excitement. There one is displaying his "power." There one is preening himself with borrowed vitality. There one is delighting to exist simultaneously as himself and as an idol very unlike himself. There one is warming himself at the blaze of what has fallen to his lot. There one is experimenting. And so on and on—all the manifold monologists with their mirrors, in the apartment of the most intimate dialogue! (Buber, 1985, pp. 28f.)

"They are all beating the air," Buber concludes. One receives the world in the other only when one turns to her and opens oneself to her. Only if I accept her otherness and live in the face of it, only if she and I say to each other, "It is Thou," does Present Being dwell between us. The true Eros of dialogue means a knowing of the beloved in the biblical sense of mutual relationship. True lovers have a bipolar experience, a contemporaneity at rest. They receive the common event from both sides at once "and thus for the first time understand in a bodily way what an event is." The lover feels the inclination of the head on the neck of his beloved as an answer to the word of his own silence without losing the feeling of his own self. He does not assimilate the beloved into his own soul or attempt to posses her freedom. He vows her faithfully to himself and turns to her in her otherness, her self-reality, with all the power of intention of his own heart.

This is not Sartre's otherness of the object, or even of the alien subject that makes me into an object, or of the other whose freedom I make subject to my freedom. It is the otherness of the other who lives with me as Thou, who faces me as partner, who affirms me and contends with me, but vows me faithfully to being as I vow her. The ancient Hindu teaching of identity in which "Husband is not dear because of husband but because of the Self in the husband" is not the basis for authentic relationship between the sexes; rather the basis is the full acceptance of otherness. Uncurtailed personal existence first appears when wife says to husband or husband says to wife, not "I am you," but "I accept you as you are." In avoiding sex and marriage as temptation to finitude, Kierkegaard sidestepped the possibility of authentic existence. What is exemplary in marriage is the fact that in it one must mean one's partner in her real otherness because one affirms her as the particular person she is. Indeed, there is scarcely a substitute for marriage for teaching us the "vital acknowledgement of many-faced otherness"—that the other not only has a different mind, way of thinking or feeling, conviction or attitude, "but has also a different perception of the world, a different recognition and order of meaning, a different touch from the regions of existence, a different faith, a different soil." Through its crises and the overcoming of these crises that arise out of the organic depths, marriage enables us to affirm and withstand otherness (Buber, 1985, pp. 61f.).

Buber carries "inclusion," or experiencing of the other side of the relationship, into the sexual act itself. He defines "imagining the real" in *The Knowledge of Man* (1988c) as a bold swinging into the other which demands the intensest action of my being and which enables me to imagine quite concretely what the other is feeling, willing, thinking—to make her present in her wholeness and uniqueness. In love this takes place, not as some Emersonian meeting of soul and soul, but with the whole body-soul person, and includes an experiencing of the other's reaction to the sexual act far more radical than Sartre's incarnation of the other's freedom:

A man caresses a woman, who lets herself be caressed. Then let us assume that he feels the contact from two sides—with the palm of his hand still, and also with the woman's skin. The twofold nature of the gesture, as one that takes place between two persons, thrills through the depth of enjoyment in his heart and stirs it. If he does not deafen his heart he will have—not to renounce the enjoyment—to love.

I do not in the least mean that the man who has had such an experience would from then on have this two-sided sensation in every such meeting—that would perhaps destroy his instinct. But the one extreme experience makes the other person present to him for all time. A transfusion has taken place after which a mere elaboration of subjectivity is never again possible or tolerable to him. (Buber, 1985, pp. 96f.)

Erich Fromm follows Buber in emphasizing love as responsibility, but he tends to overvalue will and commitment so much that he leaves no proper room for the erotic. "Every man is Adam, every woman Eve," writes Fromm (1956) in *The Art of Loving* implying that if one commits oneself to the other, one can love any person. This would hardly be compatible with Buber's emphasis on affirming the other as the particular person she is, for in matters of sexual love this affirmation cannot be made with everyone, anymore than every sexual attraction can be the ground for an enduring relationship. The Viennese logotherapist Viktor Frankl comes much closer to Buber when he writes:

There is not the least thing to be objected to in the sexual drive as long as it is included in the personal realm: as soon and as long as the sexuality is *personalized*, personalized through us to grasp another man in his being, in his suchness, in his uniqueness and particularity, but not only in his being and his suchness but also in his value, in what he shall become, and that means to affirm him. Love may be defined now as: being able to say Thou to someone—and beyond that to be able to say Yes to him; personal love must now join the sexual drive to the spiritual person, it must personalize it. *Only an I that means a Thou can integrate the It.* (Frankl, 1959, p. 91, my translation)

In his widely read book *Love and Will* (1969), Rollo May, in contrast to both Sartre and Buber, shows us sex precisely in the fusion of I-It and I-Thou: "To be human means to exist on the boundary between the anonymous and the personal" (May, 1969, p. 163). The "normal" person in our society finds, amid a plethora of sex, that very sterility that Eliot's *The Waste Land* foresaw. If the Victorian was guilty for experiencing sex, we are guilty if we do not. The removal of all limits has only increased inner conflict; for "the sexual freedom to which we were devoted fell short of being fully human." The same may be said of the relatively greater education in sexual facts and techniques of our contemporaries, compared with the generations that preceded us. Our bookish approach to "ideal marriage" has boomeranged, and the emphasis upon technique in sex has given us a mechanistic attitude toward lovemaking that has left us all the more alienated, lonely, and depersonalized. By a curious inversion, people become more wary of the sharing of tenderness than of physical nakedness and sexual intimacy!

The reasons that May advances for the obsession with sex in our culture are a depressing commentary both on our lack of love and on the emptiness of our lives. In "desperate endeavor to escape feelings of emptiness and the threat of apathy, partners pant and quiver hoping to find an answering quiver in someone else's body" (May, 1969, p. 54). This search for a responding and longing in the other through which to prove their own feelings alive is called love, but it has nothing to do with it. And no real love is present in that compulsion to demonstrate one's potency that leads one to treat the most intimate and personal of all acts "as a performance to be judged by exterior requirements." The ironic result of viewing oneself as a machine to be turned on, adjusted, and steered is the loss of feeling for oneself and one's partner to the point where "the lover who is most efficient will also be the one who is important." Another cause of impotence is our compulsively hurried relationship to time. In the age of "short-order sex," sex itself gets shortchanged. "The fact that many people tend not to give themselves *time* to know each other in love affairs is a general symptom of the malaise of our day," says May (1969, p. 282). Carried far enough, this leads to actual impotence—the body's statement that it has been left behind in the compulsive rush to carry out an idea of what we are supposed to want. We *fly* to sex in order to avoid passion, pushed by an anxiety that cannot know even in the moment of intercourse itself any real present-ness. Sex in our society, says May, is a technique for a gigantic repression of true passion. Or our obsession with sex results from our repression of death. "Sex is the easiest way to prove our vitality, to demonstrate we are still 'young,' attractive, and virile, to prove we are not dead yet" (May, 1969, p. 107).

Passion, then, is not identical with sex but is a separate, deeper force. It may be expressed through sex, but it also may be pushed under by it. What gives the special depth-dimension to passion, according to May, is the "daimonic," which he de-fines not as something evil but as any force capable of taking over the whole personality. In the daimonic is an affirmation of one's self that gives one the power to put one's self into the relationship. Without such self-assertion, one is unable to par-ticipate in a genuine relationship, a reciprocity in which each acts upon the other. Although May says that this relationship "always skates on the edge of the exploitation of the partner" (May, 1969, p. 146), the give-and-take, the experiencing of the other side of the relationship, prevents it from going over that edge while retaining the vitality of the relationship. It is only when love and will come together that we attain the truly per-sonal, and the personal is never something I possess alone but only in a person-to-person relationship. The "human being has to make the creature with whom he has sexual relations in some way personal, even if only in fantasy, or else suffer deper-sonalization himself" (May, 1969, p. 211). The need for sex is not so powerful as the need for relationship, intimacy, accep-tance, and affirmation. Therefore, exploitation, seduction, and the domination of another's freedom cannot, both Freud and Sartre to the contrary, be the last word in sex and love. In atti-tude, as well as in physical fact, sex means that posture of the ultimate baring of one's self. This mutual baring is not *despite* but *with* and *through* the fact that we are creatures destined to die. "Love is not only enriched by our sense of mortality," writes May, "but constituted by it" (May, 1969, p. 102).

Even our feelings are not private but are part of the dialogue that takes place in love. They "are ways of communicating and sharing something meaningful from us to the world." "Our feelings not only take into consideration the other person," writes May, "but are in a real sense partially *formed by the feelings of the other persons present*" (May, 1969, p. 91). Every successful lover knows by instinct to pick up the magnetic field of the feelings of the person he or she is with. Even the wish is not simply individual, as Freud thought, but is a reality *between*: "The wish in interpersonal relationships requires mutuality" (May, 1969, p. 216).

To open oneself to another in love means to be confronted with a vastly widened world, including regions of which we never dreamed. This experience produces a vertigo in which we may genuinely wonder whether we are "capable of giving ourselves to our beloved and still preserving what center of autonomy we have" (May, 1969, p. 83). Sartre would answer no; for he has made opposites of real giving to the other and self-preservation. May, using Tillich's language of the "centered self" which transcends itself, goes beyond Sartre. "Contrary to the usual assumption, we all begin life not as individuals, but as 'we' " (May, 1969, p. 316). Only because this is so, can love push us toward a new dimension of consciousness in which we transcend our isolation.

What this does not tell us is whether we will have the resources in any particular situation "to meet others and hold our ground when we meet them." Still less can we say with confidence of ourselves what May says in a commentary on a traditional people, namely, that "the community gives a humanly trustworthy, interpersonal world in which one can struggle against the negative forces" (May, 1969, p. 133). On the contrary, it may be just the absence of this "humanly trustworthy, interpersonal world" that leads to the "crisis of confidence" that sets the stage for the modern split between libidinal passion and superego, which Freud took to be human nature. "The unaffectedness of wishing is stifled by mistrust," writes Buber. "The divorce between spirit and instincts is here, as often, the consequence of the divorce between man and man."

The special form of the divorce between person and person in our day, says the psychoanalyst Leslie Farber, is the "disordered will," that willfulness that wants to handle both sides of the dialogue. If this willfulness expresses itself in the "life of suicide," it is found even more regularly in the contemporary approach to sex. Indeed, Farber goes so far as to state as his conviction "that over the last fifty years sex has, for the most part, lost its viability as a human experience." The emphasis here is on the word *human*. Sexual activity itself has not decreased, but the human possibilities of sex are becoming ever more elusive, and the couplings that take place are "poultices after the fact" which "further extend the degradation of sex that has resulted from its ever-increasing bondage to the modern will." Sex has been emancipated, to be sure, but its "emancipation" is really an abstraction from all of life—except the will—and its exaltation as the very measure of existence. As a result, what sex once brought us—the possibility of that mutual knowing and being known within which we regain *our own* body through knowing the body of the loved one—is lost in favor of an empty *knowing about* in which both bodies again escape us. Farber traces this decline in a series of steps: viewing nature as a variety of energies to be harnessed and utilized, a machine to be kept healthy so that it might lead to never-ending progress and prosperity; coming to regard the human body as just such a machine; the decision that the dominant energy of the human machine is sex; the claim of the erotic life as the exclusive province of sexology and psychoanalysis; and the abstraction and isolation of sex into the function of the sexual organs (Farber, 1976, chap. 8).

The true *reductio ad absurdum* of this historical process is William H. Masters's study of the female orgasm in an actual laboratory situation, excluding all subjects who could not produce orgasm at will, relying principally on automanipulation, or masturbation, and recording the results with color movies. Whatever else may have been discovered in this way, Farber suggests, nothing could be discovered about the human relationship between persons in sexual love. We might go farther and say that here the paradox has reached its point of greatest tension: the uttermost hiding and eclipse of the human image brought about by what claims to be the farthest outpost of the revelation of the human! Although many Feminists have lined up behind Masters and Johnson, as if the clitoral orgasm were the very bastion of feminine freedom, and have characterized Farber as a "male chauvinist," Germaine Greer has rejected this emphasis on the very same grounds as Farber; that it reduces human sexuality to something partial and mechanical rather than whole and personal. She sees in Masters and Johnson a basically authoritarian attempt to tame sex, "the blueprint for standard, low-agitation, cool-out monogamy. If women are to avoid this last reduction of their humanity, they must hold out not just for orgasm but for ecstasy." Only the domination of "the performance ethic" can explain women's finding the clitoris "the only site of their pleasure" instead of its "acting as a kind of sexual overdrive in a more general response." This stress on the clitoral orgasm is but part of a larger picture in which "Sex for many has become a sorry business, a mechanical release involving neither discovery nor triumph, stressing human isolation more dishearteningly than ever before." Greer, like Rollo May, sees the modern ideal of sex as really being mechanized sex, "laboriously and inhumanly computerized," just as "the male sexual idea of virility without languor or amorousness" is a profoundly desolating illustration of how the expression of the release in mechanical terms leads to seeking it mechanically. "Sex becomes masturbation in the vagina." That is sex for the man. But the overstress on the man's massaging of the clitoris to produce orgasm is no less masturbation for the woman (Greer, 1971).

Though we cannot return to the unawareness of the past, neither can we remain standing in the pseudoclinical situation of the present, in which frigidity is seen as something *in* the woman, impotence as something *in* the man. Both frigidity and impotence, as well as male and female orgasms, are essential aspects of an interhuman betweenness in which *both man and woman must work together on the sexual problems*, as on the financial and other problems, of the relationship. I do not mean that both should deal together with *her* problem of frigidity and/or *his* problem of impotence. I mean that the problems themselves do not belong to and cannot be simply located in one partner in the relationship, for they are a function of the relationship itself.

When and if the mutual trust that upholds the relationship is broken, especially if the separation is traumatic, it is inevitable in most cases that sexual "hang-ups" will be relegated by each partner to the other. One protects oneself from one's former closeness by turning the other into a caricature of a person—an object possessing such and such characteristics. Actually, one does not know what the other might be in another relationship. I am not denying that some relationships are too difficult to work out. But I am saying that precisely when we know exactly what is wrong with our former partner and wonder why we wasted 10 years of our lives with such a person, precisely when we seem to have reached an objective and secure ground, is the point when we have ceased to make him or her present to us as a person and are protecting ourselves from feeling any concern— from living in and with that person.

When I was 13, my young brother-in-law replaced my almost total ignorance of sex with the philosophy of the "man of action"—a philosophy that I did not put into practice for many years to come, if at all, but that left me, nonetheless, with the idea that sex was a Good Thing, regardless of whom one made love to or what one's relation was to one's partner. Later I came to recognize this same relationship not only in the college-boy boastings of "laying a girl" or "having a piece," but even in the morality of a society that claimed all premarital or extramarital sexuality to be wrong in abstraction from both the particular relationship and the concrete situation. When this morality was unmasked as the hypocritical double standard that it is, it was replaced for a great many by a no less immoral approval of sex as a "natural" act, again in abstraction from the actual relationship and the actual situation. Sex has been sought in our society as an "experience," as sensation somehow supposed to be of value in itself. Only this power of abstraction could lead so many to spend so much of their strength and effort trying to prove their "potency" with ever-fresh partners or trying to extend the variety and scope of their experience by the exchange of partners.

The mark of success in our society, the distinguished American psychiatrist Harry Stack Sullivan once said, is what you can do with your genitals to someone else's genitals. I would go even farther and say that most men and women in our society are ridden by a deep anxiety concerning their sexual adequacy, that no amount of actual sexual "conquest" or "experience" can ever really allay that anxiety, and that even those with the most self-satisfying sexual prowess live with dread of that day when their powers begin to fail. This day comes all the sooner, in fact, because of this anxiety, because of the compulsive need to allay it by sexual activity, and because of the dread of its someday proving the master. People are afraid of fumbling and faltering in sexual relations, for they do not wish to appear un*masterly*. Their harsh self-judgment is, of course, accompanied by an equally harsh judgment of others, for if things do not work out according to the ideal of the sex books, then the blame must be placed on *his* "impotence" or *her* "frigidity." Some people manage to place all the blame upon their partners, some take all the blame to themselves, and most go back and forth between blaming their partners and blaming themselves. Few take seriously the extent to which "good sexual functioning" is itself a function of good relationship or the fact that even good relationship, including all the anxieties and worries and fatigues of real life, is not on call to produce good sex at stated periods!

We are flooded with false images—caricatures—of manliness and femininity—from the John Wayne type of "he-man" to any of a number of sexy, voluptuous, clinging, or dream-girl-soft women. We fear in our sexual relationships themselves that consideration—failure to press our case to the very verge of exploitation—will be considered weakness or a lack of vitality. It takes courage to falter, to hesitate, to show bewilderment, confusion, and self-doubt. Naturally, we are vulnerable here as in perhaps no other sphere of our lives, and our most personal confirmation is at stake. "Love is being psychically wide-open to another," says Shulamith Firestone. "It is a situation of total emotional vulnerability. Therefore it must be not only the incorporation of the other, but an *exchange* of selves. Anything short of mutual exchange will hurt one or the other party" (Firestone, 1971, pp. 128f.).

Without the mutual revelation of weakness, of humanness, of hope and doubt, of faith and despair, of the very ground in which each of us is rooted, and of the strengths and foibles of our unique stances, no revelation of the hidden human image in sexual love can take place. And when the human image remains hidden, it does not flower in the darkness. It withers and atrophies and all the masks and pretenses of our smiling faces cannot dispel the growing stink of putrefaction that arises from the depths. Only when we cease to be concerned with our own images as masculine and feminine and trust ourselves to the *between* itself—allowing ourselves to be changed by the other, by the relationship—will the human image be revealed.

12

---

*Personal Freedom, Psychological Compulsion,
and the Divided Self*

One of the most important aspects of the problematic of modern man is the complex intermixture of personal freedom and psychological compulsion, a paradoxical phenomenon that can be understood only from within. The characters of Melville, Dostoievsky, and Kafka show more clearly than any case history the impossibility of ignoring the reality of such compulsion, on the one hand, or of reducing the human being to a deterministic system, on the other hand.

Ahab

What makes Captain Ahab, the central figure of Herman Melville's novel *Moby Dick*, really modern is the deep inner division in him. We are told that Ahab's intense thinking has made him into a Prometheus whose own mind creates a vulture that feeds upon his heart. In Ahab, Melville has depicted the problematic of Modern Man—the alienation, the divided nature, the unresolved tension between personal freedom and psychological compulsion which follow the "death of God."

Melville himself never lets us forget how much of Ahab's Prometheanism must be ascribed to psychological illness. Ahab cannot be dismissed as *merely* projecting evil on the non-human world; for Ishmael himself provides us with an enormous accumulation of suggestions that the world is hostile to man either in a personal-malignant or a cold-indifferent way. What makes Ahab "crazy" is the fact that he personifies this evil in Moby Dick. Melville explicitly ascribes this association of all evil with the White Whale to Ahab's delirium and his "transference," a term that Melville uses in a manner not unlike its modern psychoanalytical usage.

In "Moby Dick" (chap. XLI) Melville actually appears to "psychoanalyze" his hero. We are told of the stages of Ahab's monomania, being reassured constantly throughout that this *is* a monomania. The first stage was the "sudden, passionate, corporal animosity," which led him to drive his knife into the whale; the second stage was "the agonizing bodily laceration" that he felt when his leg was sheared off; the third came when "Ahab and anguish lay stretched together in one hammock" for "long months of days and weeks"; the fourth was that period when "his torn body and gashed soul bled into one another; and so interfusing made him mad"; by the fifth stage he became "a raving lunatic . . . unlimbed of a leg," yet possessing enormous "vital strength." This coupling of impotence and vital strength recurs again and again with Ahab. His sense of impotence is expressed in his terrible rage and frustration, but he is the only really vital person in the whole boat, the only one with full depths of vitality, and this is why everything centers on him. In the sixth stage Ahab hid his madness. "The direful madness" was gone from the outside, but "Ahab, in his hidden self, raved on." His "full lunacy subsided not but deepeningly contracted," and yet, at the same time as his "broad madness" had not been left behind, so "not one jot of his great natural intellect had perished." His vital intelligence is not only preserved in madness but enormously enhanced: "Far from having lost his strength, Ahab, to that one end, did now possess a thousand-fold more potency than ever he had sanely brought to bear upon any one reasonable object."

Ahab's madness has given him sources of almost unlimited strength: He has gone down to a deeper level not only than ordinary persons can reach, but than he himself could reach so long as he was sane. He is, in fact, a sort of negative superman; he has achieved what the rest of humanity vainly strives for: the full working of the mind, the great clarity of intellect, the fullness of passion and vitality—all harnessed in one direction. And the whole process is mad. Yet, at just this point we are told: "This is much, yet Ahab's larger, darker, deeper part remains unhinted. But vain to popularize profundities, and all truth is profound" (chap. XLI). Here, despite all the disclaimers about Ahab's madness, Ishmael clearly tells us that there is reality in this man that, far from our being able to dismiss it, is too deep for us to begin to comprehend.

Ahab's inner division and the complex relation between his personality and his psychological illness come to the surface most clearly during that brief interlude in "The Symphony" in which Ahab recognizes his compulsion for what it is. There he identifies himself, for once, not with the monomaniacal drive to chase the whale, the rage and passion to pursue, but with the person who is driven by that compulsion, the man who is old and tired and knows it. "What mad thing has made me run the seas these forty years!" he exclaims. The very nature of the compulsion that possesses Ahab has always in the past made him identify with it. The symptoms of his inner dualism that he manifests until now are not so much a sign of weakness of his resolve, we are told in "The Chart" (chap. XLIV), "but the plainest tokens of its intensity." When Ahab's intolerably vivid nightmares become an insufferable anguish that forces him to "burst from his stateroom, as though escaping from a bed that was on fire," the agent is not "crazy Ahab, the scheming, unappeasedly steadfast hunter of the White Whale" who had gone to the hammock. The agent is "the eternal, living principle or soul in him" that, becoming dissociated in sleep, "spontaneously sought escape from the scorching contiguity" of the supreme purpose that "by its own sheer inveteracy of will, forced itself . . . into a kind of self-assured, independent being of its own" which "could grimly live and burn, while the common vitality to which it was conjoined, fled horror-stricken from the unbidden and unfathered birth."

> Therefore, the tormented spirit that glared out of bodily eyes, when what seemed Ahab rushed from his room, was for the time but a vacated thing, a formless somnambulistic being, a ray of living light, to be sure, but without an object to color, and therefore a blankness in itself. (chap. XLIV, "The Chart")

Now, however, in "The Symphony," it is the fully conscious Ahab, rather than a dissociated vacant, inner blankness, who does not identify himself with his compulsion.

> The madness, the frenzy, the boiling blood and the smoking brow with which for a thousand lowerings old Ahab has furiously, foamingly chased his prey—more a demon than a man!—aye, aye! What a forty years' fool—old fool, has old Ahab been! Why this strife of the chase?" (chap. CXXXII, "The Symphony")

"Locks so grey did never grow but from out some ashes," Ahab adds, reinforcing the image of an extinct volcano implicit in Melville's earlier phrase, "the burnt-out crater of his brain." Perhaps it is because his volcanic fire has gone out temporarily, or at least burnt low, that Ahab now knows his compulsion for what it is. Ahab's inner compulsion is fate itself for him. "With little external to constrain us," says Ishmael, commenting on Ahab, "the innermost necessities in our being, these still drive us on." After Ahab has ceased to identify with his compulsion and before he projects it upon God, he has a moment of genuine doubt as to his own self that makes him question whether there really is an "I," a person behind his actions and not some objective, impersonal force.

> "What is it, what nameless, inscrutable, unearthly thing is it, what cozening, hidden lord and master, and cruel, remorseless emperor commands me; that against all natural lovings and longings, I so keep pushing, and crowding, and jamming myself on all the time; recklessly making me ready to do what *in my own proper, natural heart, I durst*

not so much as dare? Is Ahab, Ahab? Is it I, God, or who, that lifts this arm?"
(chap. CXXXII, "The Symphony")

How startling this confession of weakness on the lips of the
man who said, "Who's over me? Truth hath no confines"!

Dostoievsky

The problem of the relation of personal freedom to psychological compulsion cannot be solved by the attempt to reduce
the human being to a bundle of instinctual drives, unconscious
complexes, the need for security, or any other single factor.
Each psychoanalytic school has attempted to find a key to the
human, and each, in so doing, has lost the human. Motivation
is inextricably bound up with the wholeness of the person,
with one's direction of movement, with one's struggles to authenticate oneself. This wholeness of the person in one's dynamic interrelation with other persons Dostoievsky guards as
no psychoanalytic theory ever has. In Dostoievsky we never
see a metaphysical freedom or free will separate from conditioning factors; rather, we see the free will shining through and
refracted by the sickness that shapes and exasperates so many
of Dostoievsky's characters.[10] At the age of 18 Dostoievsky
wrote to his brother: "Man is a mystery. Even if you were to
spend your whole life unraveling it, you ought not to say that
you had wasted your life. I occupy myself with this mystery,
for I want to be a man" (quoted in Maurina, 1952, p. 129, my
translation). The fact that so many psychiatrists, including
Freud, have praised Dostoievsky for his psychological acumen
has led some to assume that Dostoievsky either holds a theory
of psychological determinism himself or provides evidence for
it. Dostoievsky is interested in mental sickness, as Samuel
Smith and Andrei Isotoff have pointed out, but not in its genesis à la Freud.

> So far from holding to the doctrine of closed-linked . . . causation for
> psychic events, he emphasizes the waywardness and unpredictabil-
> ity of impulse which motivates the actions of his persons. . . . The

closeness of his observations, since borne out by psychiatrists, is no
evidence that he had the same notions on causation in psychic dynamics as the analysts have developed. (Smith & Isotoff, 1935, pp. 390f.)

To Dostoievsky the view that reduces free will to psychological determinism is as untrue as that which accords persons a
metaphysical free will untouched by conditioning forces. The
Underground Man is both free and not free at once. No general
theory of psychogenesis and no general knowledge of persons
will tell us in advance what will be their actual mixture of spontaneity and compulsion in any particular situation. Hence,
Dostoievsky's contribution to the problematic of Modern Man
is in this respect superior to Freud's psychogenic determinism.
This does not mean that Dostoievsky's characters must be
taken at face value or even as Dostoievsky himself may have
intended them. On the contrary, even in those characters that
he intended to make most ideal, like Myshkin, and in those
ideas that he most cherished, like suffering, guilt, and the responsibility of each for all, abysses open before us that lead us
into the problematic of Modern Man.

Stavrogin and Versilov

Nikolai Stavrogin, the hero of Dostoievsky's novel *The Devils*
or *The Possessed*, (1953) has his inner division revealed by his
devil-doubles. The question that haunts us throughout *The
Devils*, however, is whether Stavrogin's enigmatic character
and antisocial actions are to be explained as madness or as attitudes for which he is responsible. After 6 months in the society of the town where the story takes place, Stavrogin suddenly
breaks loose and pulls a gentleman by the nose at his club,
kisses the wife of another man at a party in the latter's house,
and bites the ear of the governor, who is trying to help him in
a fatherly way. These actions offend local society all the more
because they seem a tangible expression of the insufferable
pride and contempt that people sense in him. When it is discovered that he has "brain fever" and these incidents are retroac-
tively attributed to his "not being himself," people receive his

apologies sympathetically but are still embarrassed, and some remain "convinced that the blackguard was merely having a good laugh at us all and that his illness had nothing to do with it."

Stavrogin, like Ivan Karamazov, has a lackey devil with whom he talks, though almost all indications of this have been omitted from the finished version. Stavrogin assures Dasha in a deleted passage that he does not believe in the existence of this devil, that his devil is himself in different form, that, in fact, he splits himself and talks with himself (Fülop-Müller & Eckstein, 1926, pp. 355-357, 371-373). But in his conversation with Tikhon, which Dostoievsky also omitted, he not only tells him that he has had hallucinations of the devil for a year, but suggests that even though he speaks of it as aspects of himself, he wonders whether it is not really the devil. In fact, he declares categorically, "I do believe in the devil, I believe canonically, in a personal, not allegorical devil," and raises the same question as his lackey devil—whether one can believe in the devil without believing in God. These hallucinations again pose the problem of the extent to which Stavrogin's actions are to be attributed to madness, and Stavrogin himself says that he should see a doctor, to which Father Tikhon immediately assents. The form of the hallucination is even more important than the fact—the heightening of the "double" that reveals not only the extent of Stavrogin's inner split but also the demonic and even diabolical character of that ignoble and not at all heroic part of himself that confronts him in Peter and still more in his lackey devil.

In his last letter to Dasha, Stavrogin seems to equate losing one's reason with an uncompromising belief in an idea. He does not see that a personality split into opposing extremes, like his own, might also mean madness, though in a different way from the monomania of Kirilov. When he apologizes for the supposedly irresistible impulses that led him to pull Gaganov by the nose and bite the governor's ear, he says he was "not himself," and when Liputin implies he was, he turns pale and cries, "Good Lord . . . do you really think that I'm capable of attacking people while in the full possession of my senses?" Stavrogin turns pale every time someone scores a direct hit. It is easier for him to face the idea that he acted on impulse, under the influence of "brain fever," than the idea that it is his very self that is split so that one part of him acts out these impulses while the other fully knows what it does.

In the St. Petersburg version of the confession, Stavrogin says, "I suspect that this is all a sickness," and the narrator himself says, "This document is, in my opinion, a product of sickness, a work of the devil that has gained mastery over this gentleman" (Fülop-Müller & Eckstein, 1926, pp. 403, 409). In the finished Moscow version of the Tikhon chapter, Stavrogin opines that his hallucination of the devil is a product of his inner split. But he repeatedly insists that his actions in relation to Matryosha and Mary were *not* the products of madness. And his evidence for this is always of the same nature, namely, that no idea ever took full hold of him, that he could always control himself "if he wanted to," that he was always completely aware of what he was doing.

> "I tell all this in order that every one may know that the feeling never absorbed the whole of me absolutely, but there always remained the most perfect consciousness (on that consciousness indeed it was all based). And although it would take hold of me to the pitch of madness, . . . it would never reach the point of making me forget myself. . . . I could at the same time overcome it completely, even stop it at its climax, only I never wished to stop it." (Dostoievsky, 1922, pp. 44f).

While he waits for Matryosha to hang herself, Stavrogin's breathing stops and his heart beats violently but, at the same time, he looks at his watch and notes the time "with perfect accuracy" and has a heightened awareness of every detail around him. When he sits by the window and looks at the little red spider, he thinks of how he will "stand on tiptoe and peer through this very chink" to see if Matryosha has hanged herself. "I mention this detail because I wish to prove fully to what an extent I was obviously in possession of my mental faculties and I hold myself responsible for everything" (Dostoievsky, 1922, pp. 62f.). A more sophisticated awareness of mental illness would have led Stavrogin not to dismiss so conclusively the possibility that the reputation of being mad that he had in his town was right. His heightened awareness of everything and his complete consciousness of what he is doing and his sense of perfect control might as easily be the mark of some type of schizophrenia, or even of paranoid schizophrenia, as of being responsible and in his right mind. Like Dostoievsky's Underground Man, he makes the mistakes of equating consciousness and will and of thinking that because he knows that is happening he is free to stop it.

> "I know I can dismiss the thought of Matryosha even now whenever I want to. I am as completely master of my will as ever. But the whole point is that I never wanted to do it; I myself do not want to, and never shall. So it will go on until I go mad." (Dostoievsky, 1922, p. 69)

The fact that he never wants to stop what is happening, even though it leads to madness, may cause us to suspect that his perfect mastery of his will is an illusion.

Stavrogin's split is nowhere more clearly manifested, in fact, than in these scenes in which one part of him acts out to the last extreme his tormented impulses while the other looks on with clinical detachment. In addition, his constant insistence that his statements prove that he is "of sound mind" are in themselves enough to raise the question of whether he is. This is a question that Dostoievsky wants to leave in our minds, and it is significant that the final comment of the book, after "the citizen of the canton of Uri" is found "hanging there behind the door," is again upon just this matter of Stavrogin's sanity:

> On the table lay a scrap of paper with the words: "No one is to blame, I did it myself." Beside it on the table lay a hammer, a piece of soap, and a large nail, evidently prepared in case of need. The strong silk cord with which Stavrogin had hanged himself had evidently also been prepared and chosen beforehand. It was thickly smeared with soap. All this was evidence of premeditation and consciousness to the last minute.
>
> The verdict of our doctors after the post-mortem was that it was most definitely not a case of insanity. (Dostoievsky, 1953, pp. 663f.)

What does Dostoievsky want us to believe—that Stavrogin was insane or that he was not insane? Neither the one nor the

other. He wants us to understand Stavrogin as precisely that
compound of freedom and compulsion, personal responsibility
and impersonal determinism that we find in Dostoievsky's Underground Man and in Ivan Karamazov. Like the Underground
Man, Stavrogin confronts us not only with his sickness but with
the fact that he is aware of it himself, and this means that
Stavrogin is more than the psychological categories that he
himself offers us. Dostoievsky has created in Stavrogin a truly
independent character who has the right to give us his own
conclusions about himself and to demand of us that we meet
him as a person—an existential subject—and not just as the object of his or our analyses. We have the right to draw our own
conclusions about Stavrogin and in so doing to make use of all
the material that Stavrogin and his author offer us, but we do
not have the right to substitute our own conclusions for the
wholeness and uniqueness of the person who is before us.
Stavrogin is not a real person, to be sure, but neither is he a
"case." He is a literary creation *and* an image of the human created by an author who has succeeded, as few others have, in
using literature as a medium for bringing us man the human
being in his or her wholeness. Both Stavrogin's despair and
his self-awareness show that he is more than any psychological categories can explain—that he is a real human being.
Dostoievsky clearly wants us to consider the possibility of
Stavrogin's madness, or he would not revert so often to this
theme, but he does not want us to conclude that he is mad, for
this would mean dismissing him as a person and diminishing
his stature as an image of the human. What he wishes us to
understand, rather, is the *problematic* of Stavrogin, which
cannot be resolved into the easy either-or's of sane or insane,
free or compulsive, responsible or irresponsible.

Versilov, the paradoxical central figure of *The Raw Youth*
(1947), illuminates Dostoievsky's attitude toward Stavrogin
still further; for Versilov inherits many of Stavrogin's traits,
including his pride and his uncontrollable impulses, and his
personality is as clearly split and subject to extremes as
Stavrogin's. When Versilov breaks in two the ikon that the
saintly pilgrim Makar Ivanovitch has left to him and his
wife, he explains his action in advance, as an almost irresistible

impulse brought about by the presence in him of a "second self." Versilov does not mean by his "two selves" merely two opposing tendencies, such as Faust's "two souls," one of which pulls him up to heaven while the other drags him down to earth, but one self that is rational and another that is definitely irrational. His description of this state is similar to Stavrogin's self-analysis with one significant difference: Versilov does not believe that his rational self can control his irrational one.

> "I am really split in two mentally, and I'm horribly afraid of it. It's just as though one's second self were standing beside one. One is sensible and rational oneself, but the other self is impelled to do something perfectly senseless, and sometimes very funny, and suddenly you notice that you are longing to do that amusing thing, goodness knows why. That is, you want to, as it were, against your will: though you fight against it with all your might, you want to." (Dostoievsky, 1947, pp. 552f.)

When Versilov breaks the ikon, his pale face suddenly flushes red, almost purple, and every feature in his face quivers and works. Versilov's bastard son Arkady Dolgoruky interprets this event at the time as a symbolic way of showing that Versilov is putting an end to everything. Yet he adds, "But that second self was unmistakably beside him, too, of that there could be no doubt." In the last chapter Arkady, who is also the narrator, dismisses the notion of "actual madness" on Versilov's part but accepts the theory of "the second self" as "the first stage of serious mental derangement, which may lead to something very bad." His conclusion is again precisely that mixed state of freedom and compulsion, responsibility and sickness that we have seen in Stavrogin. It is indeed the place in which the image of the human and psychotherapy meet:

> Though that scene at Mother's and that broken ikon were undoubtedly partly due to the influence of a real "second self," yet I have ever since been haunted by the fancy that there was in it an element of a sort of vindictive symbolism, a sort of resentment against the expectations of those women, a sort of angry revolt against their rights and their criticism. And so hand in hand with the "second self" he broke the ikon, as though to say, "That's how your expectations will be

shattered!" In fact, even though the "second self" did come in, it was partly simply a whim. . . . But all this is only my theory, it would be hard to decide for certain. (Dostoievsky, 1947, pp. 602f.)

It *would* be hard to decide for certain, but what appears clear is that it is not a question of an either-or; in Versilov, as in Stavrogin, we see the sick self and the whimsical person together, inextricably mixed. If we contrast Versilov's analysis of his "second self" with Arkady's, we can see not only what Dostoievsky thinks about the problematic of Versilov and Stavrogin, but also his understanding of the human as such. Versilov assumes that the sane and free self is the sensible and rational one and that the "senseless," "funny," and "amusing" things that he feels impelled to do are the product of a sick and unfree self. Thus, he equates the rational with the sane, the irrational with the sick. Arkady, in contrast, sees the "whim" as a product not of the sick "second self" but of the free person. Like the Underground Man, he knows that the human self is just as much irrational as it is rational and that the very essence of that self is the freedom to do the arbitrary and whimsical, what is *not* sensible and rational. Hence, in a perfectly clear and precise formulation, Arkady states, "And so hand in hand with the 'second self' he broke the ikon," in which sentence the "he" refers to the free and responsible self, in contrast to the unfree "second self." In the same way, when he says, "Even though the 'second self' did come in, it was partly simply a whim," he is contrasting the lack of freedom of the "second self" with the freedom of the self that acts on whims, whereas Versilov identifies acting on a whim with being compelled by impulses from his real self. Without question, Dostoievsky's view of the human in general—and of Versilov and Stavrogin, in particular—coincides with Arkady's analysis and not with Versilov's.

Fathers and Sons: The Divided Self

That deep inner division that characterizes the problematic of Modern Man can be illumined only partially through understanding the intermixture of personal freedom and psychological compulsion, for this tells us only of the psychological accompaniment and not of the interhuman reality of which that psychological division is the product. A deeper insight into the divided self can be obtained through understanding its close connection with the image of the human and the relationship between parent and child in which that image first arises.

The father is the first and often the most lasting image of man for the son. It not infrequently happens, however, that the father is not really present for the son, either because he is dead or absent or inattentive, or because he is in no sense a father, or because he is too weak or despicable for a son to be able to emulate him. In such a case the need for the father as the image of man remains and often leads to a lifetime search for a father who will supply an image of man as the actual father has not. Freud and modern psychoanalysts in general have seen only one aspect of this father-son relationship and have reduced it to fear of castration, introjection of the father's ideals and conscience, or even identification. The aspect that they have missed is the need that the son has for a relationship with the father that will help him find direction in the choices he must make between one way of life and another.[11] This need is not for identification but dialogue, and it is not a conditioned formation or reaction but a free and even spontaneous response. At the same time, the other, conditioned reaction does enter in, and the relationship of father to son, even in the most "normal" cases, must be seen also as a blend of the conditioned and the free, the "psychological" and the personal, as is the problematic of Stavrogin and Versilov, of which we have spoken.

It is illuminating to consider the extent to which the relationship to the father has been at the center of both the life and the writings of the three men with whose work I was particularly concerned in *Problematic Rebel*: Melville, Dostoievsky, and Kafka. Throughout almost all their works, one theme remains constant—that of the son in search of a father who is either dead or absent or who has betrayed him or does betray him. In Newton Arvin's view, Melville, who lost his father at an early age and went to sea to escape from the women in his family, was seeking the father in all his writings. Melville's own relation to his dead father is mirrored, certainly, in Ishmael and Ahab, Pierre and his father, Bartleby and his employer, Billy Budd and Captain Vere. This is not to say, however, that these relationships have a merely psychological significance. On the contrary, the absence of the father so deeply affected Melville's world view that the most profound metaphysical and existential questions take root in this soil. Ultimately, the absence of the father meant for Melville the shattering of trust, the search for the father, and the search for renewal of trust.

The Raw Youth and The Brothers Karamazov

The theme of fathers and sons is central to *The Raw Youth* and *The Brothers Karamazov*, but it is present also in *Crime and Punishment* and *The Devils*. When Dostoievsky's father was murdered by serfs, Dostoievsky, who knew, like Ivan Karamazov, that he had wished for his father's death, was left with a burden of guilt. Hence, his relationship was less to the absent father whom he longed for and sought, like Melville, or the present father whom he both loved and hated, like Kafka, than to the absent father toward whom he felt hatred and guilt—and also, no doubt, resentment that he was not the father whom he would have wished.

The wish is a recurrent bifurcation of the father figure into a hated figure and a respected one, an image that repels and an image that attracts, or a problematic image and a clear one. Raskolnikov relates to both Porfiry and Svidrigailov as father figures; Stavrogin, who also lost his father when he was a child, to both Stepan Trofimovitch and Father Tikhon. In *The Raw Youth* (1947), Arkady Dolgoruky is the bastard son of the nobleman Versilov while legally the son of Versilov's former serf Makar Ivanovitch. During the time he was growing up, Arkady had almost no contact with the aloof and enigmatic Versilov. The plot of the novel is centered largely on his coming to live near Versilov and his attempts to penetrate the mystery and solve the riddle of this fascinating, divided man. His need to do this is the need to provide himself with a sense of patrimony. But it is even more clearly the search by an intense and troubled young man for an image of the father who will give him some guidance and sense of direction. Yet the deeper he enters into relationship with Versilov, the more baffled and put off he is by the contradictions in Versilov's character and in his relationship to the other members of the family. As a result, not only does Arkady find himself reacting against Versilov and periodically breaking with him "forever," but he also becomes aware of a very different quest in his soul: the quest for "seemliness."

This quest is answered by the man who is legally his father—Makar Ivanovitch. After relinquishing his wife to his master Versilov, Makar has spent 20 years as a pilgrim and now comes home to the family to die. Like his desire to become rich through self-control, Arkady's conversations with Makar Ivanovitch derive directly from Dostoievsky's plan for "The Life of a Great Sinner." Dostoievsky portrayed a discussion similar to that between Tikhon and the boy three times, in fact: in the meeting of Stavrogin and Father Tikhon, in the conversations of Arkady and the pilgrim Makar, and in the relationship of Alyosha to Father Zossima in *The Brothers Karamazov*. In the original drafts of this last novel, moreover, Dostoievsky even planned a meeting between the learned brother, Ivan, and the *staretz*, or the holy man. Father Tikhon, the pilgrim Makar, and Father Zossima are successive attempts by Dostoievsky to represent the "god-man," and in each case this "god-man" serves as father and image of the human for a young man in the process of becoming.

The relation of father and sons is as central to *The Brothers Karamazov* (Dostoievsky, undated) as it is to *The Raw Youth*. Here, too, the father figure is bifurcated—into the depraved sensualist Fyodor Karamazov and the god-man Father Zossima, with the Grand Inquisitor as something of an ideal father figure to Ivan. Fyodor Karamazov, the father of Ivan, Dmitri, and Alyosha, characterizes himself aptly as "the old buffoon." He is sly, greedy, rapacious, sensual, dishonest, and masochistic. It is significant that we are introduced to Fyodor at the same time as we are introduced to the other father who dominates the book, the *staretz* Zossima, and that we meet them both at a gathering in the latter's cell in which all three sons are present and in which all the main, interrelated themes of the novel are brought out: Dmitri and the desire to murder the father, Ivan and the death of God, Alyosha and his holy Zossima. The two worlds of *The Brothers Karamazov* are the village and the monastery. These are the natural worlds of Russian rural life of that time, but, at the same time, they are also the symbolic worlds in which the drama unfolds. Fyodor Karamazov is the father of the village world and Father Zossima of the world of the monastery. In the confrontation of these two men in Father Zossima's cell, these two worlds are also brought into confrontation. This meeting takes place in unadulterated fashion, not as that of the sacred and the secular, but as that of the sacred and the profane. Fyodor Karamazov plays out his buffoonery to the full and shows that he is able to bring a challenge of equal force, not in the traditional sense of evil opposing good, but in the much more dreadful sense of meaninglessness opposing meaning, directionlessness opposing direction, a mask opposing a person.

Terrible as he is—and he is one of the most terrible and fully unsympathetic figures in literature—Fyodor Karamazov has a stature in some sense greater than that of anyone else in the book. He is elemental passion, the base Karamazov energy and will to live. Out of him come all three of the sons, even Alyosha, and the cold, inhuman, emasculate bastard Smerdyakov, son of the idiot girl Stinking Lizaveta, whom Fyodor raped as the last stage of depraved sensuality. Fyodor has an energy that exceeds that of any of his sons, but in him it lies formless, stagnant, and corrupt. Although he neither rears his sons nor provides for them and even cheats them out of what is rightfully theirs, he bequeaths this elemental Karamazov passion to each of them and with it the abyss of shame and the sordid depths of existence. This heritage can be either overcome, as in Alyosha, through going the way of Father Zossima and the "god-man"; or affirmed, as in Ivan, through throwing off every demand that is placed upon him and becoming himself the higher law; or acted out, as in Dmitri, by one minute following a lofty impulse and the next minute a base one.

"Why is such a man alive? . . . Tell me, can he be allowed to go on defiling the earth?" cries Dmitri at the meeting at the monastery in which his father, instead of accepting the reconciliation with Dmitri that was to have been the purpose of the meeting, shamelessly baits him. "Listen, monks, to the patricide," Fyodor cries in response to Dmitri's words. Patricide, the murder of the father, is indeed the primary motif of the novel—a motif that involves in the closest possible way not only Dmitri, who almost murders his father, but Ivan, who wishes his father dead and half knowingly encourages the murder, and the bastard son, Smerdyakov, who actually commits the murder. Ivan, as Smerdyakov says, is more like the father than either of the other two brothers. On his intellectual side he remains grand and noble, bold and courageous, with only the loftiest passions admitted to his self-image. But the other side of him remains nasty and mean. One part of him identifies with his father and, for that reason, passionately hates him, whereas the other part of him is simply detached or at best emotional only in a lofty and abstract manner. Although he likes to think that his whole being is placed at the service of his ideals, the truth is that the other, baser part of him uses both his ideals and his detachment in its own service.

The superior Ivan, who is above conventional morality, regards his brother Dmitri not merely as a "reptile," but as a "scoundrel," a "murderer," a "patricide," and a "monster" and constantly refers to him as such. When Katya says to Ivan, "It was you, you who persuaded me that he murdered his father. It's only you I believed!" and informs him she has been to see Smerdyakov, Ivan is unable to bear it and rushes off to see Smerdyakov to force him to tell what transpired between him and Katya. Ivan's irrational hatred of Dmitri is as much connected with his own feeling of guilt for desiring his father's death as with his jealousy of his rival for Katya's love. At one point Alyosha says to Ivan that he has been sent by God to tell him that it was not he, Ivan, who killed his father even though he has several times told himself that he and no one else is the murderer. Trembling all over, Ivan accuses Alyosha of having been in his room and having seen his "visitor." Once earlier, when troubled by doubts, Ivan asks whether Alyosha had thought that he desired his father's death. When Alyosha softly answers, "I did think so," Ivan says, "It was so, too; it was not a matter of guessing." Yet when he goes to see Smerdyakov and the latter also says that Ivan desired his father's death, Ivan jumps up and strikes the sick man on the shoulder with all his might. After Alyosha confesses that he thought that Ivan wished Dmitri to kill their father and was even prepared to help bring it about, Ivan takes a dislike to Alyosha and avoids seeing him. Ivan is too honest to rationalize his actions altogether, but he is too shaky in his own self-image to bear the truth. A large part of Ivan's thought, in fact—from his saying that "all is lawful" to his sin-carrying and sinless Grand Inquisitor and his all-forgiving Christ—can be seen as arising from his inability to accept guilt and his need to sublimate his guilt-feeling into the semblance of noble motives that will satisfy his conscious mind.

The dialectical and intellectual Ivan is so divided that he cannot admit to his conscious mind what has gone on. He keeps that part of himself that he does not care to recognize in a separate compartment, and he uses his hysteria as a relief from the nervous tension that comes from his inner division and from the fact that he is choosing to let things happen rather than make a real decision. Only in this murky, half-conscious world can he persist in this decisionless state of not taking responsibility and at the same time giving a negative "go ahead" to what one part of him, at least, must know is going on. He hates Dmitri as the murderer of his father, but he is impelled to plan his escape because of the burning and rankling sensation that he is "as much a murderer at heart."

Ivan is unable to cast off his guilt by identifying his self with his *conscious* self only or to accept his guilt by identifying himself with that other, surprising self that emerges into thought and action before his eyes. Ivan cannot bear to look into the foul pit of his own inner life; neither can he turn away from it. Versilov's theory of the second self applies equally to Ivan and with it the ambiguities of responsible freedom and impersonal compulsion that Versilov does not see but his son Dolgoruky does. Ivan is not Smerdyakov, able to act without conscience and without guilt, but neither is he Dmitri, ready to receive the suffering that comes to him as a way of working out of dividedness and guilt to some sort of personal wholeness. After the conflict within him between "god-man" and lackey devil has wreacked its havoc, Ivan is left less rebel than simply divided man. The bifurcation of the father figure means the bifurcation of the son.[12]

13

The Crisis of Motives,
the Problematic of Guilt, and
Existential Shame, Guilt, and Trust

The Crisis of Motives

The inner division that results from the alienation of fathers
and sons from each other is as much a commentary on the absence of a modern image of the human as on the breakdown of
the specific father-son relationship. At the heart of this breakdown, in fact, is the inability of the father to give his son a
direction-giving image of meaningful and authentic human existence. The inner division in the son that results expresses itself at times, as we have seen, in the bifurcation into opposing
selves and opposing father images. It may also, as we have
seen, express itself in a crisis of motives when the son, unable
to accept the father, suppresses his awareness of the side of him
that resembles his father in favor of an ideal self-image. Ivan
Karamazov has two contradictory images of the human, two incompatible sets of motivations: the one represented by his "Grand
Inquisitor," a noble man with high humanitarian motives; the
other by the lackey devil of his hallucinations, who embodies

all the mean and trivial emotions and attitudes that he has not wanted to recognize in himself. In all Dostoievsky's divided men, the inner conflict takes the form of a crisis of motives. Motives that in the past might have been taken at their face value—humility, love, friendship—must now be looked at more carefully. For, as Dostoievsky saw even before Freud, they may, in fact, mask resentment, hatred, or hostility. When Modern Man thinks of the humility of St. Francis, he may see also the masochistic Marmeladov allowing his wife to drag him by the beard, or Dostoievsky's "Eternal Husband" who, after ministering to the sick friend who has taken his wife, tries to kill him in his sleep.

For Nietzsche, too, men dissemble without knowing it, unaware of the ignoble lust that conceals itself behind the noble ideal. Zarathustra labels as "Tarantulas" those socialist and humanitarian "preachers of equality" whose demand for "justice" masks a secret desire for revenge. The man "who will never defend himself" is the man of *ressentiment* who "swalloweth down poisoneth spittle and bad looks, the all-too-patient one, the all-endurer." The chaste are those who seek in chastity the satisfaction that has been denied them elsewhere.

> And how nicely the bitch, sensuality, knows how to beg for a piece of spirit, when denied a piece of meat. . . .

> Your eyes are too cruel, and you search lustfully for sufferers. It is not merely your lust that has disguised itself and now calls itself pity? (Nietzsche, 1978, p. 55)

Friendship, similarly, is often merely an attempt to overleap envy, and the love of one's neighbor nothing but the bad love of oneself.

> You invite a witness when ye want to speak well of yourselves; and when you have seduced him to think well of you, then you think well of yourselves . . .

> One man goes to his neighbor because he seeks himself; another because he would lose himself. (Nietzsche, 1978, p. 61)

That modern psychoanalysis has attempted to find a rational pattern behind these hidden motivations that Dostoievsky and Nietzsche have unmasked in no way reduces the problematic nature of the mistrust that impels such unmasking and of the bad faith—with others and with oneself—that is unmasked. Both the bad faith and the mistrust mean essentially the fragmentation of the self. Modern Man knows his alienation nowhere so intensely as in the alienation from oneself that results from this inner division and conflict. In the modern age it is no longer possible to accept any person, not even oneself, at "face value." Yet, it is equally impossible simply to explain away the reality of a person by reducing that person to the psychologically determined being pictured by one of another school of psychoanalysis. What confronts us again and again in others and in ourselves, in the characters of our literature and in the authors who create them, is the bewildering intermixture of personal freedom and psychological compulsion; and the specific form that this intermixture takes differs with each person and with each unique situation.

Jean-Baptiste Clamence

Perhaps the best illustration in contemporary literature of the crisis of motives that results from this inner division is in Albert Camus's last novel, *The Fall* (1957). Jean-Baptiste Clamence, the hero of *The Fall*, was once a respected lawyer who contributed his services to worthy causes, loved one woman after another, and felt secure in the approval of himself and the world. Then, as with Franz Kafka's K., the world breaks in upon his self-assured existence, in this case in the form of a young woman whom he sees leaning against a bridge on the Seine and does not try to save when she jumps in and cries for help after he walks by. This event so undermines his faith in his own motivation that he leaves his work and the society of those he knows and becomes a "judge penitent," confessing to others in order to get them to confess to him. Unable to assert his own innocence, he takes refuge in the common guilt: "We cannot assert the innocence of anyone, whereas we can state with certainty the

guilt of all. Every man testifies to the crime of all the others—
that is my faith and my hope." To Clamence, as to Kafka, the Last
Judgment takes place every day. The foundation of his world is
social guilt, and he tries to bring others with him into "the closed
little universe of which I am the king, the pope, the judge."

Like Dostoievsky's Underground Man, Ivan's Inquisitor, and
T. S. Eliot's Prufrock, Camus's "false prophet" is making a confession from hell. Hell is the nonexistence to which he retired
when he found existence insupportable; it is the world without
reality and without grace into which he tries to attract others,
who he knows will have more nasty things to confess in the end
than those he himself has told. He identifies himself, in both his
past and present unwillingness to commit himself, to risk his
life, with the "you" to whom he has talked throughout the book
and who we realize at the end is ourselves:

> Are we not all alike . . . ? Then please tell me what happened to you
> one night on the quays of the Seine and how you managed never to
> risk your life. You yourself utter the words that for years have never
> ceased echoing through your mouth: "O young woman, throw your-
> self into the water again so that I may a second time have the chance
> of saving both of us!" A second time, eh, what a risky suggestion!
> Suppose, *chèr maitre*, that we should be taken literally? We'd have to
> go through with it. Brrr . . . ! The water's so cold! But let's not worry!
> It's too late now. It will always be too late. Fortunately! (Camus, 1957,
> p. 147)

Jean-Baptiste Clamence's affirmation of guilt is deeply dis-
quieting because in his very acceptance of the split between
what he had once pretended to be and what he is, he surrenders
that tension that might have led him back to some form of real
existence. Thus, in the end the crisis of motives becomes inseparable from the problematic of guilt.

Franz Kafka's The Trial: The Problematic of Guilt

Our fullest insight into guilt as an interhuman reality and
into the problematic of guilt that grows out of it comes to us

from the works of Franz Kafka. Kafka's treatment of guilt unquestionably includes a strong neurotic component, as the relation of son to father in Kafka's writings strongly suggests.[13] Yet, it is equally clear that Kafka is concerned not only with neurotic guilt but also with real guilt that arises as a corollary of one's personal situation and one's personal responsibility.

"Although he imagines that he knows more about himself than did the man of any earlier time," writes Buber, "it has become more difficult for the man of our age than any earlier one to venture self-illumination with awake and unafraid spirit." Buber sees this modern problem of guilt illustrated in two of the figures whom we have seen as representative of the problematic of Modern Man—Stavrogin and Joseph K. Stavrogin, "the man on the outermost rim of the age," " 'commits' the confession as he commits his crimes: as an attempt to snatch the genuine existence which he does not possess." Joseph K. is not able to make confession at all. "Not merely before the world, but also before himself, he refuses to concern himself with an ostensible state of guilt. . . . Indeed, it now passes as proved, in this his generation, that no real guilt exists; only guilt-feeling and guilt convention" (Buber, 1988c, p. 136). Each man in so doing is faithful to the stage that the problematic of Modern Man had reached in his author's lifetime:

> *The Possessed* was written in 1879, Kafka's *Trial* in 1915. The two books represent two basically different but closely connected situations of human history from which their authors suffered: the one the uncanny negative certainty, "Human values are beginning to shatter," and the other the still more uncanny uncertainty, "Do world-meaning and world-order still have any connection at all with this nonsense and this disorder of the human world?"—an uncertainty that appears to have arisen out of that negative certainty. (Buber, 1988c, p. 130)

Although the Court that K. is confronted by is "wild, crude, and senselessly disordered through and through," writes Buber, "Joseph K. is himself, in all his actions, of hardly less indefiniteness . . . as charged with guilt, he confusedly carries on day after day a life as directionless as before." He refuses to confess, not because he is proud, like Stavrogin, but because he does not distinguish himself from others. His statement, "And, if it comes to that, how can any man be called guilty? We are all simply men here, one as much as the other," is his way of denying the existence of personal guilt and escaping "the demand to bear into his inner darkness (of which Kafka speaks in his diaries) the cruel and salutary light." In denying "the ontic character of guilt, the depth of existential guilt beyond all mere violations of taboos," writes Buber, Joseph K. is doing just what Freud wished to do "when he undertook to relativize guilt-feeling genetically" (Buber, 1988c, p. 132).[14]

Guilt, to Kafka, must be understood within the context of two discernible stages in Kafka's thought: the world breaking in upon the self, and the self seeking to answer a call. To say that guilt originates with the world breaking into the self is to say that the world in some sense calls one to become oneself through fulfilling one's "calling," that to which one is called, and that it calls one to account when one does not do so. Kafka understands this calling to account, however, in a thoroughly problematic way. The central problem of *The Trial*, that of guilt, cannot be referred simply to K.'s subjectivity or to the frighteningly irregular and corrupt bureaucracy that has him in its "clutches," but to the encounter between the two. The world of Joseph K. gradually changes from the everyday business world that he takes for granted into a mysterious Gnostic hierarchy that, like some gigantic octopus, wraps its tentacles around the whole of reality until it finally crushes him to death—and, most startling of all, does so with his compliance!

"Someone must have traduced Joseph K., for without having done anything wrong he was arrested one fine morning" (Kafka, 1957, p. 10). Thus begins a book that, while it never brings to light even the most trivial offense for which K. might be arrested and punished, increasingly places in question the unambiguous insistence of the hero that he is simply the innocent victim of injustice. K. is arrested on his 30th birthday and executed on his 31st, biographical coincidences that suggest already that his "trial" is not a judgment on what he has specifically done or left undone but on his life itself. When he is told that the Law does not hunt for crime but is drawn to the guilty, K. says, "I don't know this Law," to which the warder who has arrested him replies, "All the worse for you." When K. then says, "And it probably exists nowhere but in your own head," the warder responds, "You'll come up against it yet," while the other warder comments, "See, Willem, he admits that he doesn't know the Law and yet he claims he's innocent." K.'s very guilt, we may surmise, lies in the fact that he does not know the Law, that his life is closed to the *hearing* of the Law.

Joseph K. has constructed successfully, in fact, a life that excludes "hearing." Between the meaningless routine of his work at the Bank, where he is the chief clerk, and the meaningless routine of his "bachelor pleasures," is no room for any kind of self-examination. This is the case with his life before his arrest. It is also the case after his "arrest" when he cannot bring himself to take the time needed for recalling his past life in detail. Since after his arrest K. is allowed to carry on his business as usual and since he "cannot recall the slightest offense that might be charged against" him, he begins by dismissing his arrest as an affair of no great importance. The warders cannot say that he is charged with any offense, but they advise him: "Think less about us and of what is going to happen to you, think more about yourself instead" (Kafka, 1957, p. 17). This advice directs us away from any specific guilt on K.'s part to his existence as such. In striking contrast to Kafka himself, however, K. acknowledges no guilt whatsoever and persists in regarding his trial as real only if he recognizes it as such.

The significance of K.'s ignorance of the Law—of his having no time for hearing and for self-examination—is indicated not merely by the routine character of his work and his pleasures but still more by his attempt to turn his whole existence into one of professional smoothness and efficiency. K. must always "be prepared," he must always be in control. What makes his arrest a special nightmare to him is that it comes to him when he is unprepared, at home, in bed, not ready to master the situation with smooth professional skill without involving himself personally.

Throughout the opening stages of the trial, K. preserves the demeanor of the detached observer who is somehow not really involved in his own case. Other people seem to him mad and incomprehensible; he is always sane and cool. By the same token, he is impelled constantly to contrast the orderly nature of his own life and the disorderly character of the Court. The conclusion he draws from this is that what is needed is the sort of strengthening of self-confidence through autosuggestion that is preached regularly to the modern businessman as the gospel of success: "The right tactics were to avoid letting one's thoughts stray to one's own possible shortcomings, and to cling as firmly as one could to the thought of one's advantage" (Kafka, 1957, p. 159). The Court would encounter in him a formidable opponent, a man with "know-how": "These tactics must be pursued unremittingly, everything must be organized and supervised; the Court would encounter for once an accused man who knew how to stick up for his rights."

K.'s guilt, in other words, so far as we can glimpse it, is neither legal nor social, but existential. By this we do not mean, as so many existentialists do, that his guilt is only or even primarily in relation to himself; for his existence is inseparable from his relations to others. But we do mean that he is accountable as a person and not just as someone who fulfills a social role. When the novel opens, he knows his existence only as that of the chief clerk of the Bank. By drawing him forth from the social confirmation that such a role gives him to the solitude in which he has to face his trial just as the person he is, with no help from others, his "arrest" has forced him to become aware of a personal dimension of existence that he would never have noticed of his own free will. The persons with whom K. comes in contact cannot be his allies since he has built his life on the exclusion of the reality of other people and wants to relate to them only insofar as he has mastered them. Every person who meets him is a potential judge, for that person has a reality quite alien to his own existence, a reality that confronts his existence and calls it into question.

The situation of K., who is torn out of the security of his social role into the anxiety of personal accountability, is to some extent the situation of everyone who at one time or another suddenly finds oneself standing alone without those supports of family, position, and name that are so familiar to one that one has come to take them for granted. So, too, everyone stands, whether one knows it or not, in a situation of continuous personal accountability as long as one lives. No person achieves a place where one not only may approve of all one has been but may take for granted one's responses to the new, unforeseen situation that awaits one. Our existence in time is characterized above all else by just this necessity of meeting the new face that the moment wears. In other words, the possibility of a final decision that is true of an ordinary trial is not true of our existence itself. "Only our concept of time makes it possible for us to speak of the Day of Judgment by that name," says Kafka in one of his aphorisms; "in reality it is a summary court in perpetual session" (Kafka, 1946, p. 263, no. 38). If one thinks of guilt not in legal but in personal and existential terms, then it becomes impossible to say, as K. says, that one is completely innocent. The question of whether one's existence is authentic or inauthentic cannot be answered by the sum of one's actions, as K. wishes, or by any objective standard that detaches guilt from one's personal existence itself. It is not merely a subjective or arbitrary matter, but the responsibility of the self in relation to the world. This responsibility cannot be judged from the standpoint of the world alone or of the self alone or from the standpoint of any third party looking at the world and the self, but only within the relationship itself. "Only he who is a party can really judge," reads another Kafka aphorism, "but as a party he cannot judge. Hence it follows that there is no possibility of judgment in the world, only a glimpse of it" (Kafka, 1954, p. 76). This means, too, that one is accountable for one's existence and is accountable alone, without any possibility of a "joint defense." "You are the problem. No scholar to be found far and wide," says Kafka in a remarkably Zenlike aphorism (Kafka, 1946, p. 258, no. 19).

In the course of the book, K. experiences a growing anxiety about his case, an anxiety arising from the failure of his attempts to master the situation. His trial works on K. as an ever greater distraction so that he is no longer able to concentrate upon his business or to be really present to the external world that was his life. Speaking psychologically, one might say that Kafka describes a person whose unconscious impulses or anxieties block one's conscious drive for success, a person whose life is more and more preoccupied with and distracted by a guilt that one cannot face. The proceedings and the verdict have an organic continuity with each other since what is in question here is no single crime but a line of inauthentic existence that gradually crystallizes into its own judgment on itself.

The Law is not available to every person at every moment for the simple reason that in the reality of one's personal existence one is not approached at every moment and one is not always ready to go forth to meet what comes. Something is required of one before a decisive meeting can take place, something that K. is unwilling to do, namely, involving one's whole person in one's actions in such a way that one becomes genuinely responsible for them. This in no way contradicts the statement in the "Parable of the Law" that the door is intended just for this person, for what is in question here is not some universal law that applies to people in general, but a unique relationship to reality that is available to no one else. The door is shut at the time the man from the country dies because with the end of his existence the possibility of the realization of this unique relationship also disappears.

In *The Trial* Kafka is clearly as concerned about the grotesque absurdity of the world that K. encounters as about K.'s existential guilt. But he is concerned most of all about the confrontation of these two, about what happens when the world breaks in upon the self as it does upon K. Although the world that confronts the self is absurd, it places a real demand upon the self that the latter must meet. The self can find meaning in its existence neither through rationalizing away the absurdity of the world nor through rejecting the world's demand because of this absurdity, but through answering with its existence the demand that comes to it through the absurd and that can reach it in no other way. This is the ultimate meaning of the self breaking in upon the world, as Kafka develops the theme.

Kafka emphatically denies that his view of life as a judgment is merely a psychological matter. On the contrary, he sees life itself as erected upon inner justification, and the task of such a justification as essential to human existence. By "inner justification" Kafka in no sense means an act of arbitrary self-confirmation or the self's free choice of its own image of the human in responsibility only to itself. On the contrary, he holds that time itself, and our own existence in time, must be justified before eternity. The very fact of being asked about one's life and having to answer—of being called and responding to the call—is the inner meaning of the justification that Kafka sees as the underpinning of human existence. We may even say that this call is at the same time a "calling to account," in the sense that it makes us accountable for our lives. Moreover, when we have tried to avoid this accountability, like Joseph K., the judgment that follows is a calling to account for our failure to answer the call.

We know ourselves as called, but we do not know who calls or the direction from which the call comes or the way in which we must answer it. This is the problematic of Modern Man. It is possible, therefore, to say, at one and the same time, that life is a commission and a task and that we do not know who commissions or what our task is. The conclusion from this is not, as Joseph K. thinks, that we are all absolved from guilt, but that we are accountable for our existence in a way that eludes our rational grasp of guilt and innocence. We are guilty for not answering or for answering in the wrong way the call that we could never clearly hear. "Only those fear to be put to the proof who have a bad conscience," said Kafka. "They are the ones who do not fulfill the tasks of the present. Yet who knows precisely what his task is? No one. So that every one of us has a bad conscience."[15]

Existential Shame, Guilt, and Trust

In *On Shame and the Search for Identity*, Helen Lynd presents a phenomenology of shame especially valuable in that it traces shame to something irreducibly concrete and particular. Dmitri in Dostoievsky's *The Brothers Karamazov* is ashamed not because he has stolen money or bludgeoned his father and his old servant over the head; he is ashamed because he has to take his shoes off during the examination and let others see his big toe with its blunt toenail curving out to the right. By such examples Lynd captures the opaque, essentially unrationalizable immediacy of much experience of shame and one's sense of one's self, including bodily self—one's self in the fullest and most concrete sense. Shame is associated closely with anxiety, she writes, but it is not merely anxiety caused by fear of public exposure. "The public exposure of even a very private part of one's physical or mental character could not in itself have brought about shame unless one had already felt within oneself, not only dislike, but shame for these traits" (Lynd, 1958, p. 29).

To understand shame, human goals and capacities cannot be too narrowly conceived, for "shame is an experience that affects and is affected by the whole self," and it is this that makes it a clue to identity. Shame is associated often with actions that are not only blameless but also trivial. Yet, these incidents "have importance because in this moment of *self*-consciousness, the self stands revealed." Whether our gesture toward another was inappropriate or was simply not reciprocated, the experience of shame that it causes throws "a flooding light on what and who we are and what the world we live in is." This self-illumination, in fact, is the cause, as well as the effect, of the shame—the anxiety and sense of inadequacy—that becomes manifest in a situation in which we have totally involved ourselves: "One is overtaken by shame because one's whole life has been a preparation for putting one in this situation" (Lynd, 1958, p. 49).

Lynd builds much of her treatment of shame upon Eric Erikson (1950, 1953, 1954, 1956). Shame, in Helen Lynd's understanding of it, is bound closely with the loss of trust. The loss of early trust may, of course, help determine in important ways a child's future sense of identity, because for most people trust is not altogether lost so much as "it is transmuted into more mature and understanding confidence" (Lynd, 1958, p. 49). But each loss of trust may go beyond the early shocks experienced by every child to a question of trust in existence itself. "Basic trust in one's world and especially in the persons who are its interpreters is crucial to one's sense of identity" (Lynd, 1958, p. 207). If this is so, then shame as a function of a loss of trust surely points in the first instance to the relations between person and person as a dimension as basic as that "inner" realm that Lynd assigns to shame.

Lynd does not fail to make explicit the relation of shame to the problem of human resources and the tragic limitations imposed by "man's fate." "Failure to reach our own aspirations . . . leads to the question of how far disappointment and the failure of human effort lie in the unalterable nature of things" (Lynd, 1958, p. 63). Disappointment and shame test the limits of one's faith in the possibilities of life and may even lead to the conviction that not only one's own life but that of all persons is empty, isolated, void of significance. "Experience of shame may call into question, not only one's own adequacy and the validity of codes of one's immediate society, but the meaning of the universe itself" (Lynd, 1958, p. 57).

Experiences of shame are communicated only with the greatest difficulty, Lynd points out. Just because shame exposes the self—and beyond the self, the society to which one belongs—a person may respond to shame by "refusing to recognize the wound, covering the isolating effect of shame through depersonalization and adaptation to any approved codes." But another alternative is open to us—fully to face the experiences of shame and realize their import. If we do this, they may "become a revelation of oneself, of one's society, and of the human situation" (Lynd, 1958, p. 71). One means of dealing with shame is an identification with other persons in situations that make them feel ashamed. This confrontation of the shame of others may be the beginning of the realization of shame as revelation *and* of the transcending of shame. Equally as important as the identification with the shame of others is the mutual love through which one risks the exposure of shame and enters into the mind and feeling of another person.

> If . . . one can sufficiently risk uncovering oneself and sufficiently trust another person, to seek means of communicating shame, the risking of exposure can be in itself an experience of release, expansion, self-revelation, a coming forward of belief in oneself, and entering into the mind and feeling of another person. (Lynd, 1958, p. 249)

Helen Lynd touches here on two profound paradoxes of shame—first that, unbearable as shame often seems, it perhaps can be endured if one taps deeper resources and becomes in so doing a wholer, greater person, by which she means a person more open to mutual, responsive, interhuman relations. Hence, the second paradox: The isolating quality of shame cannot be altogether removed. How could it, since shame puts its finger upon us not as part of some general category but as the unique, particular persons that we are? Yet, mutual love can help us not only risk exposure and communicate our shame but also experience from the side of the other, the person whom we love, how she, too, lives in the recurrent shame of being the person that she is. When this takes place, our shame remains real, yet we are no longer so terrifyingly alone in it. It is no longer the shame of Dostoievsky's Underground Man—the shame at being the sole exception to the "happy breed" of humankind.

Though larger identifications—"with a group of other persons, a scientific investigation or an art form, a purpose or a belief"—one can, says Helen Lynd, transcend shame, for through them one attains an enlarged perspective, a Hegelian "comic frame of reference," a "sense of proportion that is the outcome of taking the individual self and the world in their widest reach of all that they can be" (Lynd, 1958, p. 256). This confronting of shame makes "way for living beyond the conventions of a particular culture" and makes possible, by the same token, "the discovery of an integrity that is peculiarly one's own and of those characteristically human qualities that are at the same time most universal" (Lynd, 1958, p. 257). Lynd comes very close to my use of the human image when she writes of "Amos, Socrates, Tycho Brahe, Galileo, Martin Luther, Freud, Cézanne, Rilke, Stephen Hero, Black Boy . . . whose sense of self is related to ideals that they conceive as widely human and at the same time peculiarly their own" (Lynd, 1958, p. 227). Thus, she moves from shame as an irreducibly particular, cruelly isolating experience to universal ideals that transcend not only the isolated self but the limits of societies and cultures; at the same time, she retains the connection between these ideals and the individual person in his or her particularity and uniqueness.

By withdrawing shame and its overcoming from the "outer" social sphere and placing it into the "inner" personal sphere, on the one hand, and the universal, on the other hand, Helen Lynd is in danger of missing what, even from her own examples, is the real center and problematic of shame—the meeting point of the personal and the social. No sense of inner or universal values can ever quite remove the shame of exposure, of inappropriateness, of an unreciprocated gesture. Even Dostoievsky's Christlike Prince Myshkin is a figure of shame to himself, as well as to others, just *because* he acts in ways inappropriate to the social group in which he moves. One may question, therefore, whether Lynd has taken sufficiently seriously the problem she herself has set up—the relation between personal identity and social reality. Ludwig Binswanger in *Existence* (May, 1958) makes a criticism of Erwin Straus's distinction between existential, or protecting, shame and purely concealing shame that might well be applied to Lynd's treatment of shame, even though her categories are different from Straus's. In concealing shame, according to Straus, it is not a question of primal shame, originally intrinsic to being human (and not acquired in the course of the life history), but of the public shame stemming from one's own reflection thrown upon the others. At bottom, however, writes Binswanger, existential and concealing shame belong together, just as being-oneself and being-with-others belong together. Existential shame, too, shows itself in blushing, thus revealing to the other precisely what it wants to hide (Binswanger in May, 1958, p. 337).

The most serious question that *On Shame and the Search for Identity* (Lynd, 1958) raises concerns the contrast between shame and guilt that Lynd places at the center of the book. Following Gerhart Piers and Franz Alexander, Lynd sees guilt as the transgression of the taboos of society, shame as falling short of the self-ideal; guilt as related to the superego imposed or taught by others, shame as one's own line of direction discovered by oneself; guilt as connected with specific, detachable acts, shame as connected with the whole self and, therefore, as general and nondetachable. Guilt is connected with fear—the fear of mutilation; shame is connected with anxiety—the anxiety of abandonment. In guilt one lives in terms of conventions; shame leads beyond convention and one's immediate culture. In guilt one person can see another as merely external and instrumental, whereas in shame they can be a part of each other.

Out of all these contrasts Lynd forms a basic contrast between a "guilt axis" and a "shame axis." Guilt involves "an additive process," shame "total response that includes insight";
guilt "competition, measurement on a scale, performing the
acts prescribed as desirable," shame "pervasive qualitative demands of oneself, more rigorous than external codes." On the
guilt axis is "being a good, loyal friend, husband, wife, parent",
on the shame axis, "having an overflowing feeling for friend,
husband, wife, children which makes goodness and loyalty a
part of the whole experience with no need for separate emphasis." Guilt entails "emphasis on decision-making: any decision
is better than none," whereas shame entails "ability to live with
some indecisiveness (multiple possibilities) even though it
means living with some anxiety." "Surmounting of guilt," the
last item states, "leads to righteousness," whereas "transcending of shame may lead to a sense of identity, freedom." The conclusion that Lynd draws is "that a sense of identity cannot be
reached along the guilt axis alone."

Lynd expresses the belief that "in a society more directly and
variously expressive of human desires" than our own, "the
guilt axis and the shame axis, role fulfillment and personal fulfillment, might more nearly coincide." Even though role fulfillment and personal fulfillment may not coincide in our society,
neither can they be separated in the way that Lynd seems to
separate them. One's identity cannot be envisaged apart from
one's interpersonal and interhuman relations, including, in
some important measure, one's social role. One may question,
too, her certainty that shame goes deeper than guilt because it
leads us to question trust: "It is worse to be inferior and isolated than to be wrong" (Lynd, 1958, p. 207). Unless we assume
that the self is *not* centrally concerned with its relations with
others, we can hardly relegate guilt to a subordinate position.
If shame may help us see the world through the eyes of another,
so that we become both "more separated from and more related
to others," it certainly does not follow that guilt means treating
others merely as external and instrumental.

The greatest weakness in Lynd's approach is her assumption that guilt is merely a social product. Certainly
purely social and even neurotic guilt can be derived from a set

of mores and taboos imposed upon the individual by parents and society and incorporated into an internalized "superego." But there is also real guilt, guilt that has to do with one's actual stance in the world and the way in which one goes out to relate to other people from that stance. If such a thing as real or existential guilt exists, then it cannot be merely additive and atomistic, as Lynd has held, but, like shame, must be grounded in the whole self and never entirely detachable from it. What is more, since they both are involved in the problem of personal wholeness and direction, somewhere in the depths of the self, existential guilt and existential shame must meet and interrelate.

One must question also, for those reasons, Lynd's assertion that guilt does not exclude communication, whereas shame is isolating. Certainly a completely objective, external, detachable guilt can be objectively communicated, but that is neither real guilt nor real communication. One is as alone with true guilt as with true shame, and it is no easier to confess the one than the other. Both Kierkegaard and Kafka have stressed the fact that personal guilt is incommunicable.

In Kafka's novel *The Trial*, Joseph K. can never even discover why he is arrested and what he is charged with. His guilt cannot be reduced to isolated, detachable, additive acts but concerns his existence as a whole. He himself, to be sure, wishes to reduce his responsibility to being answerable only for his external actions:

> He had often considered whether it would not be better to draw up a written defense and hand it in to the Court. In this defense he would give a short account of his life, and when he came to an event of any importance explain for what reason he had acted as he did, intimate whether he approved or condemned his way of action in retrospect, and adduce ground for the condemnation or approval. (Kafka, 1957, chap. VII, p. 142)

K. wants to see himself as accountable only in his actions and not as a person. But, as I have shown in *Problematic Rebel*, everything in *The Trial* suggests that it is not his detached actions but precisely his existence that is on trial and that his insistence upon regarding his life as no more than the sum of his actions is itself, perhaps, his chief guilt. This means that his guilt, so far as we can glimpse it, is neither legal nor social, but existential, that he is accountable, even in his social relationships, as a person and not just as someone who fulfills a social role.

When K. is taken to a vacant lot by two tenth-rate actors and a knife is plunged into his heart, he exclaims, "Like a dog!" to which the author adds, in the last words of the novel, "It was as if the shame of it must outlive him." In his "Letter to His Father," Kafka identifies these words with the "boundless" sense of guilt inculcated in him since his childhood. If one takes seriously these last words of The Trial, one may question whether the deepest level of *The Trial* is not guilt but shame. Why, after all, do Kafka and his hero speak of a shame so great that it might outlive one if it were not that deeper than any sense of personal guilt, and certainly than any sense of guilt for a specific action, lay shame for his father and for himself? Following Helen Lynd, we should not find it difficult to interpret much of Kafka's attitude toward his parents and himself as an expression of that sort of irreducible, unrationalizable shame so closely associated with the body and the sense of self, with the relation of the child to its parents and to itself.

This would not mean that we should have to choose shame *instead* of guilt, as Lynd does, unless we followed her in treating guilt as a totally identifiable with the taboos and restrictions of a particular culture. If we think in terms of existential shame and existential guilt, then the ending of *The Trial*, as I suggest in *Problematic Rebel*, will point to the meeting and interfusion of these two responses rather than to a choice between them:

A man may defend himself against specific accusations of guilt, but when he has a sense of "boundless guilt" rooted in a deep feeling of worthlessness, a shame for his very existence, he can only take all accusations on himself. Everything that happens to such a person confirms his essential shame at being himself, and no amount of external success or social confirmation will do more than enable him to forget it temporarily. The only "immortality" such a man may know is the very shame which may do him to death but will not die itself, so much is it the very air that he breathes, the all too narrow and constricting ground upon which he walks! This "boundless guilt" represents that area in the depths where existential shame and existential guilt meet and interfuse. Kafka and Joseph K. are ashamed for their very existences: Being killed like a dog leads one to question not just the specific actions that lead one into this cul-de-sac but one's whole life. But by the same token, it means a recognition of personal existential guilt for what one's life has been. Since this guilt is not just a matter of specific acts, there is no point where one can accurately draw a line and say, "These acts were avoidable and these not; these acts are a subject for guilt and these for shame." (Friedman, 1970, pp. 475f.)

Existential guilt is as closely tied to existential, or basic, trust, or the lack of it, as is existential shame and for the same reason: They both are rooted in basic, existential trust. A remarkably lucid example of how real guilt grows out of the presence and absence of existential trust is Hermann Hesse's novella, "A Child's Heart." In it the 11-year-old boy in need of comfort goes up to his father's room. When he finds it empty, he is compelled by his disappointment to steal some pen points and figs from his father's drawers. He spends the whole day in tormented anguish, longing for a punishment that does not arrive until the following day when he is already in another place emotionally.

He needs to penetrate his father's secrets, to find out something about him. But though he understands this unconsciously, he cannot bring it into words for his father, and instead the boy lets his fate carry him in solitary defiance into an ever worse position in which he "watched with pain and strange gloating delight . . . how he suffered and was disappointed, how he appealed in vain to all my better instincts." He would do no more than nod when his father asked him whether he was sorry and marveled at how "this big intelligent man" could fail to see how the whole affair hurt him and twisted his heart. What he learns from all this is how utterly two well-intentioned human beings can torment each other, creating new tortures, wounds, and errors. Finally, his father makes peace with him, and he goes to bed with the certainty that "my father had completely forgiven me—more than I had forgiven him" (Hesse, 1970, pp. 3-42). The basic trust of childhood is broken by a shame and guilt that try each partner in the relationship but that also in the end reestablish existential trust on a more mature, if less perfect, level.

Existential trust cannot be identified with the basic trust of childhood, even though it originally is grounded in it. It is not a secure possession of the "normal" adult. It is something that is shattered and renewed as long as we live, and shame and guilt, both neurotic and existential, are interwoven inextricably with its loss and its renewal. Existential trust is related integrally to the "partnership of existence," the life of dialogue. The beginning of dialogue is the acceptance of the reality of separation, of that ever-renewed distancing that is the prerequisite for all relationship. Dialogue begins with reality, with trust. I can go forth again to meet present reality, but I cannot control the form in which I shall meet it. We continue to care about and be responsible for the person who has been our partner even when we are not in actual dialogue with him or her. But we cannot *insist* that he or she remain a partner for us. This does not mean that every meeting must be brand new or that we do not look forward eagerly to seeing our friends and those we love. But when we insist that it has to be in a certain form when we try to control it, then our friendship, love, or marriage will wither because we shall not allow it to be what it can become in the moment.

The existential trust that enables us to live from moment to moment and to go out to meet what the new moment brings is the trust that makes it possible that in new meeting we again become whole, alive, present. If I trust in a person, a relationship, this means that despite what may and will happen, I shall enter into relationship again and bring all the past moments of meeting into present meeting. The particular person who is my partner may die, become sick, disturbed; he or she may betray me, rupture the relationship, or simply turn away and fail to respond. Sooner or later something of this does happen for most of us. When it does, it is trust that enables us to remain open and to respond to the address of the new situation. If we lose our existential trust, conversely, we are no longer able to enter anew into real dialogue.

It is our existential trust that ultimately gives actuality and continuity to our discontinuous and often merely potential relationships to our human partners. And it is this trust, too, that gives continuity and reality to our own existence as persons, for in itself personality is neither continuous nor always actual. If it is the confirmation of others and our own self-confirmation that gets us over the gaps and breaks in the first instance, it is our existential trust that enables this individual course to become a personal direction rather than a meaningless flux.

Trusting persons accept the fact that a genuine relationship is two-sided and, therefore, beyond the control of their will. It is a readiness to go forth with such resources as you have and, if you do not receive any response, to be ready another time to go out to the meeting. Many people imagine that they are justified in a settled mistrust or even despair because once or twice they ventured forth and encountered a stone wall or a cold shoulder. After this they anticipate rejection and even bring it about, or they protect themselves from it by never risking themselves. Genuine trust recognizes as its corollary "existential grace," the grace that comes to us from the other who meets us but also from our own resources, which are not simply waiting for us to use them but come and go, only partially subject to our will. We cannot control our response by an act of will power, or if we do, we are falling into that willfulness that misuses and cuts back our potentialities, making spontaneity impossible. Thus, spontaneity and genuine responsibility are two sides of the same coin.

We need the courage to address and the courage to respond, a courage that recognizes no formulae for when and how to address and to respond, and that includes the courage *not* to respond when we cannot do so in this situation as a whole person in a meaningful way. Our response should be to a true address to us; it ought not to be a mere reaction that is triggered off. If it is important not to allow ourselves to be "triggered off," it is equally essential not to withhold ourselves. One of the forms we have of withholding ourselves is the protective silence that makes us feel we never have to speak out, that we are merely observers in the group, that nothing is demanded of us. Another form of withholding ourselves, however, is the anxious verbosity that overwhelms the situation so that we are not present and we do not allow anyone else to be present either.

Still another form of withholding ourselves is substituting technique for trust.

We address others not by conscious mind or will but by who we are. We address them with more than we know, and they respond—if they really respond—with more than they know. Address and response never can be identified merely with conscious intent or even with "intentionality." Our resources have to do with what calls us and with the way we bring or do not bring ourselves into wholeness in response to this call. The courage to respond begins with openness and listening. Conversely, when we habitually fail to listen, we reach the place where we are not able to hear.

Even when we are still able to hear, the address is not always clear or even present, and we cannot always find the resources to respond when a voice does call. We live in an era of existential mistrust—a mistrust that arises from the loss of trust in our meeting with other persons in the interhuman, social, and political realms. We not only expect that the other is trying to put something over on us, we even suspect our own motivation as untrustworthy. (Abraham Heschel wrote that the modern golden rule is, "Suspect they neighbor as thyself.") We no longer really believe that we can confirm others or they us, for we do not really mean them and they do not really mean us. In such a situation, only healing through meeting can restore our crippled capacity for existential trust.

14

The Image of the Human and Psychotherapy

On the basis of the "death instinct," which he ranges alongside the "love instinct" as equally primary in *Civilization and Its Discontents* (1958), Sigmund Freud presents a devastating image of the human that no person living in the world today can afford to ignore:

> Not merely is the stranger on the whole not worthy of love, but, to be honest, I must confess he has more claim to my hostility, even to my hatred. He does not seem to have the least trace of love for me, does not show me the slightest consideration. If it will do him any good, he has no hesitation in injuring me, never even asking himself whether the amount of advantage he gains by it bears any proportion to the amount of wrong done to me. What is more, he does not even need to get an advantage from it; if he can merely get a little pleasure out of it, he thinks nothing of jeering at me, insulting me, slandering me, showing his power over me; and the more secure he feels himself, or the more helpless I am, with so much more certainty can I expect this behavior from him towards me. . . .

> The bit of truth behind all this—one so eagerly denied—is that men are not gentle, friendly creatures wishing for love, who simply defend themselves if they are attacked, but that a *powerful measure of desire for*

aggression has to be reckoned as a part of their instinctual endowment
[italics added]. The result is that their neighbor is to them not only a
possible helper or sexual object, but also a temptation to them to
gratify their aggressiveness on him, to exploit his capacity for work
without recompense, to use him sexually without his consent, to seize
his possessions, to humiliate him, to cause him pain, to torture and
to kill him. (Freud, 1958, pp. 59-61)

Homo homini lupus, Freud concludes: "Man is a wolf to man."
"Who has the courage to dispute it in the face of all the evidence in his own life and in history?"

Who indeed? In the years since Freud's death in 1939, as
much new evidence of "man's inhumanity to man" has come
to light as in the whole of recorded history up until that time:
the Nazi extermination of six million Jews and a million gyp-
sies, the Allied bombing of German cities, the atomic destruction of Hiroshima and Nagasaki by America, the slave-labor
camps of the Soviet Union, the wars and uprisings and systematic exterminations. The view of the human being as an essentially good, rational creature who will gladly cooperate with
others in his or her own self-interest is no longer a live option.
Such evidence cannot be excluded from any serious contemporary image of the human.

It is evidence, nonetheless, of how the human being *acts* and
not of what he or she *is*. Like the myths that Freud uses, it is a
plausible, perhaps even a convincing, hypothesis—but one that
can never be scientifically verified. Because we cannot know
either instinct or human nature outside a historical context, we
cannot categorically assert, as Freud has, that the desire for aggression is a part of the human being's instinctual nature.[16] It
would be equally possible to say with Erich Fromm that the
destructiveness that human beings vent upon one another is
the product of an authoritarian character structure that is, in
turn, the product of one or another type of authoritarian society. What is *not* possible is to ignore the enormous amount of
hostility and destructiveness that human beings have dis-
played toward one another in history and in our own day.
Rousseau held that the human being is by nature good and that
it is only civilization that makes him bad. Freud, with much
greater realism, recognizes that civilization is inseparable from

man. In his sense, it is meaningless to ask what man is "by nature," because we only know man as a social and civilized being. For the same reason, it is not necessary or even possible to accept Freud's view of "human nature" at face value. But it *is* necessary to confront his view of the human with utter seriousness and to take it into our own, (it is to be hoped) larger, human image.

Jung criticizes Freud for seeing the human being as basically evil, and he himself characterizes the "evil" side of the self as the "shadow," the complement of the good. If it is not suppressed, this "evil" can be brought as such into the very integration that Jung calls the "self," thus achieving a type of wholeness in which the individual knowingly succumbs to evil "in part." Good and evil both are relativized here to mere functions of wholeness. Human values are transcended by "the voice of Nature, the all-sustainer and all-destroyer." "If she appears inveterately evil to us," says Jung, "this is mainly due to the old truth that the good is always the enemy of the better." But what is this "better" of which he speaks? It is the "individuation," or wholeness in the unconscious, that has no reference, check, or court other than itself, no direction, guide, or criterion by which to distinguish one voice of the archetypal unconscious from another. If we still recognize apparent evil in the unconscious, then it is our task, for the sake of this "better," to succumb to it in part so that we may realize our destiny:

> The inner voice brings the evil before us in a very tempting and convincing way in order to make us succumb. If we do not partially succumb, nothing of this apparent evil enters into us, and no regeneration or healing can take place. (I say "apparent," though this may sound too optimistic.) If we succumb only in part, and if by self-assertion the ego can save itself from being completely swallowed, then it can assimilate the voice, and we realize that the evil was, after all, only a semblance of evil, but in reality a bringer of healing and illumination. (Jung, 1954, p. 185)

What sort of "healing and illumination" does this "semblance of evil" bring? Jung's immediate answer is that "the inner voice is a 'Lucifer' in the strictest and most unequivocal sense of the word, and it faces people with ultimate moral decisions without which they can never achieve full consciousness and become personalities." But Jung's concept of a "moral decision" is very different from the old distinctions between right and wrong, just as the court of conscience is replaced for him by the criterion of wholeness and the address of the inner voice.

If the healing that such "moral decision" leads to is not obvious, still less is the "illumination" it provides: "The highest and the lowest, the best and the vilest, the truest and the most deceptive things," reads the very next sentence, "are often blended together in the inner voice in the most baffling way, thus opening up in us an abyss of confusion, falsehood, and despair" (Jung, 1931, p. 80). What is the way out of this "confusion, falsehood, and despair"? It is succumbing in part to evil, or, as Jung puts it in a later writing, not succumbing to either good or evil, but rising above them, which means, once again, to relativize them. Jung means by this, of course, that evil must be confronted in order to be integrated. The Carpocratian Gnostic teaching of going along with one's own body in its instinctive demands is cited favorably by Jung in *Psychology and Religion* and is freely read by him into Taoism as what *must*, according to his own insights, be the secret of Taoist detachment:

> Have we, perhaps, an inkling that a mental attitude which can direct the glance inward to that extent owes its detachment from the world to the fact that *those men have so completely fulfilled the instinctive demands of their natures* that little or nothing prevents them from perceiving the invisible essence of the world? Can it be, perhaps, that the condition of such knowledge is freedom from those desires, ambitions, and passions, which bind us to the visible world, and *must not this freedom result from the intelligent fulfillment of instinctive demands*, rather than from a premature repression, or one growing out of fear? (Jung, 1931, p. 80f.)

In his critique of Jung in *Eclipse of God*, Buber (1988a) confesses that he is concerned particularly by Jung's Modern Gnostic resumption, under the guise of psychotherapy, of the Carpocratian motif of mystically deifying the instincts instead of hallowing them in faith. "The soul which is integrated in the Self as the unification in an all-encompassing wholeness of the opposites, especially of the opposites good and evil, dispenses

with the conscience as the court which distinguishes and decides between the right and the wrong. It itself arbitrates an
adjustment between the principles." This "narrow as a knife's
edge" way leads Jung to the positive function of evil. Evil is
integrated in the "bridal unification of opposite halves" in the
soul, which is the goal of the process of individuation. The self
that is indistinguishable in its totality from a divine image and
the self-realization that Jung describes as "the incarnation of
God" goes back, Buber points out, to "a Gnostic figure, which
probably is to be traced back ultimately to the ancient Iranian
divinity Zurvan (not mentioned, as far as I know, among Jung's
numerous references to the history of religions) as that out of
which the light god and his dark counterpart arise" (Buber,
1988a, p. 90).

In his distinguished book *The Symbolic Quest* (1969), the
American Jungian analyst Edward Whitmont asserts that
Buber has seriously misunderstood and misquoted Jung. What
Whitmont actually offers is not evidence of misquoting or even
necessarily of a misunderstanding but an alternate interpreta-
tion of Jung's statements, one that may see Jung more from
within than Buber did, though modified at the same time by
Whitmont's own personal extensions of Jung's theories:

> When he says that we have to experiment with evil—Martin Buber
> attacks him for this—he means that we must experiment with what
> may appear to be evil to our ego-identified attitude and to our
> collectivized value system, because it is still the primitive daimon.
> But we must struggle with, accept, follow it, not identify with it. This
> means paying attention to our own deepest conscience and guarding
> against falling in with that which this deepest conscience reveals to
> us as destructive. (Whitmont, 1969, p. 227)

Whitmont's disclaimer on Jung's behalf is less effective than it
might be because of the ambiguity of the distinction between
accepting and following evil and identifying with it. What
makes it still more problematic is the reference to "our own
deepest conscience"; for, in Jungian terms this may refer not to
conscience at all in the ordinary sense but the process of individuation. Similarly, the force of the word *destructive* depends

upon what is assumed to be "constructive"—one's relations with others or the integration and individuation of the self in the depths of the personal unconscious.

Perhaps the most important issue between Jung and Buber is the question of what happens to the drives toward evil, what the Talmud and the Hasidim call the "evil urge." Jung says we give in to them intelligently and in part. Buber calls this "mystically deifying the instincts instead of hallowing them in faith." Whitmont, not at all in the context of the Buber-Jung interchange but very much to the point for that interchange, insists that they are constructively transformed:

> Transformation, however, postulates a change of the drives themselves so that there is no longer any need for sublimation. As a result of the transformation the drives would cease to be threatening and destructive and would become converted into helpful elements. This goal is to be brought about by a widening of the ego's position and approach to the drives which opens new channels of expression. (Whitmont, 1969, p. 296)

If this is an accurate interpretation of Jung and not a modification, then Buber's, and my own, criticism of him on this point may indeed need to be modified.

Erich Fromm criticizes Freud for seeing human beings as antisocial by nature and only secondarily in relationship. Fromm holds, as does Harry Stack Sullivan, that one becomes destructive only when one's neurosis turns one aside from a creative relationship with other people and with one's work. For Fromm, human nature is potentially good or evil, with health on the side of good. It is significant, however, that Fromm was not content with this explanation of the evil of Nazism as the product of authoritarian society and character structure in *Escape from Freedom* (Fromm, 1941) and went on to ever deeper and more extensive analysis of human evil in *The Heart of Man* (Fromm, 1964) and his voluminous study, *The Anatomy of Human Destructiveness* (Fromm, 1973).

For the American psychologist Carl R. Rogers, in contrast to Freud, Jung, and Fromm, human nature is unqualifiedly good. Rogers's theory of the complete acceptance of the "client" by the therapist is based upon the assumption that the client is "good" in his or her depths, that one is by nature social and constructive, that all one needs is to be accepted by the therapist so that one may accept oneself and one will make manifest the socially good person that one really is. Martin Buber's reply to Rogers on this point suggests, as we have seen, that a third alternative exists to seeing the human being as "evil," to be controlled, or "good," to be trusted, and that is seeing the person as "polar" and in need of personal direction.

Contemporary man's image of himself and of authentic human existence meets psychotherapy at the precise point at which this image enters into the process of his becoming. Recognition of the importance of philosophy and the human studies for the full understanding of the methods and goals of psychotherapy is growing. When the Washington School of Psychiatry brought Martin Buber from Jerusalem in 1957 to give the fourth William Alanson White Memorial Lectures, the title of the series was "What Can Philosophical Anthropology Contribute to Psychiatry?" In his introduction to these lectures, Leslie H. Farber, M.D., the chairman of the faculty, pointed out that none of the sciences have asked the question about man in his *wholeness* that is the concern of philosophical anthropology.

> The medical and biological sciences were asking, What is man in his relation to nature—to natural history, the evolution of organisms, and the physical forces regulating his body? . . . And it was upon this natural basis that all the other sciences of man—anthropology, sociology, political science, and finally the new Freudian science of psychoanalysis—asked their question. . . . None of the sciences were asking the *whole* question, What is man? Nor were they asking the unique question, Who am I, in my uniquely human essence? . . . These are not smaller or more personal questions; they are larger and more comprehensive than the ones which science has been asking. They include . . . man's personal being—my personal experience and knowledge of myself—as well as my philosophical and scientific knowledge of what *"man* is." (Farber, 1957, pp. 95f.)

Especially helpful in Helen Merrell Lynd's *On Shame and the Search for Identity* are her clear insights into the implications of various personality theories for the image of man which a particular psychology or psychoanalytic theory assumes, and her recognition that such images are matters of basic assumption even more than of scientific evidence and methodology.

> It does make a difference whether the individual is considered as eager, curious, and trusting until specific experience in a given society and historical period lead him to be anxious, cautious, and aggressive, or whether he is regarded as born with hostility, aggression, and fear which specific experiences may modify only to a limited degree in the direction of trust, sympathy, and interest. (Lynd, 1958, p. 142)

The possibility of mutual relations "between persons as an enlargement, not a contradiction of individual freedom," is compatible with personality theories "that see men primarily as need-satisfying objects, or in terms of their particular status or role relations to oneself" quite as much as with those theories centering in "release of tension, return to quiescence, and self-preservation." "Much depends," she writes, "upon whether one believes that isolation and alienation are inevitable in man's fate or that openness of communication between persons, mutual discovery, and love are actual possibilities" (Lynd, 1958, p. 237).

"The aim of therapy is often that of helping the person to be better adjusted to existing circumstances," says Fromm (1962) in *Beyond the Chains of Illusion*. "Mental health is often considered to be nothing but this adjustment, or to put it differently, a state of mind in which one's individual unhappiness is reduced to the level of the general unhappiness. The real problem . . . need not even be touched in this type of psychoanalysis" (Fromm, 1962, pp. 139f.). "Psychologists and psychoanalysts," writes Helen Merrell Lynd, "have given more encouragement to the adjustment of individuals to the realities of a given society than to personal differentiation and deviation from them."

> They frequently fail to give explicit recognition to the distinction between normal or healthy in terms of what are the generally accepted norms of the society and in terms of what is humanly desirable. If the psychoanalyst . . . does not rigorously examine his own

values in relation to those of society, he almost inevitably tends to accept tacitly the dominant values of the society as the norm of behavior, and to measure health and illness by these. Scientific objectivity, then, becomes indistinguishable from acceptance of social determinants. (Lynd, 1958, p. 212)

Even if psychoanalysts do rigorously reexamine their values, as Lynd suggests, they are still likely to impose them under the mask of objectivity; for they are not going to lose their values through examining them. It is true, as Fromm (1947) says in *Man for Himself*, that it matters whether therapists encourage their patients to adapt or strengthen them in their unwillingness to compromise their integrity. It is also true, as other therapists would point out, that patients are sometimes so tied up in their neurotic rebellion against the culture that they could do little else anyway. In either case, therapists cannot take the risk of encouraging patients to oppose society and to undergo privation unless they have a sure enough sense of those persons in their uniqueness. They must feel sure that their clients have a ground upon which to stand as persons and that they stand there in some real and creative relationship to the society that they are going to oppose. Otherwise, therapists cannot help encouraging patients to adjust to this particular society, for the therapists will see their patients' health and sickness in terms of that adjustment.

Frieda Fromm-Reichmann offers us a special insight into the problem of adjustment from her years of direct work with schizophrenics. Therapists who want to guide patients successfully toward discovering what degree of cultural adjustment is adequate to their personal needs must be persons with personal security and must have inner independence from the authoritarian values of the culture, including undue concern about their prestige as therapists.

The recovery of many schizophrenics and schizoid personalities, for example, depends upon the psychotherapist's freedom from convention and prejudice. These patients cannot and should not be asked to accept guidance toward a conventional adjustment to the customary requirements of our culture, much less to what the individual therapist personally considers these requirements to be. (Fromm-Reichmann, 1950, p. 32f.)

Another central problem is the relationship between therapist and client and its implications for both of their images of the human. In *Beyond the Chains of Illusion* Erich Fromm (1962) tells how he began at first with the "strictly orthodox Freudian procedure of analyzing a patient while sitting behind him and listening to his associations." This procedure turned the patient into the object of a laboratory experiment, says Fromm. He was able to fit the patient's dreams into his theoretical expectations, but he was still talking *about* the patient rather than *to* him. Eventually, he found a new way: "Instead of being an observer, I had to become a participant; to be engaged with the patient; from center to center, rather than from periphery to periphery." That this means an even more radical departure from the traditional method than Sullivan's "participant observer" is suggested by Fromm's remark to me that he not only sees therapy as "healing through meeting" but that he believes the therapist himself is healed in the process. This stress on participation does not mean that Fromm is under any illusion about therapy being fully mutual. Even while he felt himself fully engaged, as he had never been before, and learned that he could understand his patient rather than interpret what he said, he discovered that he could at the same time remain fully objective—seeing the patient as he is, and not as Fromm might want him to be. "To be objective is only possible if one does not want anything for oneself, neither the patient's admiration, nor his submission, nor even his 'cure' " (Fromm, 1962, p. 152). The therapy takes place for the sake of the cure, but a genuine wish to help will protect the therapist from being hurt in his self-esteem when the patient does not improve or elated about "his" achievement when he gets well.

Many psychotherapists today would join Fromm in taking issue with Freud's approach to psychotherapy. Looking on man in a purely "scientific" way similar to what we bring to a nonhuman entity is not sufficient to understand man. It is necessary for the therapist to understand the person facing him from within through his own participation, through the fact that he himself is a person who must make basic decisions, that he confronts the other as a person and not merely as a scientific observer. Jung in *The Undiscovered Self* points out the difference between the psychotherapist when he is concerned with man in general and, therefore, with statistical and scientific knowledge of man, and the same psychotherapist when he is concerned with the particular, unique individual before him and his concrete problems. The therapist, says Jung,

> is faced with the task of treating a sick person, who, especially in the case of psychic suffering, requires *individual understanding*. The more schematic the treatment is, the more resistances it—quite rightly—calls up in the patient, and the more the cure is jeopardized. . . . Today, over the whole field of medicine, it is recognized that the task of the doctor consists in treating the sick patient, not an abstract illness. (Jung, 1958, p. 12)

Freud found meaning in everything—in dreams, in slips of the tongue, in the psychopathology of everyday life. But it was only meaning as seen by the scientist from the outside, not the meaning of the personal life seen from within. Freud's one-time disciple, Jung, offers the possibility of deep inner meaning beyond our ordinary imaginings. His goal is not merely curing sickness; it is "individuation" in which the four functions—thought, sensation, feeling, and intuition—are united into a whole, integrated personality. Jung went much further than Freud did in the direction of a real mutuality between patient and therapist. He recognized before Freud that a therapist should be analyzed himself. He recognized that the therapist must risk himself, that he cannot hide behind his professional superiority. At the same time, Jung's "analytical psychology" is so focused upon the patient's inwardness that the outer person tends to be seen as a mask or mere social role. A danger also exists of relating to the other not as a person but as an "anima" or an "animus" (the feminine and masculine aspects of the psyche) or as the "shadow." Jung holds that the aim of his therapy is to bring the patient back into relationship with the world freed from the "shadow" that has turned negative because it is repressed and is then projected onto the other. Only then, says

Jung, can he have real relationships with others. Jung assumes that the person becomes whole first and only then enters into a genuine relationship. One of the dangers of this assumption is the tendency for the other person to become the function of your becoming, as you of his. Another is the precarious nature of a "personal integration" attained apart from lived mutuality and the direction found in going out to meet what is not yourself.

The human image has more to do with therapy itself than it does with our theories about therapy, important as the theories may be; for the danger exists of the theory becoming a construct in which the therapist settles down. "Young therapists often regard the dreams of their patient as examinations," Fromm said to me. "They feel that they must be ready to give some theoretical interpretations, and as a result they do not really hear the dreams." When he was working with 30 of us in Washington, DC, in a series of seminars on dreams and the unconscious, Martin Buber said that a therapist has two kinds of relationship to dreams—one in which he puts them into the categories of his school and the other in which he responds to them spontaneously and wholly in a "musical floating relationship." "I am for the latter," Buber (1990, pp. 167f.) added. This musical relationship in which the therapist really hears the unique person and experiences his side of the relationship is crucial for all therapy, regardless of the school. No matter what school the therapist comes from and no matter what knowledge and experience he has, the basic question is still *when* his insights apply to this particular patient and when not. To answer this question, he must use the categories of his school in a flexible, "musical" way in order to try again and again to arrive at this person's uniqueness. To do this, the therapist must practice what Buber calls the act of "inclusion," experiencing the patient's side of the relationship, as well as his own. Rollo May, as we have seen, stresses the centrality of such inclusion in terms of what might be called a "field theory" of the emotions:

> Our feelings, like the artist's paints and brush, are ways of communicating and sharing something meaningful from us to the world.

> Our feelings not only take into consideration the other person but are in a real sense partially *formed by the feelings of the other person present*. We *feel* in a magnetic field. A sensitive person learns, often without being conscious of doing so, to pick up the feelings of the persons around him, as a violin string resonates to the vibration of every other musical string in the room. . . . Every successful lover knows this by "instinct." It is an essential—if not *the* essential—quality of the good therapist. (May, 1969, p. 91)

Even the patient's "sickness" is part of his uniqueness, for even his sickness tells of the road he has not gone and has to go. If, instead, the therapist makes the patient into an object to himself, as well as to the therapist, he will have robbed him of part of his human potential and growth. This is not a question of a choice between the scientific generalization and the concrete individual, but of which direction is the primary one. Is the individual regarded as a collection of symptoms to be registered in the categories of a particular school, or are the theories of the school regarded as primarily a means of returning again and again to the understanding of his unique person and his relationship with his therapist? An increasingly important trend in psychotherapy suggests that the basic direction of movement should be toward the concrete person and his uniqueness and not toward subsuming the patient's symptoms under theoretical categories or adjusting him to some socially derived view of the "ideal" man. This trend emphasizes the *image* of man as opposed to the *construct* of man. The image of man retains the understanding of man in his concrete uniqueness; it retains the wholeness of the person.

Sigmund Freud is one of the great Promethean explorers of our age who has pushed back the limits of human knowledge. No one in our age can have an image of the human that has not been in some decisive way influenced by Freud. In the same year in which Martin Buber published his classic *Ich und Du* ("I and Thou")—1923—Freud published his famous book *Das Ich und das Es* (literally "The I and the It" but Latinized in English translation into *The Ego and the Id*). The person comes into being as person, Freud suggested, through libidinal "cathexes" in relation first to his mother and later his father. Through these psychobiological relations the whole psychic economy of id, ego, and superego arises. The superego, which even takes into itself some of the libidinal energy of the id, represents the introjected father figure, "conscience" being nothing other than the man-child's fear of castration by the father.[17] Certainly some justification can be given to Ludwig Binswanger's complaint that Freud's genetic approach reduces human history to natural history and that this reduction is based upon "a complete taking apart of being-human as such and a natural-scientific-biological reconstruction of it." "The real battle," says Ludwig Binswanger of his argument with his lifelong friend Sigmund Freud, "is the battle over the image of man." "Only human existence is genuinely historical," writes Binswanger. Hence, Freud misses that in man which is specifically human. Psychoanalysis has developed its entire critique and interpretation on the basis of Freud's *homo natura*, whose nature is driven instinctively and whose history is essentially formed by sexuality. (Binswagner, 1958, p. 314f.)

One of the decisive aspects of this "battle over the image of man" is the problem of the relation between psychological necessity and personal freedom. Kierkegaard once remarked that one cannot judge another person, for no one knows how much of his action is suffering—a compulsion he must bear—and how much is temptation—a matter about which he has some real choice. This is not a theoretical question of "free will" versus "determinism," but a concrete question of the resources of a particular person in a particular situation. Probably even he himself will not know afterward to what extent he was able to respond to the situation with the spontaneity of the whole person and to what extent his action was the product of fragmentary and conditioned response. He will have lost the situation in its presentness, its concreteness, its need for decision, lost it, perhaps, in a cloud of refashioned and rationalized memory. Psychotherapy has contributed an enormous amount to the understanding of the importance of determining factors, but also, because it is therapy and concerned with healing, it aims at freedom, at freeing man for a real response in the present situation to what the therapist and the client can recognize as reality. This is the place where the meeting of therapy and the image of man becomes truly decisive. Even such phenomena as repression and resistance must be understood from the aspect of the mixture of necessity and freedom, writes Rollo May.

Through its awareness that "the battle is over the image of man," existential psychotherapy has made a decisive contribution to our understanding of the interrelationship of the image of man and psychotherapy. It has opened up genuine new directions of exploration, ranging from phenomenological analyses and the exploration of the world of the psychotic to a different understanding of the very meaning of such basic therapeutic terms as transference and healing. "Existential psychotherapy," says May in his introductory essays to *Existence*, "is based on the assumption that it is possible to have a science of man which does not fragmentize man and destroy his humanity at the same moment as it studies him" (May, 1958, p. 36). In contrast to the tendency to make technique an end in itself, "existential technique should have flexibility and versatility," writes May, "varying from patient to patient and from one phase to another in treatment with the same patient" (May, 1958, p. 78). This means the recognition that the patient's commitment, his basic decision about his life, precedes his knowledge of himself. In fact, he cannot even permit himself to get insight or knowledge until he is ready to take a decisive orientation to life and has made the preliminary decisions along the way (May, 1958, p. 87).

Analysis of existence is not identical with existence: Concern with existence does not give ready-made phenomenological categories a privileged position over the categories of Freud or any other psychologist. "The temptation to use existential concepts in the service of intellectualizing tendencies is especially to be guarded against," Rollo May rightly points out, "since, because they refer to things that have to do with the center of personal reality, these concepts can the more seductively give the illusion of dealing with reality" (May, 1958, p. 90). The configuration of self and world or self to self is not existential, Paul Goodman has remarked. "It is interpretation just in the Freudian sense. Real existential psychotherapy would try to do as far as possible without interpretations and stick to particular situations." Irvin Yalom, on the other hand, as Charles Brice observes, uses interpretations very well within an existential framework.

Both Ludwig Binswanger and Hans Trüb adopt the language of "I and Thou" under the influence of Martin Buber, but the one uses it primarily in the service of phenomenological analysis of the patient's "world-design" (who in the case of Ellen West is not even his own patient), whereas the other uses it as a means of *pointing* to the existential situation of the patient and the concrete meeting between patient and therapist. Binswanger's existential analysis tends to lead to still another *construct of man* to set over against those given us by the older schools of psychotherapy. Only a psychotherapy that begins with the concrete existence of persons, with their wholeness and uniqueness, and with the healing that takes place through the meeting of therapist and client will point us toward the image of the human. In the last analysis the issue that faces all the schools of psychotherapy is whether the *starting point* of therapy is to be found in the analytical category or the unique person—in the *construct* or the *image* of the human.

The revelation of the human image—its coming forth from its hiding—is a revelation that takes place *between* therapist and client or *among* the members of a group. It cannot be equated with the image of the human that each holds or comes to hold separately. The coming into the light of the hidden human image is inseparable from the dialogue itself—a dialogue of mutual contact, trust, and shared humanity. In this sense, "healing through meeting" is identical with the revelation of the hidden human image. This revelation is more than an individual finding an image of the human. It is a *becoming* of the human in relationship—becoming human with such resources as the relationship affords, including the possibility of tragedy when such resources are lacking. It is not the diploma on the wall that assures clients that they have the right therapist. The "rightness" of the relationship depends upon mutual existential trust—and upon an existential grace that is not *in* the therapist or *in* the client but moves *between* the two. When these are not present, or not sufficiently so, then the ground of tragedy has been reached—whether or not the relationship ends in suicide. This touching of the tragic itself unfolds the hidden possibilities of the human, as well as shows the real limitations in which we stand.

Notes

1. Quoted with no reference in Leonard, 1968, p. 24.

2. For a full-scale discussion of Fromm in this context, see Friedman, 1967, chapter 13, "Erich Fromm and 'Self-Realization.' "

3. This chapter is based largely upon a much longer article entitled "Aiming at the Self: The Paradox of Encounter and the Human Potential Movement" (Friedman, 1976a, pp. 5-34).

4. A full-scale discussion of Ludwig Binswanger and Ronald Laing will be found in Friedman, 1984; and of Viktor von Weizsäcker, Rollo May, Medard Boss, Leslie Farber, Erving and Miriam Polster, and Hans Trüb in Friedman, 1985.

5. Maurice Friedman, *The Worlds of Existentialism (Ludwig Binswanger, "Basic Forms and Knowledge of Human Existence")*. This selection, trans. Jacob Needleham for this volume, is the only English translation of Binswanger's *Grundformen und Erkenntnis menshlichen Daseins.*

6. These selections were translated for Friedman 1991 by William Hallo and are the only published translations in English of Trüb 1952.

7. This chapter is a summation of the essential conclusions of my book *The Healing Dialogue in Psychotherapy* (Friedman, 1985). As such, it also serves as a conclusion for Part III on "Dialogue" in this present book.

8. For a full-scale interpretation of T. S. Eliot's *The Waste Land*, see Friedman, 1978, chapter 2, "Images of Inauthenticity," pp. 31-38.

9. Charles Brice points out quite rightly that the above passage is a simplification of Freud's view: "You neglect Freud's emphasis on the ego as the organization that makes a *healthy* compromise between passion and sterility, id and superego" (C. W. Brice, personal communication, 1990).

10. Vyacheslav Ivanov sees the relation of compulsion to freedom in Dostoievsky as a lower level of empirical determination and a higher level of free will that simply uses but is in no wise determined by the lower.

> Dostoievsky presents each individual destiny as a single, coherent event taking place simultaneously on three different levels.... On the two lower levels is displayed the whole labyrinthine diversity of life ... the changeability of the empirical character even within the bounds of its determination from without. On the uppermost, or metaphysical, level ... there is no more complexity or subjection to circumstance: here reigns the great, bare simplicity of the final ... decision ... for being in God; or for ... flight from God into Not-being. The whole tragedy played out on the two lower levels provides only the materials for the construction, and the symbols for the interpretation of the sovereign tragedy of the God-like spiritual being's final self-determination: an act which is solely that of the free will. (Ivanov, 1957, pp. 38f.)

Ivanov's material and metaphysical levels do not so much solve the problem that Dostoievsky presents us as sidestep it. Although we may agree with Ivanov that Dostoievsky's "searching ... has a single aim: to ascertain that part played by the intelligible act of will in the empirical deed," we cannot agree with any a priori formulation that answers this question in the abstract rather than in terms of each character and each situation. Dostoievsky does not present us with "empirical" and "metaphysical levels," but with an image of the wholeness of Man in all his complexity and contradictoriness.

11. Commenting on this passage, Charles Brice refers us to *The Ego and the Id* (Freud, 1947), "especially the part about the 'negative' Oedipal Complex in which Freud states the importance of the relationship with the father and the positive incorporation as the Ego Ideal" (C. W. Brice, personal communications, 1990).

12. This chapter is based upon Friedman, 1970, pp. 469-472, 129-133, 220-227, 472f., 238-251.

13. "Nowhere in twentieth-century letters is there a better case for the Freudian," writes Frederick J. Hoffman. "The writings of Franz Kafka are ... persistent demonstrations of an anxiety neurosis—a constant flight from anticipated affective danger." Hoffman links this anxiety with the guilt arising from Kafka's Oedipus complex ("Escape From Father," in *The Kafka Problem*, ed. Angel Flores, 1946, pp. 214, 246).

14. Buber answers the question of "how the absurd confusion that rules in the court is to be reconciled with the justice of the accusation and the demand" with the assertion that Kafka lets "the just accusation of an inaccessible highest judgment be conveyed by a disorderly and cruel court." For Kafka the meaning that reaches one and demands response from one comes to one only through

the absurd. Buber's conclusion, nonetheless, has to do not with one's encounter with the absurd but with oneself and one's illumination of one's personal guilt: "Only that man can escape the arm of this court who, out of his own knowledge, fulfills the demand for confession of guilt according to its truth through executing the primal confession, the self-illumination. Only he enters the interior of the Law" (Buber, 1988c, p. 135). Buber's discussion of existential guilt includes an emphasis upon concrete and specific acts of guilt that seems quite foreign to *The Trial*, where no specific action is ever in question. By the same token, Buber's emphasis upon illumination and confession of one's personal guilt has a far more particular ring than anything in Kafka. Even when Kafka speaks of confession in his diaries, it is doubtful that he means confession of particular acts. Kafka was a man who lived all his life in a shadow world of guilt in which "the profound ambiguity between good and evil," to use Tillich's phrase, far outweighed any specific sense of sin.

15. This section of this chapter on the crisis of motives and the problematic of guilt is based upon Friedman, 1970, pp. 473-475, 425-427, and chapter 15, "*The Trial*: The Problematic of Guilt," pp. 346-356, 360-364, 367-369, 372f.

16. "But we can observe infants, and if we do, the notion of an aggressive drive is inescapable" (C. W. Brice, personal communication, 1990).

17. "Freud explicitly states that (1) a pre-Oedipal identification exists which ushers in conscience and (2) the person continues to identify with other authority figures and cultural institutions which continue to form his superego. Also, you neglect his theory that both male and female fear loss of love and that makes up aspects of the superego" (C. W. Brice, personal communications, 1990).

References

Apfelbaum, B., & Apfelbaum, C. (1973). Encountering encounter groups: A reply to Koch and Haigh. *Journal of Humanistic Psychology, 13*(1), 53-67.

Binswanger, L. (1963). *Being-in-the world: Selected papers of Ludwig Binswanger* (J. Needleman, Ed. and Trans.). New York: Basic Books.

Boss, M. (1963). *Psychoanalysis and Daseinsanalysis* (L. Lefebre, Trans.). New York: Basic Books.

Boszormenyi-Nagy, I. (1965). Intensive family therapy as process. In I. Boszormenyi-Nagy & J. L. Framo (Eds.), *Intensive family therapy: Theoretical and practical aspects* (pp. 87-142). New York: Harper & Row.

Boszormenyi-Nagy, I. (1987). *Foundations of contextual therapy: Collected papers of Ivan Boszormenyi-Nagy, M.D.* New York: Brunner/Mazel.

Boszormenyi-Nagy, I., & Krasner, B. R. (1986). *Between give and take: A clinical guide to contextual therapy.* New York: Brunner/Mazel.

Boszormenyi-Nagy, I., & Spark, G. (1984). *Invisible loyalties: Reciprocity in intergenerational family therapy.* New York: Brunner/Mazel. (Original work published 1973)

Boszormenyi-Nagy, I., & Ulrich, D. (1981). Contextual family therapy. In A. S. Gurman & D. P. Kniskern (Eds.), *Handbook of family therapy* (pp. 159-186). New York: Brunner/Mazel.

Brice, C. W. (1984). Pathological modes of human relating and therapeutic mutuality: A dialogue between Buber's existential relational theory and object-relations theory. *Psychiatry, 47*(2), 109-123.

Buber, M. (1958). *I and Thou* (2nd rev. ed.) (R.G. Smith, Trans). New York: Scribner.

Buber, M. (1985). *Between Man and Man* (2nd ed). (R. G. Smith, Trans.). New York: Macmillan.

Buber, M. (1988a). *Eclipse of God: Studies in the relation between religion and philosophy* (M. S. Friedman et al., Trans.). Atlantic Highlands, NJ: Humanities Press.

Buber, M. (1988b). *Hasidism and modern man* (M. S. Friedman, Ed. and Trans.). Atlantic Highlands, NJ: Humanities Press.

Buber, M. (1988c). *The knowledge of man: A philosophy of the interhuman.* (M.S. Friedman, Ed.; M. S. Friedman & R. G. Smith, Trans.). Atlantic Highlands, NJ: Humanities Press.

Buber, M. (1990). *A believing humanism: My testament, 1902-1965* (M. S. Friedman, Trans.). Atlantic Highlands, NJ: Humanities Press.

Bugental, J. F. T. (1976). *Search for existential identity: Patient-therapist dialogues in humanistic psychology.* San Francisco: Jossey-Bass.

Bugental, J. F. T. (1987). *The art of the psychotherapist.* New York: Norton.

Camus, A. (1957). *The fall* (J. O'Brien, Trans.). New York: Knopf.

Chein, I. (1972). *The science of behavior and the image of man.* New York: Basic Books.

Coulon, W. R. (1972). *Groups, gimmicks, and instant gurus.* New York: Harper & Row.

Dostoievsky, F. (undated), *The brothers Karamazov.* (C. Garnett, Trans.). New York: Modern Library.

Dostoievsky, F. (1922). *Stavrogin's confession and the plan for the life of a great sinner* (S. S. Kotelianksy & V. Woolf, Trans.). Richmond, England: L. & V. Woolf.

Dostoievsky, F. (1947). *The raw youth* (C. Garnett, Trans.). New York: Dial Press.

Dostoievsky, F. (1953). *The devils (The possessed)* (D. Magarschak, Trans.). Harmsworth, England: Penguin Classics.

Erikson, E. (1950). *Childhood and society.* New York: Norton.

Erikson, E. (1953). Growth and crises of the "healthy personality." In C. Klucholn & H. Murray (Eds.), *Personality in nature, society, and culture.* New York: Knopf.

Erikson, E. (1954). On the sense of inner identity. In R. P. Knight & C. R. Friedman (Eds.), *Psychoanalytic psychiatry and psychology: Clinical and theoretical papers* (Vol. I). New York: International Universities Press.

Erikson, E. (1956). The problem of ego identity. *Journal of the American Psychoanalytic Association, 4*(1), 56-121.

Farber, L. H. (1957). Introduction to Martin Buber, The William Alanson White memorial lectures, fourth series. *Psychiatry, 20*(2), pp. 95f.

Farber, L. H. (1966). *The ways of the will: Essays toward a psychology and psychopathology of the will.* New York: Basic Books.

Farber, L. H. (1976). *Lying, despair, jealousy, envy, sex, suicide, drugs, and the good life.* New York: Basic Books.

Firestone, S. (1971). *The dialectic of sex: The case for feminine revolution.* New York: Bantam Books.

Flores, A. (Ed.). (1946). *The Kafka problem.* New York: New Directions.

Frankl, V. E. (1959). *Das menschenbild der seelenheilkunde: Kritik des dynamischen psychologismus.* Stuttgart: Hippokrates Verlag.

Frankl, V. E. (1960). Beyond self-actualization and self-expression. *Journal of Existential Psychiatry, 1*(1), 5-20.

Freud, S. (1947). *The ego and the id* (J. Riviere, Trans.). In E. Jones (Ed.), *The International Psycho-Analytical Library* (No. 12, 4th ed.). London: The Hogarth Press and The Institute of Psychoanalysis.

Freud, S. (1958). *Civilization and its discontents* (J. Riviere, Trans.). New York: Doubleday.

Friedman, M. S. (1967). *To deny our nothingness: Contemporary images of man*. New York: Delacorte.

Friedman, M. S. (1970). *Problematic rebel: Melville, Dostoievsky, Kafka, Camus* (2nd rev. ed.). Chicago: University of Chicago Press, Phoenix Books.

Friedman, M. S. (1972). *Touchstones of reality: Existential trust and the community of peace*. New York: E. P. Dutton.

Friedman, M. S. (1974). *The hidden human image*. New York: Delacorte.

Friedman, M. S. (1976a). Aiming at the self: The paradox of encounter and the human potential movement. *Journal of Humanistic Psychology 16*(2), 5-34.

Friedman, M. S. (1976b). *Martin Buber: The life of dialogue* (3rd rev. ed.). Chicago: University of Chicago Press, Phoenix Books.

Friedman, M. S. (1978). *To deny our nothingness: Contemporary images of man* (3rd rev. ed.). Chicago: University of Chicago Press, Phoenix and Midway Books.

Friedman, M. S. (1983). *The confirmation of otherness: In family, community, and society*. New York: Pilgrim.

Friedman, M. S. (1984). *Contemporary psychology: Revealing and obscuring the human*. Pittsburgh, PA: Duquesne University Press.

Friedman, M. S. (1985). *The healing dialogue in psychotherapy*. New York: Jason Aronson.

Friedman, M. S. (1988). Introductory essay (Chapter 1). In M. Buber, *The knowledge of man: A philosophy of the interhuman*. Atlantic Highlands, NJ: Humanities Press.

Friedman, M. S. (1989). Elemente einer neuen humanistischen psychologie: Dialog und bestaetigung und das bild vom menschen. *Report Psychologie, Zeitschrift des Berufsvergances Deutscher Psychologen (BDP), 14* (Juli), 29-33.

Friedman, M. S. (Ed.). (1991). *The worlds of existentialism: A critical reader*. Atlantic Highlands, NJ: Humanities Press.

Fromm, E. (1941). *Escape from freedom*. New York: Rinehart.

Fromm, E. (1947). *Man for himself: An inquiry into the psychology of ethics*. New York: Rinehart.

Fromm, E. (1956). *The art of loving*. New York: Harper & Row.

Fromm, E. (1962). *Beyond the chains of illusion: My encounter with Marx and Freud*. The Credo Series. New York: Simon & Schuster.

Fromm, E. (1964). *Religious perspectives: Vol. 12. The heart of man: Its genius for good and evil* (R.N. Anshen, Ed.). New York: Harper & Row.

Fromm, E. (1973). *The anatomy of human destructiveness*. New York: Holt, Rinehart & Winston.

Fromm-Reichmann, F. (1950). *Principles of intensive psychotherapy*. Chicago: University of Chicago Press.

Fülop-Müller, R., & Eckstein, A. (Eds.). (1926). *Der unbekannten Dostojewski*. Munich: Piper Verlag.

Gardner, M. (1952). *In the name of science*. New York: Putnam.

Giorgi, A. (1969). Psychology: A human science. *Social Research, 36*(3), 412-432.

Giorgi, A. (1970a). *Psychology as a human science: A phenomenologically based approach*. New York: Harper & Row.

Giorgi, A. (1970b, May 15-16). *Science and scientism: The human sciences.* Symposium conducted at Trinity College, Dublin, Ireland.

Goldstein, K. (1963). *Human nature in the light of psychotherapy.* New York: Schocken.

Greening, T. C. (1971). Encounter groups from the perspective of existential human-ism. In T. C. Greening (Ed.), *Existential humanistic psychology.* Belmont, CA: Brooks/Cole.

Greer, G. (1971). *The female eunuch.* New York: McGraw-Hill.

Guntrip, H. (1969). *Schizoid phenomena: Object relations and the self.* New York: International Universities Press.

Haigh, G. V. (1971). Responses to Koch's assumptions about group process. *Journal of Humanistic Psychology, 11*(2), pp. 129-132.

Hesse, H. (1970). *Klingsor's last summer* (R. Winston & C. Winston, Trans.). New York: Farrar, Straus & Giroux, Noonday Books.

Horney, K. (1950). *Neurosis and human growth: The struggle toward self-realization.* New York: Norton.

Hycner, R. H. (1985). Dialogical gestalt therapy: An initial proposal. *Gestalt Therapy Journal, 8*(1), pp. 23-49.

Hycner, R. H. (1989). *The therapeutic relationship: Interviews with existential-humanistic psychotherapists Ivan Boszormenyi-Nagy, James F. T. Bugental, Rollo May, Erving and Miriam Polster, Virginia Sapir, and Irvin Yalom* (work in progress).

Hycner, R. H. (1991). *Between person and person: Toward a dialogical psychotherapy.* Highland, NY: Center for Gestalt Development.

Ivanov, V. (1957). *Freedom and the tragic life: A study in Dostoievsky.* New York: Noonday Press.

Jourard, S. M. (1968). *Disclosing man to himself.* New York: D. Van Nostrand.

Jourard, S. M. (1971). *The transparent self* (2nd ed.). New York: Van Nostrand Reinhold.

Jung, C. G. (1931). *European commentary: T'ai-i, The secret of the golden flower* (R. Wilhelm & C. F. Baynes, Trans.). London: Kegan Paul, Trench, Trubner.

Jung, C. G. (1954). *The development of the personality.* (R.F.C. Hull, Trans.). New York: Pantheon.

Jung, C. G. (1958). *The undiscovered self.* (R.F.C. Hull, Trans.). Boston: Little, Brown.

Kafka, F. (1946). *The great wall of China: Stories and reflections* (W. Muir & E. Muir, Trans.). New York: Schocken.

Kafka, F. (1954). *Dearest father: Stories and other writings.* (M. Brod, Ed.; E. Kaiser & E. Wilkins, Trans.). New York: Schocken.

Kafka, F. (1957). *The Trial* (W. Muir & E. Muir, Trans.). New York: Knopf.

Kierkegaard, S. (1980). *The concept of anxiety* (R. Thomte, Ed. and Trans.). Princeton, NJ: Princeton University Press.

Kiesler, S. (1973). Emotion in groups. *Journal of Humanistic Psychology, 13*(3), 19-31.

Koch, S. (1971). The image of man implicit in encounter group theory. *Journal of Humanistic Psychology, 11*(2), pp. 112-127.

Kuhn, T. (1962). *Structure of scientific revolutions.* Chicago: University of Chicago Press.

Laing, R. D. (1969). *The divided self: An existential study in sanity and madness.* Middlesex, England: Penguin.

Leonard, G. B. (1968). *Education and ecstasy.* New York: Delacorte.

Löwith, K. (1964). *From Hegel to Nietzsche: The revolution in nineteenth century thought.* New York: Holt, Rinehart & Winston.

Lynd, H. M. (1958). *On shame and the search for identity.* New York: Harcourt Brace.

Maurina, Z. (1952). *Dostojewskij, Menschengestalter und Gottessucher.* Memmingen, Germany: Maximillian Dietrich Verlag.

May, R. (1958). [Introductory essays (chapters 1 and 2)]. In R. May, E. Angell, & H. F. Ellenberger (Eds.), *Existence: A new dimension in psychiatry and psychology.* New York: Basic Books.

May, R. (1969). *Love and will.* New York: Norton.

Nietzsche, F. (1978). *Thus spake Zarathustra* (W. Kaufmann, Trans.). New York: Penguin.

Pfuetze, P. E. (1973). *Self, society, and existence: Human nature and dialogue in the thought of G. H. Mead and Martin Buber.* Westport, CT: Greenwood.

Polster, E., & Polster, M. (1974). *Gestalt therapy integrated: Contours of theory and practice.* New York: Vintage.

Rogers, C. R. (1951). *Client-centered therapy: Its current practice, implications, and theory.* Boston: Houghton Mifflin.

Rogers, C. R. (1961). *On becoming a person: A therapist's view of psychotherapy.* Boston: Houghton Mifflin.

Rogers, C. R. (1967a). The interpersonal relationship: The core of guidance and Learning to be free. In C. R. Rogers & B. Stevens (Eds.), *Person to person: The problem of being human. A new trend in psychology* (pp. 89-103). Lafayette, CA: Real People.

Rogers, C. R. (1967b). Some learnings from a study of psychotherapy with schizophrenics. In C. R. Rogers & B. Stevens (Eds.), *Person to Person: The problem of being human. A new trend in psychology.* Lafayette, CA: Real People.

Rogers, C. R. (1967c, summer). Article in *Voices.*

Rogers, C. R. (1970). *Carl Rogers on encounter groups.* New York: Harper & Row.

Rogers, C. R. (1980). *A way of being.* Boston: Houghton Mifflin.

Rogers, C. R. (undated). *Ethical perspectives of the 21st century.* Paper presented at the Humanist Institute, San Francisco.

Sartre, J. P. (1973). *The age of reason.* New York: Vintage.

Smith, S. S., & Isotoff, A. (1935). The abnormal from within. *Psychoanalytic Review, 22*, pp. 361-391.

Spiegelman, M. J. (1965). Some implications of the transference. In *Speculum Psychologiae: Festschrift fur C. A. Meier.* Zurich: Raschon Verlag.

Straus, E. W. (1963). *The primary world of senses* (J. Needleman, Trans.). New York: The Free Press of Glencoe.

Trüb, H. (1952). *Heilung aus der Begegnung. Eine Auseinandersetzung mit der Psychologie G. G. Jung* (E. Michel & A. Sborowitz, Eds.). Stuttgart: Ernest Klett Verlag.

Wertz, F. J. (1981). The birth of the infant: A developmental perspective. *Journal of Phenomenological Psychology, 12*(2), 205-220.

Whitmont, E. C. (1969). *The symbolic quest: Basic attitudes of analytical psychology.* New York: G. P. Putnam.

Yalom, I. D. (1980). *Existential psychotherapy.* New York: Basic Books.
Yalom, I. D. (1989). *Love's executioner and other tales of psychotherapy.* New York: Basic Books.

Author Index

Subject Index

Abraham, K., 136
Agee, J., 15
Age regression, 77
Alexander, F.: and guilt, 197; and shame, 197
American Psychiatric Association, 90
American Psychological Association, annual convention of, vii
Analysts, existential: Binswanger, 62, 67-68, 220; Boss, 66-67
Anthropologists, philosophical, 127-128, 130
Anthropology, philosophical, 42, 127-131; and the image of the human, 125-137; phenomenology and, 128
Anxiety, 137; age of, 138-146; and will, 145; psychology and, 135
Apfelbaum, B., and encounter groups, 24-25
Apfelbaum, C., and encounter groups, 24-25
Association for Humanistic Psychology, 29
Auden, W. H., and the age of anxiety, 138

Behaviorism, 28
Between, the, 19, 108, 109, 158, 163. *See also* Buber, Martin
Binswanger, L., 35, 62; and Boss, 68; and Buber, 68, 220; and communal love, 67; and concealing shame, 197; and existential shame, 197; and Freud, 218; and manics, 67; and schizophrenia, 67; and Straus, 197; and therapy as love and friendship, 67-68; as existential analyst, 62, 67-68
Boss, M.: and Binswanger, 68; and social relationships, 66; as dasein-analyst, 67; as existential analyst, 66-67
Boszormenyi-Nagy, I.: and Buber, 92-107; and centrifugal concern, 98; and centripetal concern, 98; and contextual therapy, 92-107; and destructive entitlement, 104; and dialogue in family therapy, 92-107, 109; and entitlement, 96, 100, 101; and fair acknowledgment, 99; and goal of therapy of, 106;

232

About the Author

MAURICE STANLEY FRIEDMAN

From 1973 to 1991 Maurice Friedman was Professor of Religious Studies, Philosophy, and Comparative Literature at San Diego State University. From 1973 to 1975 he was a member of the Core Faculty and Coordinator of Non-Statistical Dissertations at the California School of Professional Psychology-San Diego. He belonged to the Guild of Tutors, International College (Los Angeles), and is on the faculty of Williamson University. Professor Friedman is Co-Director of the Institute for Dialogical Psychotherapy (San Diego) and is on the faculty of its training program. In the summer of 1975 he was the first Visiting Scholar of Religion in Hawaii and Visiting Professor at the University of Hawaii in Honolulu. In 1972 he was Visiting Distinguished Professor of Religious Studies at San Diego State College and Visiting Fellow of the Center for the Study of the Person, La Jolla. From 1967 to 1973 he was Professor of Religion at Temple University, Philadelphia, where he was the Director of both the PhD Program in Religion and Literature and the PhD Program in Religion and Psychology. He was at the same time on the regular faculty of Pendle Hill, the Quaker Study

Center in Wallingford, Pennsylvania. From 1966 to 1967 he was Professor of Philosophy at Manhattanville College of the Sacred Heart, Purchase, New York. From 1954 to 1966 he was on the Faculty of Philosophy and Literature at the New School for Social Research, New York City. From 1951 to 1964 he was Professor of Philosophy, Religion, and Literature at Sarah Lawrence College. He has also taught at the University of Chicago, Columbia University, Washington University (St. Louis), Ohio State University, Vassar College, the Hebrew Union College-Cincinnati, Union Theological Seminary (New York City), the Washington (DC) School of Psychiatry, and the William Alanson White Institute of Psychiatry, Psychoanalysis, and Psychology (New York City). He is in *Who's Who in America*.

Professor Friedman is the author of *Martin Buber: The Life of Dialogue* (1955); *Problematic Rebel: Melville, Dostoievsky, Kafka, Camus* (1970); *The Worlds of Existentialism: A Critical Reader* (1964); *To Deny Our Nothingness; Contemporary Images of Man* (1967); *Touchstones of Reality: Existential Trust and the Community of Peace* (1972); *The Hidden Human Image* (1974); *The Human Way: A Dialogical Approach to Religion and Human Experience* (1982); *Martin Buber's Life and Work: The Early Years—18 78-1923* (1982); *The Middle Years— 1923-1945* (1983), and *The Later Years—1945-1965* (1984); *The Confirmation of Otherness: In Family, Community, and Society* (1983); *Contemporary Psychology: Revealing and Obscuring the Human* (1984); *The Healing Dialogue in Psychotherapy* (1985); *Martin Buber and the Eternal* (1986); *Abraham Joshua Heschel and Elie Wiesel: "You Are My Witnesses"* (1987); *A Dialogue with Hasidic Tales: Hallowing the Everyday* (1988); *Encounter on the Narrow Ridge: A Life of Martin Buber* (1991); *Religion and Psychology: A Dialogical Approach* (1992); and *A Heart of Wisdom: Religon and Human Wholeness* (1992).

Professor Friedman holds an S.B. *magna cum laude* in Economics from Harvard University (1943); an MA in English from The Ohio State University (1947); a PhD in the History of Culture from the University of Chicago (1950); an honorary LLD from the University of Vermont (1961); and a Doctor of Humane Letters from the Professional School of Psychological Studies, San Diego (1986). In 1983 he received an MA in Psychology from International College. Since 1982 he has been in private practice as a psychotherapist. In 1982 he gave the keynote paper for the five-day seminar "Women's

Image Making and Shaping," Pune, India. From 1984 to 1985 he was San Diego State University's first University Research Lecturer. In 1985 Professor Friedman received the Jewish National Book Award for biography for 1984 for his *Martin Buber's Life and Work: The Later Years*. From 1987 to 1988 he was Senior Fulbright Lecturer at The Hebrew University of Jerusalem in Israel.

In October 1991 Professor Friedman was director of the three-day International Interdisciplinary Conference on "Martin Buber's Impact on the Human Sciences" at San Diego State University. In January-February 1992 he was visiting lecturer at the Indira Gandhi National Center for the Arts, New Delhi, India.